Samuel Lewis Gracey

Annals of the Sixth Pennsylvania Cavalry

Samuel Lewis Gracey

Annals of the Sixth Pennsylvania Cavalry

ISBN/EAN: 9783337814137

Printed in Europe, USA, Canada, Australia, Japan

Cover: Foto ©ninafisch / pixelio.de

More available books at **www.hansebooks.com**

ANNALS

OF THE

Sixth Pennsylvania Cavalry.

By Rev. S. L. GRACEY,
CHAPLAIN OF THE REGIMENT.

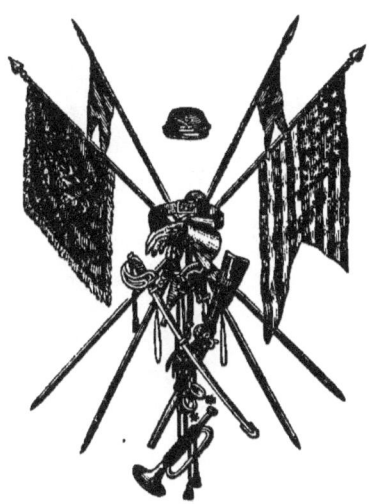

PUBLISHED FOR THE OFFICERS OF THE REGIMENT BY
E. H. BUTLER & CO.
MDCCCLXVIII.

Entered, according to act of Congreſs, in the year 1868.

By E. H. BUTLER & Co.,

In the Clerk's Office of the Diſtrict Court for the Eaſtern Diſtrict of Pennſylvania.

"Oh, great corrector of enormous times,
Shaker of o'er-rank States, thou great decider
Of dusty and old titles, that heal'ſt with blood
The earth when it is ſick .   .   .
    .   .   .   .   .   . I do take
Thy ſigns auſpiciouſly, and in thy name
March boldly on."

Entered, according to act of Congress, in the year 1868.

By E. H. Butler & Co.,

In the Clerk's Office of the District Court for the Eastern District of Pennsylvania.

"Oh, great corrector of enormous times,
 Shaker of o'er-rank States, thou great decider
 Of dusty and old titles, that heal'st with blood
 The earth when it is sick   .   .   .
 .   .   .   .   .   . I do take
 Thy signs auspiciously, and in thy name
 March boldly on."

HEADQUARTERS MILITARY DIVISION OF THE GULF,
NEW ORLEANS, LA., *February 5th*, 1866.

REV. S. L. GRACEY, *Chaplain, &c.*

DEAR SIR: Your communication of January 7th was duly received, and it is with great pleasure I hear of the intention of the officers of the 6th Pennsylvania Cavalry to prepare a history of the campaigns of that regiment.

No organization in either the regular or volunteer service enjoyed a more enviable reputation in every respect, and its services were of so valuable a character to the government that every endeavour was made by me after its muster out in 1864 to have an organization formed, the nucleus of which should be such officers and men of the original regiment as were desirous of again entering the service.

I congratulate you and the officers and men formerly connected with the 6th Pennsylvania Cavalry on the abundant pleasing material at your disposal from which to make a history.

I am, sir, very respectfully,
PHIL. H. SHERIDAN,
Major General U. S. A.

CONTENTS.

Page

CHAPTER I.—Organization—Colonel R. H. Rush receives Authority from the War Department—"Philadelphia Light Cavalry"—Companies Muſtered into the United States Service—Camp Meigs—Drilling—Flag Preſentation from the Ladies of Germantown, . . . 17

CHAPTER II.—The Lance—Street Parade—Preſentation of Regimental Standards by Governor Curtin—Speeches—Original Officers, . 26

CHAPTER III.—Off for Waſhington—Camp "Barclay"—Provoſt Duty—Sword Preſentation to Colonel Ruſh—Proſpect Hill—Mud March—Off for "Dixie"—Stormy Paſſage to Fortreſs Monroe—Hampton, 37

CHAPTER IV.—On the Peninſula—Newmarket—Yorktown—Morris's Farm—Ruffin's Farm—Reconnoiſſance—Hanover Courthouſe—Report of Colonel Ruſh—Fair Oaks—Tunſtall's Station—Stuart's Raid—Report by Colonel Ruſh, ... 43

CHAPTER V.—Cold Harbour—Fair Oaks—Beaver Dam Creek—Mechanicſville—Gaines's Mill—The Change of Baſe to James River—The Retreat—Robinſon's Battery—Savage Station—White Oak Swamp—Charles City Croſs-Roads—Glendale—Frazier's Farm, . 55

CHAPTER VI.—Malvern Hill—Reports of McClellan and Lee—Severe Fighting—July Fourth—Congratulatory Addreſs from the General Commanding—Capture of Hoſpitals—Experience in Rebel Priſons—Harriſon's Landing—Night Shelling—Adieu to the James, 72

CONTENTS.

Page

CHAPTER VII.—Through Wafhington—Into Maryland—Frederick—
South Mountain—Antietam—The Great Battle of the Fall of 1862
—Ordered to Frederick, Maryland, ... 87

CHAPTER VIII.—Pofition of the Army of the Potomac—Stuart's Raid
into Pennfylvania—The Sixth Pennfylvania fent out to Picket the
Roads to the North—Scouting Duty—The Rebel Column at Em-
mettfburg—Report of Colonel Rufh—Captain Cadwalader and his
Company near being Captured—Rebels Efcape—Army moves into
Virginia—Several Companies Rejoin the Army—Frederickfburg, . 104

CHAPTER IX.—Battle of Frederickfburg—General Hooker's Account
—General Franklin's Left Grand Divifion—General Franklin and
Meade's Reports—The Sixth as Provoft Guard of the Left Grand
Divifion—Recroffing the Rappahannock—Details from the Regi-
ment—Colonel Rufh, with Companies "B" and "G" Rejoin—They
march from Wafhington, and have a Skirmifh at Occoquan, . . 115

CHAPTER X.—A General Advance—Winter Campaign—" Burnfide's
Mud March"—Burnfide's Farewell Addrefs to the Army—Belle
Plain—The Cavalry Reviewed by Prefident Lincoln—Opening of
the Spring Campaign—Colonel Rufh leaves the Regiment and Field
Service—Major Robert Morris, Jr., ... 123

CHAPTER XI.—Stoneman's Raid—Croffing the Rappahannock—Orange
Springs—Louifa Courthoufe—A Skirmifh—Colonel Percy Wyndham—Columbia on the James—General Gregg's Expedition—Captain Lord and the Firft United States—The Fifth United States Cavalry—Thompfon's Crofs-Roads—The Return—Difmal Night Rides, 136

CHAPTER XII.—Encampments near Bealton—Morrifville and Hartwood Church—March to Brooks's Station—Dumfries—After
Guerillas—Encamped at Catlett's Station—Great Cavalry Engagement at Beverly Ford—Exciting Charge of the Sixth Pennfylvania
Cavalry, ... 153

CHAPTER XIII.—The Ninth of June—Brandy Station—Beverly Ford
—Full Reports of the Engagement—New York Herald—Philadel-

CONTENTS.

	Page
phia Evening Bulletin—New York Times—Putnam's Rebellion Record, ...	165

CHAPTER XIV.—Thoroughfare Gap—Aldie—Upperville—March into Maryland—Battle of Gettyſburg—Forced March to the Potomac—Rebel Spy—Engagement at Williamſport—Boonſboro, . . . 176

CHAPTER XV.—Engagements at Boonſboro—Funkſtown, near Hagerſtown—Our Cavalry Batteries—Operations of our Noble 100—Falling Waters—Again in "Dixie"—Wapping Heights—Brandy Station and Culpepper—Camp Buford, ... 187

CHAPTER XVI.—Major Robert Morris, Jr.—Rejoin the Army in Virginia—A Night Advance—A Fight at Briſtoe—Deſtruction of Railroad—Captain Lockwood inſide the Enemy's Lines—Guerillas at Morriſville—Murder of Lieutenant Sage—Acroſs the Rappahannock—Engaged near Culpepper, ... 197

CHAPTER XVII.—Engagement at Rappahannock Station—Mine Run Expedition—In Camp near Culpepper—Death of Major-General John Buford—Changes in Field, Staff, and Line, ... 206

CHAPTER XVIII.—Winter Quarters near Mitchell's Station—Reconnoiſſance to Robertſon's River—General Cuſter's Raid to Charlotteſville—Stormy Night Rides in Midwinter—Flight of the Contrabands, ... 221

CHAPTER XIX.—Reorganization—Spring Campaign—In the Wilderneſs—Great Flank Movement of the Army of the Potomac—Todd's Tavern—Firſt and Second Day—The Wounded—Sheridan's Raid, . 231

CHAPTER XX.—Sheridan's Raid—Captain Miller—Engagement at Yellow Tavern—Meadow Bridge—New Market—White Houſe—Mechanicſville—White Chimneys—Aylett's—Hawes's Shop—Battle at Betheſda Church, ... 241

CHAPTER XXI.—Battles at Old Church and Cold Harbour—Bottom Bridge—Raid on the Virginia Central Railroad—Battle at Trevillian Station—Return March to the White Houſe, . . . 254

CONTENTS.

Chapter XXII.—Engagement at White House—General Gregg Engaged at St. Mary's Church—March to Wilson's Wharf on James River—Wilson's Raid—Camp near Windmill Point, . . . 264

Chapter XXIII.—Feint on the Enemy's Left on the North Side of the James—Fight at Darby's House—Burnside's Mine—March to Lee's Mills—Return March to City Point and Embarkation for the Shenandoah Valley, ... 270

Chapter XXIV.—General Grant visits Hunter at Monocacy—Grant's Instructions — The Middle Military Division—Sheridan succeeds Hunter—Skirmishes at White Post and Newtown—Destruction of Baggage Train—Skirmish at Front Royal—Withdrawal to Halltown—Skirmish at Kearneysville, ... 277

Chapter XXV.—Engagements at Leetown and Smithfield—Regiment Ordered to Pleasant Valley to be Mustered Out—Death of Surgeon John B. Coover, ... 290

Chapter XXVI.—Record of Officers Mustered out in 1864, and of Promotions and Changes omitted in the Narrative, . . . 300

Chapter XXVII.—Winter Operations of the Army—The Beginning of the End—Destruction on James River—Last of Jubal Early—Charlottesville — Duguidsville—Amherst Courthouse — Arrival at White House—Rejoining the Army of the Potomac, . . . 316

Chapter XXVIII.—Reconnoissance toward Five Forks—Charge of the Regiment—Dinwiddie Courthouse—Five Forks—Last Fight of the Regiment, ... 324

Chapter XXIX.—The Pursuit and Surrender of Lee, . . . 342

Chapter XXX.—Conclusion, ... 355

ANNALS OF THE SIXTH

PENNSYLVANIA CAVALRY.

CHAPTER FIRST.

Organization—Col. R. H. Rufh receives authority from the War Department—"Philadelphia Light Cavalry"—Companies muftered into the United States Service—Camp Meigs—Drilling—Flag prefentation from the ladies of Germantown.

THE regiment whofe campaigns are here recorded was amongft the firft cavalry organizations offered for three years' fervice under the General Government. 1861. April 13th.

It will be remembered that on the 13th of April, 1861, there was announced to the world the inauguration of armed refiftance and hoftility to the authority of the United States by the attack upon Fort Sumter. Upon the performance of this overt act of rebellion, a call was iffued by the Prefident upon the loyal men of the country, to volunteer in the military fervice, to fupprefs the outbreak and fuftain the national authority.

It was at firft fuppofed that feventy-five thoufand men could eafily accomplifh this work in a fhort time;

ORGANIZATION.

1861. and that number were enrolled as a national police force for three months.

Early in their service, the rebellion assumed proportions far beyond the conception of any loyal mind, and it became evident that a much larger force must be enlisted, and for a longer period. A second call was made by the Chief Executive on the 1st day of July, 1861, for two hundred thousand troops for three years' service.

At this time, RICHARD HENRY RUSH, ESQ., of Philadelphia, a graduate of the Military Academy at West Point, and late a captain of artillery in the United States Army, offered his services to the State to raise a regiment of artillery. It was not deemed desirable, at that time, to recruit to any great extent for that arm of the service, and the proposal received no immediate response.

July 24th. On the 24th of July, an offer of his services as a grad-
July 27th. uate of the United States Military Academy, was made to the General Government at Washington, and on the 27th he received authority from the War Department to recruit, without delay, a regiment of cavalry for three years' service.

Many of the organizations that had responded to the first call of the President were now returning to their homes; and Colonel Rush, selecting from their number many who were personally known or favorably represented to him, invited their coöperation in the formation and recruiting of his regiment.

Those only were chosen for official position whose faithfulness in service already rendered, or whose education, general intelligence, social position, and moral character, gave assurance of fitness to command.

ORGANIZATION.

Early in August, rendezvous were opened in different parts of the city, with Headquarters at No. 833 Market Street, and the work of recruiting was entered upon with great vigor.

In those days but small bounties were offered—one hundred dollars only, and that payable on honorable discharge from the service. The desire of the recruit seemed to be as great to conceal his physical defects as it became in the days of the "draft" to magnify them. The war spirit was at its height, and numerous regiments for all arms of the service were recruiting at the same time, and all filling up rapidly. In despite of competition and haste, the material of the regiment was far above the average.

The first advertisements and posters announced recruiting for the "PHILADELPHIA LIGHT CAVALRY," as which the regiment was organized.

On the 15th of August, Colonel Rush received notification from Governor Curtin that he had been selected by the officers of the 1st Pennsylvania artillery regiment as their colonel, and that he would be commissioned accordingly; but, having already accepted appointment from the War Department, he declined the nomination. He was also elected Lieutenant-Colonel of the Third Pennsylvania Volunteer Regiment Infantry, Colonel Ellmaker, which was likewise declined. He was commissioned Colonel of the Sixth Pennsylvania Cavalry by Governor Curtin, with rank as such from July 27th, 1861.

On the 24th of August, Company "A" was mustered into the service of the United States by Captain John H. McArthur, Fifth United States Cavalry. W. P. C.

margin: 1861. August. Aug. 24th

1861. Treichel was muſtered as lieutenant of the company. This being the firſt troop fully formed and muſtered, it was addreſſed by Colonel Ruſh on the call of the men.

Sept. 3d.   On the 3d of September, the firſt camp of the regiment was eſtabliſhed on Second Street above Nicetown Lane, on the Logan eſtate, and was known as Camp Meigs. Companies "A" and "B" pitched their tents on this date.

Sept. 6th.   Company "G" was recruited by George E. Clymer, of Reading, Pa., who had received authority from the War Department to raiſe an independent company. It was muſtered into ſervice at Reading, on the 8th of Auguſt, by Captain W. R. Terrill, Fifth United States Artillery. In the latter part of Auguſt it was attached to the Sixth Pennſylvania Cavalry, and reported at Camp Meigs on the 6th of September. It was aſſigned its place in the regiment as Company "G."

Sept. 7th.   Diſmounted drills were commenced on the 7th, and continued each day thereafter while in this camp.

Sept. 20th.   The firſt horſes for the regiment were received on the 20th. Mounted drills began on the 25th. This attracting large numbers of viſitors from the city, it was found neceſſary to eſtabliſh a guard around the camp, to keep off the great crowds that gathered there daily, interfering with order and diſcipline, and rendering mounted drills almoſt impoſſible. Perſons were admitted to the camp on paſſes iſſued by Colonel Ruſh.

Clement C. Barclay, Eſq., took a very great intereſt in the formation of the regiment, aſſiſting in a very ſubſtantial manner. Through his influence large ſums of

money were collected to meet the neceffary expenfes of 1861.
recruiting, printing, telegraphing, renting of rendezvous,
travelling, &c., in the interefts of the regiment, and in
this connection it may be ftated that Colonel Rufh felt
greatly indebted to the active co-operation of Jofeph R.
Fry, William R. Wifter, Charles Henry Fifher, S. & W.
Welfh, and other prominent citizens.

On the 30th of October an interefting ceremony took Oct. 30th.
place at Camp Meigs, which is thus defcribed in the
Philadelphia Inquirer of Oct. 31ft:

"An interefting fcene was witneffed at Camp Meigs
yefterday, the occafion being the prefentation of a ftand
of colors, and a fet of guidons to the regiment of Philadelphia Light Cavalry. The flags were prefented by
the ladies of Germantown. At half-paft two o'clock in
the afternoon, a large number of citizens had affembled,
while vehicles of every defcription lined the road oppofite
the camp. Nearly a thoufand horfemen were drawn up
in line, and ftood with all the filence and precifion of
military difcipline. At the appointed time the regimental
band ftruck up 'Hail! Columbia!' when a committee
of ladies reprefenting the donors, left the large tent
erected for their ufe, and were efcorted to the platform,
before which the regiment was formed, one lady bearing the regimental colors, while the others carried the
guidons of red and white filk intended for the different
companies.

"When the mufic had ceafed, MR. WILLIAM ROTCH
WISTER, reprefenting the ladies, addreffed Colonel Rufh,
as follows:

1861.   "'Colonel Rufh, officers, and foldiers, of the Philadelphia Light Cavalry Regiment: The ladies of Germantown and its vicinity have requefted me, in their name, to prefent to you the ftandard and guidons which are before you. I do fo, fir, with the greateft pleafure, becaufe I have, as they have, perfect confidence that they will be faithfully and honorably maintained, and that you and your command will ftand by them, if needs be, until the laft trump founds.

"'Soldiers! You are in arms in refponfe to the call of your country. At that call you have left your peaceful avocations, your friends and your families, to defend that country and the conftitution which, for more than feventy years, has given happinefs to the people: the good name and fame of which have penetrated beyond the confines of civilization.

"'It is well, fir,—it is fitting that fuch a regiment as yours, compofed of the flower of the youth of our city and State, fhould volunteer for the defence of the country againft the ingrates and traitors that are in arms againft it.

"'Remember, foldiers, that your flag is our flag, and your caufe our caufe; and that what you may do to fuftain it in this its hour of trial, will be gratefully remembered. Bear in mind that thofe who give you your flag will anxioufly look for all reports of it, and that you carry with you their beft wifhes for your fuccefs. Their earneft prayer is that God, in His mercy, may watch over, keep and protect you; that you may one and all do your duty manfully and fearleflly; and after the rebels in arms againft us fhall have been overcome, that you may return with glory, to pafs the remainder of your lives in peace and profperity.'

"Upon the conclufion of this fpeech, the captains of the ten companies fimultaneoufly difmounted. An orderly advanced to the bridle of each horfe, while the captains, preceded by the colonel, advanced to the platform, and received from the ladies, each captain the guidon intended for his company, and the colonel the regimental ftandard.

"The captains then returned to their companies and remounted. The colonel, handing the ftandard to the regimental color-bearer, afcended the platform, and replied to Mr. Wifter as follows:

"'On behalf of the officers and men of the Philadelphia Light Cavalry, I thank you, fir, and through you the ladies of Germantown, for this gift, fo kindly and in terms fo gratifying, made to the regiment which I have the honor to command. We accept it with grateful fenfibilities and thanks. If we cannot, in the hour of trial, do all that is expected of us, we will do our beft; but I. muft requeft you not to expect too much from thofe thus willing to do their beft. It is eafy to collect men together in maffes, drefs them in uniform, and inveft them with the furroundings of military life; but it is not thus alone that foldiers are made. It is only difcipline,—regular, fteady, rigid difcipline,—which can form the foldier to be relied on in the hour of need. The difafters which have overtaken us are in a great part to be accounted for by want of this, the greateft element in military organization.

"'It will be my defire, while I am honored with this

1861. command, to give it that element of power and usefulness; but at present we are but recruits; hence I ask, in justice to the regiment, that you will not ask too much. It is to the generosity and kind interest of Philadelphians that it owes, in a great measure, the success which its friends are kind enough to say it has met with. It has not been formed under the patronage, or with the aid, of the State government. It has sprung from Philadelphia, and goes into service offered to and accepted by the General Government.

"'As the colonel of this regiment, may I be permitted to say, that it was my privilege and honor to be educated at the United States Military Academy. From the commencement of this war, I have felt that it was my duty to give all my efforts, and, if necessary, my life, to the service of my country; and I do but justice to the officers and men by whom I am surrounded, if I say that the same feeling influences them. There is, perhaps, no one who has closer ties among those who are now opposed to us in arms, than myself. But I feel, nevertheless, that the highest duty we all owe to our country, and our whole country, North and South, is to urge on the war with a wicked rebellion against our national existence until it is finally and forever crushed. As the regiment has now its preparatory orders to march, this is probably the last time we shall have the pleasure of meeting in our camp, our fellow-countrymen and countrywomen who have so often honored us with their presence, I can, therefore, only say again, sir, we will do our best. The beautiful gift of the ladies of Germantown we shall always highly value, and will strive to prove that we are not unworthy of it.'

"After this spirited and soldierly address, pronounced in a dignified and firm tone of voice, which was heard over all the field, Col. Rush returned to the front of the regiment. The regiment then went through a drill, which reflected great credit upon officers and men. The enlisted men are fine-looking, young, and athletic, and ride well. The officers are all fine horsemen, from the colonel to the youngest lieutenant, and are all men of high character and principles."

The occasion was one of great interest, and will ever be remembered with pleasure by all who were permitted to be present.

CHAPTER SECOND.

The Lance—Street Parade—Prefentation of Regimental Standards by Gov. Curtin—Speeches—Original Officers.

1861.
Nov. 30th.
IN the latter part of November, telegrams were received from Gen. Geo. B. McClellan, then commanding the Army of the Potomac, requefting that the regiment be armed with the lance, and to be ufed for fuch duty as belongs to that arm of the fervice. This was the firft fuggeftion in reference to the lance being placed in the hands of the regiment, and coming from the commanding General of the forces in the Eaft, affent was willingly given to be thus armed and ufed.

The weapon being entirely new in our fervice, great attention was given to the felection of pattern and the manufacture, as will appear in the report of Col. Rufh, hereafter.

The firft iffue was made to the command on the 30th of November.

Dec. 4th.
The regiment paraded on the ftreets of Philadelphia on the 4th of December, exciting great intereft. This was one of the fineft cavalry difplays ever witneffed in this city, and the only time that a regiment of LANCERS was ever feen on its ftreets. The lance being new and highly burnifhed; the fcarlet pennon bright and attrac-

tive; the new uniform, and the tidy appearance of men and horses, all combined to render it a brilliant and impofing pageant.

1861.

The prefentation of the State colors to the regiment took place this day. Great preparations had been made to render the occafion one of great intereft to the citizens of Philadelphia. Five regiments, all nearly filled and ready to march to the feat of war, paraded on the occafion, and received their regimental ftandards. The occurrence is thus defcribed in one of the city papers:

Dec. 6th.

"Summer feemed to have revived yefterday, as if for the exprefs purpofe of allowing our citizens to witnefs a grand military difplay under a clear fky, and in a balmy air. The announcement, which appeared in the *Inquirer* of yefterday, that five regiments would be prefent to receive their colors from Governor Curtin, attracted an immenfe crowd to the fpot defignated, which was a large field near the Odd Fellows Cemetery, on Iflington Lane, containing about ten acres.

"It was neceffary to ftation a large force of policemen around this field, to keep back the immenfe crowd there gathered. On the north fide, near Iflington Lane, a platform was erected, fufficiently elevated to command a fine view of the entire field: this was for the Governor and other diftinguifhed vifitors. The fpectators arranged themfelves along the lane, filled the fteps of the entrance to the Cemetery, and furrounding the entire field, occupied every available pofition within view of the ftand.

"About 3 o'clock, the head of the cavalry regiment, commanded by Col. Rufh, appeared in the diftance, preceded by their full band. The regiment turned into the

1861.
Dec. 6th.
field, and affumed pofition in line facing the ftand. Soon after the infantry regiments arrived, thofe of Col. Staunton, Col. Gregory, and Col. Jones, having bands. The regiments then formed in the following order, preparatory to the arrival of the Governor and his ftaff:

91ft Penn. Volunteer Infantry, Col. Gregory.
90th   "   "   "   Col. Lyle.
67th   "   "   "   Col. Staunton.
58th   "   "   "   Col. Jones.
70th   "   "   6th Cavalry, Col. Rufh.

"Governor Curtin came upon the ground in an open barouche. He was accompanied by his ftaff, and a number of invited guefts from Harrifburg, and other parts of the State. Among them were the following Pennfylvanians: Col. Ruffell, of Pittfburg, Col. Biddle, of Philadelphia, Col. Parker, of Carlifle, and Col. Potts, of Harrifburg, ftaff; Gen. Keim; Gen. Irvin, Commiffary Department; Gen. Hall, Quartermafter; Gen. Bart. Shaffer; Capt. Anderfon, 1ft Cavalry; S. B. Thomas, Deputy Secretary of State; Col. Meredith, commanding Camp Curtin, and O. W. Lee, of Harrifburg. The following citizens of Philadelphia were alfo on the platform: Maj. Gen. Patterfon, Brig. Gen. Frank Patterfon, Morton McMichael, Efq.; the State Society of Cincinnati, compofed of feven members, each wearing a blue rofette; Mrs. Col. Rufh, and other ladies. On the left of the platform were the mounted aids of Gen. Patterfon, and on the right were Gen. Pleafonton and ftaff, and other officers of the Home Guard organizations.

"The flags, confifting of the regimental ftandards for

each regiment, and a number of guidons for the cavalry, were placed in front of the platform, unfurled. The troops were then closed, *en masse*, in front of the platform, and were addressed in the following very appropriate speech by Governor Curtin:

1861. Dec. 6th.

"'I appear before you in obedience to law, to present to you before your departure in the service of your country, the regimental standards provided by the State. The duty is not new to me, nor have I grown weary from its frequent performance.

"'It is always impressive to contemplate the separation of our friends and fellow-citizens from their homes, but all the feelings which such occasions excite are intensified when those about to leave are under arms, and prepared to encounter the vicissitudes and trials of actual war. We are, in Pennsylvania, truly a peaceful people. Our genial climate, our geographical position, and our vast material resources, have led us to cultivate those arts and occupations, and those relations of social life, which are not in harmony with military discipline and pursuits, or with antagonisms or hostilities.

"'Having scarcely a military organization in the State, and our citizens having had no expectation of an attempt being made to disturb the Nation; and as we were at peace with all the world, this rebellion found us, in a measure, without military preparation. But we have what is infinitely better than mere military training: a loyal people devoted to the Government, and ready, at any moment, to take up arms in its defence.'

"He then traced the causes leading to the rebellion,

1861.
Dec. 6th.
and the necessity resting upon the Executive, and the several States, to put forth every effort for its immediate suppression. 'You go to vindicate the history of the past, and make that of the present. And as you shall save our great Government from destruction, to insure a still brighter page for its future, that liberty, civilization, and Christianity, may continue to grow and spread in all the world. All mankind have an interest in your success; all loyal men will give you countenance and support; and all good men will send up their constant prayers for your prosperity and ultimate victory. Thousands and tens of thousands of your fellow-citizens at home, will watch your progress from every part of this great Commonwealth; from all its homes and its firesides; from the family altar of the high and the low, the rich and the poor, will go up supplications in the evening and the morning, that the God of battles may strengthen and protect you by His almighty power.' . . . . .

" 'It is the duty of all good and true men to maintain legitimate authority independent of difference of opinion or personal relations. It is for the maintenance of the Constitution and the Government, and for the support of its duly constituted agents in the discharge of their duty, that you have taken up arms. It is for this that thousands have gone before you, and thousands will follow as demands are made by the Government, until peace and order prevail throughout the land, and the Government established by our fathers, and under which we have been blessed with so many years of prosperity, shall be re-established in all its original power. It is our duty to transmit to our posterity the precious legacy given to us by our fathers perfect and unimpaired. Under it we have enjoyed seventy-three years of continued enlargement and prosperity, of national power, and individual happiness. If you, and the brave men associated with you, shall re-establish and maintain it, future generations will rise up and call you blessed. .... And it is in perfect harmony with all the proceedings of the day and the occasion, as with the memories and traditions of the past, that we are honored by the presence of the remnant of the members of the "Society of Cincinnati," an association established by the immortal WASHINGTON himself, and which constitutes a link between the living and the dead, the present and the past; the dawn of liberty in the world, and the perfect unity of all good men to maintain it against the combination of bad men to destroy it.

1861. Dec. 6th.

"'The Society of Cincinnati, early in this struggle, presented me with a sum of money to be used at my discretion in arming and equipping the volunteers of the State. The subject was referred to me by the Legislature, then in session; they directed me to procure and present standards to the volunteers as they passed into the service of the United States.

"'And now, as representing the people of the State, I pray that that Providence, which has so long upheld this generation, may maintain and support you in the contest in which you are about to engage, and shield you by His divine power, that you may safely return to your friends and families.'

"During the address of Governor Curtin, the colo-

1861.
Dec. 6th.
nels of the different regiments took a position in front of the stand. They were all mounted. The five regimental standards were then unfurled and placed in the hands of the colonels, who, upon receiving them, passed them to their respective color guards, and responded in short speeches to the Governor. Col. Rush, being the first, spoke as follows:

"'GOVERNOR: On behalf of the officers and men of the 6th Pennsylvania cavalry regiment, I thank you, and through you, the Society of Cincinnati, to whose liberality we partially owe these colors, and to the people of the State of Pennsylvania. We have heard the eloquent, patriotic sentiments you have uttered. You have expressed the hope that these colors will be restored to the State, in accordance with the law, unstained and unsullied, with the promise that those actions in which it may be the good fortune of my regiment to distinguish itself shall be engraved upon the colors. I trust this hope will not be misplaced. I trust that the regiment will be worthy of the wishes expressed for it in anticipation. Nevertheless, I may be pardoned in saying that time is required to complete the thorough organization of a regiment of cavalry. The combination of horse and rider is a difficult task, and requires much training on the part of the soldier. If we do not, at an early day, give good account of ourselves in field service, due allowance should be made, and we not be judged too severely. In time we hope to be able to show success. In behalf of the officers and men of my regiment, I again thank you.'

"He was followed by the other regimental commanders in appropriate speeches; at the conclusion of which the whole force was reviewed by the Governor. 1861. Dec. 6th.

It is estimated that there were not less than twenty thousand persons present.

The following report was made to General Stoneman, commanding the Cavalry Corps of the Army of the Potomac, in response to a circular from him calling for information in reference to the "organization of the regiment, and everything giving information that may lead to the improvement of the cavalry arm of the service," presents a brief *résumé* of our early history:

"HEADQUARTERS SIXTH PENN'A CAVALRY,
CAMP NEAR WHITE OAK CHURCH, VA., Feb. 27th, 1863.

"GENERAL:

"In compliance with your communication of January 24th, I have the honor to submit the following report:

"This regiment was raised by authority given to me by the War Department, on the 27th of July, 1861, and was to consist of ten companies, or troops; but as the plan proposed was to clothe, equip, and mount the regiment in Philadelphia, before it should be reported ready for service, there was considerable delay in procuring necessary orders to accomplish it, and it was not until August 18th, that the full authority asked for was granted, and a general recruiting station and barracks were hired in Philadelphia. By this delay much good material was lost, which would have been secured from regiments of the three months' service, that had just disbanded. In the formation of the first companies, many recruits were lost from the fact that we were not permitted to muster them into service until a first lieutenant's command was recruited; the result of which was, that for every man mustered at least two were enrolled; as proof of which two hundred names were enrolled for the ninety-two mustered in as the first company. This difficulty was afterwards removed, and the men were mustered in as fast as the defective system adopted by the United States mustering officers would permit. Had this been less imperfect, the regiment would have been raised much sooner than it was. In consequence of the privileges given by the Department, the com-

1861.
Dec. 6th.
panies were each, with but little delay, fupplied with clothing, camp, and garrifon equipage, from the United States depot in Philadelphia, as foon as the minimum number was raifed. A camp of inftruction was formed about three miles from Philadelphia. The firft four companies encamped on the 3d of September, 1861; the tenth company went into camp in November. The arms and horfe equipments were furnifhed from the Frankford arfenal, and the horfes by the Quartermafter in Philadelphia, as rapidly as they were required for, except towards the completion of the regiment. The complete equipment of the regiment, before leaving Philadelphia, had been announced in the advertifements and pofters as part of the programme of its organization; and as many regiments had been hurried off unarmed and unclothed, this was confidered a great inducement. When the fuccefs of the regiment feemed fure, numerous companies, already organized and officered, under the State militia fyftem of election, were offered; and by the time the tenth company was completed, fuch applications to the number of fifteen were made; but all refufed, the regiment being officered in a very different way. One exception, however, was made in favor of a company from Reading, raifed by Captain George Clymer, who was one of the original appointees in the interval between the firft authority given me by the Department, July 27th, and the full authority given Auguft 18th, as before mentioned, he having received authority direct from the War Department to recruit an independent company. The regiment was recruited under the name of the 'Philadelphia Light Cavalry,' and was to be armed with fabre and piftol, but at the fuggeftion and requeft of Major General George B. McClellan, then commanding the Army of the Potomac, the lance was adopted, and added to thefe weapons. The piftols were Colt's army fize; the fabres were the light cavalry, but defective in temper, and, I think, of objectionable pattern. The lance being a new weapon to our fervice, and the Department having none to iffue, a careful ftudy of the weapons, as ufed in foreign fervice, was neceffary, and great attention was paid to their manufacture. Valuable advice and affiftance in this matter was received from the Duc de Chartres, Compte de Paris, and Major Von Hammerftein, all then on General McClellan's ftaff, and refulted in the adoption of the Auftrian pattern. It is about nine feet long, with an eleven inch three-edged blade; the ftaff is of Norway fir, about one and a quarter inches in diameter, with ferule and counterpoife at the heel; the whole weighing four pounds thirteen ounces, with a fcarlet fwallow-tailed pennon. They were furnifhed by the Ordnance Department, under contracts which they made from patterns fubmitted by me.

REPORT OF COLONEL RUSH.

1861.
Dec. 6th.

Experience in their ufe has fuggefted improvements in their pattern. By the ufe of hickory, the ftaff might be made lighter with equal ftrength, and the blade of the pattern of the bayonet would alfo decreafe the weight. The regiment places all confidence in this weapon, if applied to its legitimate ufe, and only regrets that an opportunity has not offered which would enable them to fhow that this confidence is not mifplaced. Recently twelve carbines to a company has been added to the armament, the neceffity for which has been proven by the large amount of picket and fcout duty which the regiment has been required to perform. The officering of the regiment, which is the all-important part of its organization, was as follows: The appointments were made chiefly upon invitation from myfelf, and the appointees were felected from men whofe pofition in life, previous character, and education, would infure difcipline in camp, courage and judgment in the field, a good example to the men, and a careful execution of the many refponfibilities of their feveral offices. Towards the clofe of the organization of the regiment, applications for pofition were very numerous, and many, well fitted for, but who could not obtain office, enlifted in the ranks. Many of the officers had already feen fervice in the three months' volunteers. The Quartermafter of the regiment had formerly been Quartermafter-Sergeant of the 2d U. S. Cavalry, and by his experience and judgment, rendered the moft valuable affiftance. He has fince become an officer in the 5th U. S. Cavalry,— Captain Maley. By this plan of officering, there was no connection between the officers and the men, no affiliations whatever, and no relations but thofe incident to military fervice. The lift of officers was nearly filled before the Central Recruiting Station was opened, and the whole force was ufed to recruit the firft company, and each fucceffive company had the fervices of the remaining officers. This was rather unfavorable to the laft companies, but they had the advantage of the fact that the exiftence and equipment of the regiment was eftablifhed. In November, the regiment was ordered to report to the Governor of the State of Pennfylvania, and received the defignation of the Seventieth Pennfylvania Volunteers, or Sixth Pennfylvania Cavalry. Between the 5th and 16th of December, the regiment, nine hundred and twenty ftrong, moved to Wafhington, and encamped on Meridian Hill, where it remained during the winter, going through fuch drilling as the unfavorable ftate of the weather and ground would permit.

ORIGINAL OFFICERS.

"The regiment being fully organized, armed, equipped, and mounted,

1861.
Dec. 6th.
awaited marching orders. At this time the officers of the regiment were as follows:

FIELD AND STAFF.

Colonel—Richard Henry Ruſh.
Lieutenant-Colonel—John H. McArthur.
Firſt Major—C. Roſs Smith.
Second Major—Robert Morris, Jr.
Adjutant—1ſt Lieut. F. C. Newhall.
Surgeon—William Moſs.
Aſſiſtant Surgeon—Charles M. Ellis.
Quartermaſter—Thomas E. Maley.
Chaplain—Waſhington B. Erben.

LINE OFFICERS.

A.

Captain—W. P. C. Treichel.
1ſt Lieut.—H. P. Muirheid.
2d Lieut.—J. Newton Dickſon.

B.

Captain—John H. Gardiner.
1ſt Lieut.—R. Walſh Mitchell.
2d Lieut.—W. W. Frazier.

C.

Captain—H. C. Whelan.
1ſt Lieut.—Charles L. Leiper.
2d Lieut.—Edwin L. Tevis.

D.

Captain—Joſeph Wright.
1ſt Lieut.—Samuel Hazzard, Jr.
2d Lieut.—Emlen N. Carpenter.

E.

Captain—J. Henry Hazeltine.
1ſt Lieut.—G. Irvine Whitehead.
2d Lieut.—Charles B. Davis.

F.

Captain—Robert Milligan.
1ſt Lieut.—Charles E. Richards.
2d Lieut.—J. Hinckley Clark.

G.

Captain—George E. Clymer.
1ſt Lieut.—Auguſtus Bertolette.
2d Lieut.— —— Call.

H.

Captain—Benoni Lockwood.
1ſt Lieut.—Chas. E. Cadwalader.
2d Lieut.—Wm. Odenheimer.

I.

Captain—James Starr.
1ſt Lieut.—Oſwald Jackſon.
2d Lieut.—Frank Furneſs.

K.

Captain—Howard Ellis.
1ſt Lieut.—John W. Williams.
2d Lieut.—Thomas W. Neill.

CHAPTER THIRD.

Off for Waſhington—Camp "Barclay"—Provoſt Duty—Sword Preſentation to Colonel Ruſh—Proſpect Hill—Mud March—Off for "Dixie"—Stormy Paſſage to Fortreſs Monroe—Hampton.

COMPANIES "A" and "B," and "C" and "F," 1861. under command of Lieutenant-Colonel McAr- Dec. 10th. thur, left Camp Meigs on the 10th, and marched to the Baltimore Depot, where they packed camp and garriſon equipage and horſes into cars provided for their conveyance, and at 8 P.M. ſtarted for Waſhington. At 7 o'clock on the morning of the 11th, they arrived at Baltimore, and after breakfaſting at the "Soldiers' Refreſhment Saloon," near the Baltimore and Ohio Railroad Depot, took cars again, and arrived at Waſhington about noon. Meals were taken at the "Soldiers' Reſt," where they remained until the following morning, when they eſtabliſhed camp out Fourteenth Street, near Columbia College, on Meridian Hill.

Four more companies joined them on the 14th. Col- Dec. 14th. onel Ruſh, with the balance of the regiment, arrived on the 16th. This encampment was called, in honor of our faithful Philadelphia friend, CAMP BARCLAY, and

1861. was about three miles north of the city. The place was
December. not unfavorable to health, compared with the furrounding country, though two circumſtances combined to counteract its natural advantages: 1ſt. Our camp was pitched on a ſpot juſt vacated by another cavalry regiment that had occupied it for ſeveral months; 2dly. A ſucceſſion of heavy rains converted our entire camping and parade ground into a deep clayey bog, in which the horſes ſank to their knees, and through which the men muſt wade in paſſing about the camp. This neceſſitated ſuch conſtant labor to ſecure proper drainage, that many of the command were unavoidably expoſed to the ſeverity of the weather, and much ſickneſs reſulted.

On the 20th, the regiment was inſpected and reviewed by General Stoneman, Chief of Cavalry of the Army of the Potomac.

1862. The regiment paraded through Waſhington City, attracting great attention, on the 1ſt of January.

Jan. 8th. Company "B" was placed on Provoſt duty in the city, where it remained with Company "A," ſent in the day following, interchanging with each other on duty until the 12th, when both companies were placed on this duty.

Feb. 5th. Companies "A" and "B" returned to camp on the 5th of February, being relieved from duty in the city by the 4th Pennſylvania Cavalry.

Feb. 6th. On Thurſday, the 6th, the monotony of camp life was varied by the intereſting ceremony of a ſword preſentation to Colonel Ruſh, by the non-commiſſioned officers of the regiment.

The ſword was one of the fineſt of Philadelphia work-

SWORD PRESENTATION. 39

manſhip, and was richly ornamented on the blade with beautiful deſigns and mottoes of ſterling patriotiſm. The grip is of ſolid ſilver, bound with gold lace; leaves of gold adorn the ſheath, and the initials "R. H. R." in raiſed ſilver, with the inſcription, "Preſented to Colonel R. H. Ruſh, of the Philadelphia Light Cavalry, by the non-commiſſioned officers of his regiment."

1862.

The men preſenting the weapon formed on the parade ground, and marched to the Colonel's headquarters, preceded by the regimental band. On arriving there the Sergeant-Major, Eugene P. Bertrand, made a neat preſentation ſpeech. The Colonel replied in his uſual happy manner. After muſic by the band, other officers were called upon, and ſhort ſpeeches were made by Lieutenant-Colonel McArthur, and Majors Smith and Morris.

Mrs. Harris, of Philadelphia, viſited our hoſpitals to-day, bringing pillows, bed-quilts, blankets, and other hoſpital comforts and luxuries, ſent by kind friends for the ſick of the regiment.

Feb. 18th.

In the Philadelphia papers of the 19th, appeared the following item, taken from communications ſent them in reference to the matter then mentioned.

Feb. 19th.

"We are requeſted, on behalf of the officers and men of Colonel Ruſh's regiment of Lancers, to offer their thanks to the ladies and gentlemen of Philadelphia, who ſo generouſly contributed the funds neceſſary to purchaſe the new pennons for their lances. Theſe, one thouſand in number, of ſcarlet cloth, have been finiſhed with great neatneſs, and reflect great credit upon the taſte of

1862. the donors. They were much needed, and thankfully received."

About the 8th of March, the fick of the command were transferred to permanent hofpitals in the city, and arrangements were made for a fhare in the active efforts of the approaching Spring campaign.

Mar. 10th. On the 10th, the effective men of the regiment, under orders from General McClellan, ftarted from Camp Barclay, to take pofition with the Army of the Potomac, then lying near Manaffas. The regiment prefented a fine appearance as, with colors flying, and band playing, they paffed through the city, and ftarted out for active fervice. The men were in buoyant fpirits as they bid farewell to winter quarters, and took the field for earneft work.

As they croffed Chain Bridge and paffed to the Virginia fide, the band, riding in the advance, ftruck up "Dixie's Land," exciting great enthufiafm among the troops. We marched out fome ten miles on the road to Manaffas, halting at Profpect Hill, Virginia, where we reported to General Keyes, then commanding the 4th corps, on the right of the army. We were engaged in fcouting to Hunter's Mills and vicinity.

Mar. 15th. On the 15th, a large part of the army moved back toward Alexandria, and our regiment, with General Keyes' corps, marched to near Chain Bridge, moving all day through wretched roads, and encamped at night in a denfe pine wood. During the night it rained heavily, and continued the entire day of the 16th. We remained in our uncomfortable bivouac, unfheltered from the

severe storm, which prevailed without intermission, all   1862.
day. Early in the evening, the men disposed themselves   Mar. 16th.
for rest around large fires, and under their gum blankets
had settled themselves for the night, when about 9 o'clock
they were aroused by the bugles sounding "boots and
saddles." The regiment was soon in the saddle, and in
line of march, in the heaviest storm and worst roads
through which they had ever marched,—passing over
Chain Bridge, through the city, to Camp Barclay again,
where they were rejoiced to find tents still standing, and
dry shelter awaiting them.

This being our first trip to "Dixie," was a very rough
introduction to field service, and has been remembered
in the regiment as the Prospect Hill "Mud March."

We left Camp Barclay finally, about 10 o'clock on   Mar. 30th.
the morning of the 30th. Crossing Long Bridge, we
marched to Alexandria, and encamped near Fort Ells-
worth. Since the 15th, a large portion of the army had
embarked from this point, on transports, for Fortress
Monroe. We were here encamped four days, awaiting
conveyance for the regiment.

On the 3d, we embarked at Alexandria. Seventeen   April 3d.
schooners and several steam tugs were required to con-
vey the command. An easterly storm of great violence
broke upon us when out but a short time, which scattered our fleet most effectually. Several of the vessels
sailed as far as Acquia Creek, where they put in at 8 P.M.
on the 4th. They left this anchorage about sunrise on
the 5th, and made about twelve hours' sail to St. Mary's

1862. Harbor. On the 6th, we left St. Mary's, and failed to Fortrefs Monroe, where we anchored at 9½ P.M.

The fchooner conveying Company "A," grounded near the Fort; her anchor chain parted, rudder broke, and becoming unmanageable, the Government fteam tug "Tempeft" was fent to her affiftance. A heavy north-eaft ftorm prevailing all night and the following day, it was found impoffible to effect a landing. For feveral days they were compelled to remain in their uncomfortable quarters, and were heartily thankful when difembarked on the 10th. After feeding horfes, and diftributing rations, they ftarted in fearch of the companies that had previoufly landed. A part of the regiment was found encamped near the ruins of the once beautiful little town of Hampton, where Colonel Rufh, with the headquarters and balance of the regiment, arrived on the 12th.

April 13th. On the 13th, we moved about four miles to Newmarket Bridge, where we eftablifhed our camp, and while here, we were brigaded with the 8th Pennfylvania Cavalry.

CHAPTER FOURTH.

On the Peninsula—Newmarket—Yorktown—Morris's Farm —Ruffin's Farm—Reconnoissance—Hanover Court-house— Report of Colonel Rush—Fair Oaks—Tunstall's Station— Stuart's Raid—Report by Colonel Rush.

MARCHED to Yorktown, where we went into camp. On the 5th, one squadron was sent, under Major Morris, to Mulberry Point, on the James River, on a reconnoissance. On the evening of the 6th, tidings were received of disaster to General Hooker's command at Williamsburg, and orders to hold the regiment in readiness to move at a moment's notice. We saddled up and "stood to horse," all night, in a drenching rain. At daylight we unsaddled, picketed the horses, and re-established our camp. We remained in this vicinity, engaged in picket and scout duty, until the 9th, when we left for Yorktown, to join General Emory's brigade, of which we had formed part since March 29th. This was the second brigade of the Cavalry Division commanded by Brigadier General Philip St. George Cooke, and was known as the "Reserve Brigade," composed of the 5th and 6th United States, and 6th Pennsylvania Cavalry Regiments.

1862.
May 4th.
May 5th.

Our march on the 11th was impeded by wagon trains,

1862. which completely filled the roads, and after moving a short distance, we halted, and bivouacked for the night. Reveille sounded at 3 o'clock on the morning of the 12th, and we again started; the roads being clear, we made a good march, and near night joined the brigade at Barnsville.

May 13th. Moved to near Cumberland, where we halted until the 15th, when we marched all day, and encamped at night upon a farm belonging to Captain Morris, of the rebel army. On the 17th, we left Morris's farm, and marched to within two miles of the White House, and encamped in a field belonging to the Washington estate.

May 18th. Moved to the Richmond and York River Railroad. On the 20th, we marched about six miles, and encamped on Ruffin's farm, near the Pamunkey River, and five miles from Tunstall's Station. On the day following, after marching some ten miles, we received instructions to make a reconnoissance towards Richmond, with a view of capturing a body of rebel cavalry, said to be hovering about the right flank of our army. We found no indication of their presence in that direction, and we returned to the brigade after a march of twenty miles.

May 22d. To-day, by order of General McClellan, we were detached from the Reserve Brigade. Marched seven miles, and encamped near Old Church. Companies "A," "B," "E," "F," "G," and "K," were placed on picket duty near Newcastle and Piping Tree Ferry.

May 23d. Made a reconnoissance with the 1st Connecticut Heavy Artillery and 5th New York Infantry (Colonel Duryea's Zouaves), all under command of Colonel Warren. We found indications of the presence of the enemy, and

according to orders deſtroyed the bridges on the Pamun- 1862.
key. On the 24th, we moved cautiouſly forward toward
Hanover Court-houſe, where we diſcovered the enemy
in force, which we reported to General Fitz John Porter, and awaited orders.

On the 25th, the Fifth Corps advanced to Hanover May 25th.
Court-houſe, our regiment accompanying. Lieutenant
Leiper, in command of Company "C," charged the advance cavalry picket of the enemy with the lance, and
drove them precipitately upon their infantry ſupport,
when the company was withdrawn without being followed or attacked.

The battle of Hanover Court-houſe occurred on the May 27th.
27th. It had been learned by reconnoiſſance, that the
enemy were in ſtrong force near the Court-houſe, threatening the right of our army, and General Fitz John
Porter was ſent out to clear the way in that direction for
the further advance of our army. General Emory firſt
became engaged with the enemy about noon; reinforcements arrived promptly upon the field, and our whole
line ſteadily advanced upon the enemy, driving them
from one poſition to another, until they were totally defeated. Their camps fell into our hands, with one piece
of artillery, caiſſons, a large number of arms, and two
trains of cars filled with ſtores and quartermaſter's
property.

The loſs of the enemy was eſtimated in killed, 200;
wounded and priſoners, 730. Our loſs did not exceed
50 killed, and 300 wounded and miſſing.

This expedition diſlodged the enemy from our right,

1862. and cut off direct communication from the rebel capital, by railroad, with Frederickſburg and Gordonſville, and was regarded as ably conducted, and reflecting great credit upon the officers commanding.

This was the firſt engagement in which any part of our regiment was recognized as being a participant, and is ſo mentioned in the report of Colonel Ruſh to Governor Curtin.

May 27th. The 6th regiment was ſent on the extreme right of the advance, and by its active demonſtrations in that quarter, ſerved to diſtract the attention of the enemy from our main infantry column. We were under fire much of the day, but no opportunity offered for the regiment to be uſed in the charge. We moved forward to Hanover Court-houſe, thence to a bridge croſſing the Pamunkey River, which we completely deſtroyed. On this purſuit we captured a large number of priſoners. Reports were received of heavy reinforcements to the enemy, and a ſevere engagement going on, and at 6 o'clock P.M. orders were received to return. We rejoined our infantry late in the evening, and bivouacked in a large wheat field, two miles from Hanover Court-houſe. During the day Lieutenant J. N. Dickſon, commanding the advance guard, confiſting of Company "A," ſucceeded in capturing a company of North Carolina infantry of ſixty men, with their officers. Private Brady, of Company "A," captured a rebel officer in a bold and daring manner.

The following report was made to Governor Curtin, of the operations of the regiment about this date:

REPORT OF COLONEL RUSH. 47

"HEADQUARTERS SIXTH PENN'A CAVALRY, 1862.
NEW BRIDGE, VA., May 31st, 1862. May.

" *To his Excellency A. G. Curtin, Governor of the State of Pennsylvania:*

"I have the honor to report to you, as Governor of the State of Pennsylvania, the active duty my regiment has been doing, knowing you would like to learn what all your Pennsylvania regiments, in the Army of the Potomac, are doing in the way of active service.

"We were detached from the Reserve Brigade of Cavalry on the 22d of May, by order of General McClellan, to make a reconnoissance along the Pamunkey River, from Piping Tree Ferry to Hanover Town Ferry. We had three squadrons on picket at these ferries, the balance of the regiment was used for scouting. We found on the 23d instant, the enemy were very strong at Hanover Court-house, and immediately sent word to General Porter, upon which information General Porter ordered us to destroy the ferries and bridges along the Pamunkey, which the squadrons picketed along the river instantly did. On the morning of the 24th, the squadrons that were on picket were ordered to move towards Hanover Court-house, and feel the enemy, which we did at daybreak, and found their first pickets about five miles from the Court-house, which our advance guard drove in, as well as their other pickets, to within three miles of Hanover Court-house, where they found the enemy were in such strong numbers they halted, and finally returned to the regiment. This information was immediately conveyed to General Porter, who concluded to send a force to capture them, if possible.

"On the morning of the 27th, we marched towards Hanover Court-house on the right to attract the enemy's attention, while General Porter brought up his force on the left and rear, the success of which you, of course, know.

"The regiment was under fire here for the first time, and all the officers and men behaved most gallantly. We followed up the retreat of the enemy, and captured eighty men and two commissioned officers, and also burned the bridge on the Pamunkey to the rear of Hanover Court-house.

"On the morning of the 30th, we were ordered to send three squadrons to make a reconnoissance towards Ashland, and burn the railroad bridge at that place, if the enemy were not too strong. We found several of their cavalry pickets on the road, which retired before us. We captured eight men and horses belonging to the 4th Virginia Cavalry, and entered Ashland without any resistance, the enemy having left for Richmond by railroad the night

1862. before. We burned the railroad bridge here as directed, and returned to our camp, where we found orders to move to New Bridge, and join the Reserve Brigade of Cavalry. This ten days' scout was a very hard one, though we lost no men. Thirty-four horses were killed or maimed.

"R. H. Rush,
"Colonel Commanding Lancers."

May 30th. Our force was pushed forward to Fair Oaks, and the south side of the Chickahominy was held as follows: Casey's Division was on the right of the Williamsburg road, at right angles to it, the centre at Fair Oaks; Couch's Division at the Seven Pines; Kearney's Division on the railroad from near Savage Station towards the river; Hooker's Division was on the borders of the White Oak Swamp. The rivers being greatly swollen by heavy rains, and the roads being very muddy and difficult to traverse, it was regarded by the enemy as a favorable period for attack, and they hoped to be able to capture or destroy that part of the army thus apparently cut off from the main force by the rapidly rising streams. They attacked Casey's Division with an overwhelming force: he was driven back, and his position taken by the enemy. A very heavy engagement was brought on, and our whole force fought most desperately. Though Casey suffered disastrously, other troops, in other parts of the field, were engaged with better success; and under cover of the night, the enemy fell back to their

June 1st. position of the morning. The rebels advanced early the next morning, and after a very severe contest, were defeated and driven back beyond their first position of the previous day. Our troops pushed rapidly forward until they gained the whole field, and the camps of the enemy in part, recovering our own wounded, and capturing those of the enemy.

On the 1st day of June, we were sent on the extreme right of the army, and were slightly engaged during the day. Early on the following morning, June 2d, the regiment was sent on picket and scout duty to Old Church, and Newcastle, Bassett's, and Piping Tree Ferries. Heard heavy musketry firing on the left of our line all day. Our pickets were withdrawn during the night, and the next morning reveille sounded at 3 o'clock. We prepared breakfast, fed our horses, saddled up, and moved by daylight. Marched about four miles, when we rejoined the brigade. The whole force was soon drawn up in line of battle, in which position we remained undisturbed until 5 o'clock in the afternoon, when we bivouacked for the night.

On the 4th, we established camp on Johnson's Farm, where we remained in quietness, and enjoying rest, until the 10th, when two squadrons, consisting of Companies "A" and "K," "H" and "I," under command of Major Morris, were sent out on a reconnoissance. They moved toward Hanover Court-house, and halted at night, after a fatiguing march, at the Richmond and Hanover Cross-Roads. They were on the road again at daylight on the morning of the 11th, scouring the country as far as Hanover Court-house, but finding nothing of importance, and capturing a few prisoners, they began the march back, and rejoined the command near morning. The regiment took its regular tour of picket duty, although not armed for that service. On the morning of the 13th, rumors were circulated of an

1862. attack upon "Tunstall's Station," in our rear. Two squadrons of 5th United States Cavalry, under command of Captain Royal, stationed near Old Church, were attacked by an overwhelming force of the enemy, numbering about fifteen hundred men, with four pieces of artillery. They were reported as moving toward the White House, where we had large quantities of stores and shipping. The regiment, save one squadron that re-
June 13th. mained on picket, was sent in pursuit of this force of rebel cavalry, now making the first great raid of the war, and being conducted by General J. E. B. Stuart, to the rear of, and, eventually, entirely around our army. We were in the saddle about noon, and marched all the afternoon and night, not halting but for a few minutes until daylight of the 14th, when we arrived at Tunstall's Station. Here we found evidences of his presence, in a general destruction of cars, wagon trains, sutler's, and commissary stores, and all Government property accumulated at the station. We here learned that when the enemy arrived at Tunstall's Station, a portion of them dismounted, and awaited the arrival of an up train, upon which they fired, killing one man, and wounding several others. The engineer, instead of halting on such a peremptory and unusual summons, crowded on all steam, and ran rapidly beyond range, thus escaping with many men, and a large train of valuable stores. The rebels then being greatly incensed at their failure, burned the station house, and several cars loaded with grain, &c.; tore up a portion of the track, and secreting themselves, awaited the arrival of another train. The Third Brigade of the Pennsylvania Reserve Corps arrived at the

ſtation in time to prevent the accompliſhment of their deſign, as they fled at the approach of the Reſerves. The purſuit was continued from this point by the cavalry only, being conducted by Generals Cook and Emory, and was not regarded as being very well managed. A general ſearch for the enemy followed, mounted troops being ſent in all directions. Major Morris, in charge of the advance of our regiment, under Captains Whelan and Starr, preſſed cloſely upon the enemy as they approached the Chickahominy, and were the only troops that enjoyed the ſatisfaction of firing upon the retreating foe. We were prevented following them farther by the deſtruction of the bridge over which they had juſt croſſed. In a very intereſting account of this raid, publiſhed in the "Edinburgh Review," and written by Baron Van Brock, chief of ſtaff for General Stuart, who accompanied him on the expedition, occurs, near its cloſe, this alluſion to the ſhare our regiment took in the purſuit:

"The rear guard, under Colonel W. H. F. Lee, had meanwhile moved down ſteadily from the high ground, and defiled acroſs the bridge. The hoofs clattered on the haſty ſtructure; the head of the column was turned toward the ford beyond; the laſt ſquadron had juſt paſſed, and the bridge was being deſtroyed, when ſhots reſounded on the oppoſite bank of the ſtream, and Colonel Ruſh thundered down with his 'Lancers' to the bank. He was exactly ten minutes too late. Stuart was over with his artillery, and the ſwollen ſtream barred the way, even if Colonel Ruſh had thought it prudent to 'knock up againſt' the one thouſand five hundred crack

1862. cavalry of Stuart. His men banged away at Colonel
June. Lee, and a parting falute whizzed through the trees as
the gray column flowly difappeared. A lady of New
Kent afterwards told me that Colonel Rufh ftopped at
her houfe on his return, looking weary, broken down,
and mad. When fhe afked him if he had 'caught Stuart,'
he replied, 'No: he has gone in at the back door;
I only faw his rear guard as it paffed the fwamp.'"

We returned to our camp at Johnfon's Farm on the
15th, when the following report was fubmitted to General
Porter:

"Headquarters Sixth Penna. Cavalry,
Camp of the Cavalry Reserve, June 15th, 1862—10 p.m.
"Captain:
"In obedience to the letter of Captain Locke, A. A. G. of General F. J.
Porter's Divifion, of this date, I have the honor to report, that on the 13th
inftant, about 3¼ o'clock, 'boots and faddles' was founded from the headquarters
of the Cavalry Referve Brigade, and I immediately got my regiment
in the faddle, and followed the 5th and 6th United States Cavalry regiments,
which were moving out of their camp-grounds in the direction of Bethefda
Church. At that point orders from General Emory, who was in the advance,
came to me to remain where I was, near Bethefda Church, and to
detach a fquadron to guard and patrol the two roads leading weftward, one
above, and the other below Bethefda Church. The remaining four fquadrons
of my regiment were then moved further down the Old Church Road,
and halted in a field, where we met General Cook. We remained here
fome time,—until near funfet,—the 1ft United States Cavalry, General
Cook, and General Emory, being all prefent. Hearing we were probably
to be gone for a day or more, I obtained permiffion to return with my regiment
to camp, which was not half a mile diftant, to get rations and forage,
and return, to march with Colonel Warren's command toward Old Church.
As we entered our camp-ground, we met Colonel Warren there, near funfet.
Whilft in camp, about funfet, I received an order from General F. J.

Porter, to send a squadron to patrol and picket the road from Cold Harbor to Old Church, and before I had time to even give the order, I received another order from General Porter to report with my regiment to General Sykes. I immediately started with my remaining squadrons,—one having been left at Bethesda Church,—and reached General Sykes's headquarters at about 9 o'clock, and there detached the squadron to patrol and picket the road to Old Church from Cold Harbor. I there waited the return of General Sykes, who was not present when I arrived. At a little before 10, General Emory arrived with orders for me to report to him with what was left of my regiment; and at 10 o'clock General Emory assumed the command, and we were sent to Tunstall's Station. At sunrise on the 14th, General Emory directed me to send a squadron to patrol the ground east of the railroad. I detached Major Morris with one squadron for this purpose, and in the course of a few hours, received information that he had got on the trail of the enemy, several hundred strong. This was the first information I had of the enemy since the attack on Old Church.

"General Emory gave me permission to reinforce Major Morris at once, and other reports soon coming, confirming his first information of the direction, force, and movement of the enemy, I sent the remaining squadrons of my regiment, and followed with a platoon of the 11th Pennsylvania Cavalry, that had come in from the White House, General Reynolds promising to reinforce me with what cavalry he could get at the White House. It was now about 10 o'clock A.M., and I pushed on to overtake Major Morris, which I did between 1 and 2 o'clock. Various and conflicting reports were obtained of the time, place, and strength of the enemy; but from careful sifting of all, I am satisfied that the enemy, with not less than fifteen hundred cavalry, and two iron guns, drawn by six horses each, reached the section of country between Garlick's Landing, Tunstall's, and White House, during the evening of the 13th, and in several detachments; that during the night they had united into one general column, with many captured and led animals and wagons, and that all had marched down, between 12 and 3½ A.M. of the 14th, on the road from Baltimore Hospital towards Jones's Bridge, passing Olivet Church; that they had stopped at the Sycamore Farm, near to the Forge Mill, until about 8 A.M., when they left Sycamore Farm, and went to the Chickahominy to cross. They repaired an old broken bridge just below the 'Forge Mills,' using the rafters and girders of an old house for that purpose: by 2 o'clock they had passed over nearly all their column. At a quarter of 3, I reached the Sycamore Farm, and seeing smoke through the

1862.
June.

woods ahead, fent forward Major Morris, with a fquadron and eight carbineers. They foon returned, reporting that a mile beyond the woods he had come to the Chickahominy, and that the bridge was burning, and men at work on its deftruction. His carbineers fired upon the difmounted troops on the other fide of the ftream, when they mounted and ran. I fcouted the woods for an hour, and in all the vicinity of the Sycamore Farm and Mill, but getting no new trail of the rebels, and being fatisfied, from all the teftimony I could get, that all had croffed the river, I returned with my command to Tunftall's Station. Three fquadrons of the 11th Pennfylvania Cavalry, from White Houfe, joined me juft as I ftarted to return. I had but four fquadrons of my regiment on this chafe. Great credit is due to Major Morris for the prompt manner in which he found and followed the trail of the retreating rebels in the morning.

(Signed) "R. H. Rush."

CHAPTER FIFTH.

Cold Harbor—Fair Oaks—Beaver Dam Creek—Mechanicsville—Gaines's Mill—The Change of Base to James River—The Retreat—Robinson's Battery—Savage Station—White Oak Swamp—Charles City Crofs-Roads—Glendale—Frazier's Farm.

ON the morning of the 16th of June, the regiment 1862. marched to Cold Harbor, and went regularly into camp: wagons were overhauled, tents put up, and arrangements made for reft. About noon, Company "A" was fent on picket beyond Old Church, where they remained until after midnight, when they were relieved, and ordered back to the regiment, arriving in camp at daylight on the 17th.

On the 18th, Major Clymer, with two fquadrons, June 18th Companies "B," "G," "C," and "H," was detached from the regiment, and ordered to report to General McCall, commanding Divifion of the Pennfylvania Referve Corps, on the extreme right of the army in front of Richmond, near Mechanicfville. He reported to General J. F. Reynolds, and picketed and patrolled the roads and approaches to the Chickahominy, from Mechanicfville northward to Atlee's Station. The detachment was encamped on the edge of a wood near Beaver

1862. Creek, about one and a half miles from Ellerſon's Mills. The 2d Pennſylvania Reſerves were encamped in an oat-field near us. In the afternoon we were entertained by balloon aſcenſions, made by Mr. Hall, in one of Profeſſor Low's balloons, from near our camp. The balloon reconnoiſſance was cut ſhort by being too cloſe to the enemy, and within range of their artillery. Several ſhots were fired at the aeronaut.

On the ſame day the above ſquadrons were detached, the two ſquadrons under Lieutenant-Colonel C. Roſs Smith, commanded by Captains Treichel and Starr, conſiſting of Companies "A," "D," and "I," "K," were on picket near Hanover Court-houſe, and were driven in by Jackſon's rapid advance. They fell back to Old Church, where they were ordered to report to General Stoneman, who was ſent with a light column to the White Houſe, to protect it until the removal of ſtores, wagon trains, &c., there accumulated. They accompanied him to the White Houſe, and thence on his ſkilful retreat, moving large wagon trains in ſafety. This movement was alſo deſigned as a feint, with a view of deceiving the enemy into the belief that the main body of the army was moving in that direction. Theſe ſquadrons accompanied General Stoneman to Williamſburg and Fortreſs Monroe, and rejoined the regiment July 10th.

June 23d. On the 23d, the regular brigade of Cavalry, under General P. St. George Cook, moved to Cold Harbor, and participated in all the active movements of the army that followed. Our regiment, by detachments, was ſerving in all parts of the eventful fields, and a general sketch of the whole operations will best present, to those 1862. participating and to their friends, this part of our service. The regiment was represented in every engagement of the Peninsula from this date until it found its new base at Harrison's Landing: though in some much more actively than in others.

On Wednesday, June 25th, an engagement occurred June 25th. between about six thousand Union troops and two divisions of the rebel army, a short distance beyond Fair Oaks. The enemy, though of superior strength, were driven back a mile or more, but from some unexplained cause, the advantage thus gained was mysteriously abandoned, when the enemy again poured back over the field. Another advance was ordered, and though stubbornly contested, they were again forced back over all the ground we originally won, and we held the position during the night, throwing out our pickets to an advanced position. Three squadrons of the Sixth participated in these engagements.

Thursday, June 26th, had been fixed upon by the June 26th. commanders of both armies as the day when each should commence aggressive operations, neither General knowing of the intention, or exact position or force of his opponent. General McClellan had received information of a contemplated early advance of the enemy, from spies, contrabands, and deserters. Early this morning, both armies were in the excitement of preparation for severe work to be done ere nightfall. General Jackson was reported as threatening our right and rear. A. P. Hill had moved northward, concentrating his division near Meadow Bridge. General Branch advanced down

1862. the northern bank of the Chickahominy. Branch and
June 26th. Hill moved down towards Mechanicsville, and about 3 o'clock, consolidated their forces near Beaver Dam Creek. They here came upon the Union lines, striking McCall's division of Pennsylvania Reserves, with which two squadrons of the Sixth were serving. Our forces occupied a strong position, as they had their left resting on the creek, curving around Mechanicsville for a mile: the water, waist deep, was about eighteen or twenty feet in width, with steep banks. It was impassable for artillery, except on bridges. The right rested on a dense wood, beyond the upper road to Mechanicsville. The passage of the creek was very difficult for any troops, and impracticable for artillery, except over the bridges at the roads crossing at Ellison's Mills, near the left, and that near the right, called the upper road. Earthworks were thrown up on the right, under Reynolds; and it was well that they were, for the main attack of the enemy was made in that direction. The rebels advanced in line of battle about 4 o'clock in the afternoon; pushed forward rapidly, delivering their fire as they came, and though passing through a murderous fire, reached the edge of the creek. A few succeeded in crossing above Reynolds, and gained a lodgment on the nearer shore, but they soon left, as elsewhere the assault was repulsed, and they retired with heavy loss.

General Ripley's (rebel) division was sent forward to A. P. Hill, who, thus reinforced, made a furious assault upon our left at Ellison's Mills, which was held by Seymour. This attack failed even more disastrously than that upon the right. The fighting over the entire field was of the moſt ſtubborn character: General Robert E. Lee preſſing, with all energy, every point of attack, giving his greateſt attention to our right. At 9 o'clock the enemy, repulſed at all points, fell back beyond artillery range, leaving us in poſſeſſion of the field. At the cloſe of the day, General McClellan decided upon an entire change of baſe, from the York to the James River. The Quartermaſter at Weſt Point was directed to ſend ſupplies to the front to the laſt moment, and to hurry the remaining ſtores up the James River, burning everything which could not be got off.

1862.

On the following morning, the right of our army fell back to Gaines's Mill, the poſition at Beaver Dam Creek being far in advance of the main force, and having its extreme right greatly expoſed. During this movement, a ſcattering fire of artillery and muſketry was kept up until the new line was eſtabliſhed five miles below. The troops of Porter's corps croſſed the Chickahominy, burning New Bridge, the upper one on that ſtream, after croſſing.

June 27th.

"The army now held a ſtrong poſition. A ſmall unnamed ſtream, curving ſickle-wiſe, empties into the Chickahominy, the banks in ſome places fringed with ſwamps, and in others riſing abruptly, the bed of the ſtream forming a ravine. On the eaſtern ſide the land riſes in a gradual ſlope, croſſed by gullies, and ſpreads into a flat table land above." Haſty preparations had been made for defence. To General Fitz John Porter, with the Fifth Corps, and all diſpoſable reinforcements, was aſſigned the taſk of keeping the enemy in check while other movements were being executed. The line

1862.
June 27th.
of battle formed an arc of a circle, on the interior edge of the denſe woods bounding the extenſive plain of cleared land, ſtretching ſome twelve or fifteen hundred yards back of the river. "Butterfield had the extreme left of this line, extending to the ſwamps of the Chickahominy; next came Martindale, both of Morell's diviſion; then Griffin's diviſion; then Sykes, with his regulars; all of theſe of Porter's corps, formed the firſt line." "Behind this was McCall's diviſion, Meade then commanding a brigade on the extreme left; next Reynolds; then Seymour,—who, a few hours before, had cruſhed Ripley and Pender at Beaver Dam Creek,—as reſerve behind the ſecond line. Stoneman, with his cavalry, were miles away to the north, under orders to retreat to the White Houſe, and from thence carry off all the ſtores poſſible, and rejoin the army as beſt he could, ſomewhere on the James."

General P. St. George Cook commanded the cavalry engaged on this day, which was placed under cover of a hill in the rear of the poſition, and was compoſed of the 4th Pennſylvania Cavalry, 5th United States, two ſquadrons of the 1ſt United States, and three ſquadrons of the 6th Pennſylvania Cavalry.

"The troops were all in poſition by noon, with the artillery on the commanding ground, and in the intervals between the diviſions and the brigades. Beſides the ordinary diviſion batteries, there was from the Artillery Reſerve, Tidball's horſe battery, poſted on the right of Sykes's diviſion, and Robinſon on the extreme left of the line in the valley of the Chickahominy." Shortly after noon, the enemy was diſcovered approaching in

force, and it soon became evident that the entire position
was to be attacked. His skirmishers advanced rapidly,
and soon the firing became heavy along the whole front.
"Longstreet was held back, because it was thought by
Lee that Jackson's approach on the left, which was
every moment expected, would cause the extension of
the Union lines in that direction. Hill's brigade dashed
across the plain, floundered through the swamp, and
pressed up the opposite slope in the face of a fierce fire
of artillery and musketry. Some brigades advanced close
to the infantry lines: a few regiments even met them,
but they were soon forced back. For two hours the
battle raged with equal obstinacy on either side." "The
Union troops gained ground, and from being the assailed
became the assailants. Hill was defeated, crushed, and
almost routed. Some of his regiments threw themselves
flat upon the ground to escape the withering fire, while
others rushed from the field in disorder." "Lee, finding Hill sorely worsted, ordered Longstreet to make a
feigned attack upon the left, hoping to divert a part of
the Union force to that direction, and thus relieve Hill.
Longstreet attacked, but found the force opposing him
very strong, and that he must make a real attack with
his whole force. Jackson now joined him; and D. H.
Hill, also, in advance on the extreme right, Ewell and
Whiting on the left, and Lawton a little to the rear.
The line was now complete, and a general advance
along its whole extent ordered. General Porter was
reinforced by Slocum's division of Franklin's corps,
which was hurried across the Chickahominy, and arrived
upon the field just as the general rebel advance was

1862.
June 27th.

1862.
June 27th.
made, at half-paſt 4 o'clock. The attack was made with great vigor, and the battle raged with terrible fury and changing fortune until dark. Our line was preſſed along its whole length by a force of almoſt two to one. The crowning attack was made half an hour before ſunſet, and was ſo irreſiſtible, that the Union lines gave way almoſt ſimultaneouſly on the right, centre, and left. Where it firſt broke no one can ſay." All were forced back toward the river. The main part of every diviſion fell back in order, but fragments were flying away on all routes to the river. "It was not a rout, though faſt threatening to become one. All, ſoldiers and fugitives, were thronging toward the bridges. All at once a great ſhout rent the murky air, and French's and Meagher's brigades,—Meagher, it is ſaid, leading in his ſhirt ſleeves,—daſhed up the bluff, driving through the ſtragglers, and advanced to what was now the front. Their preſence gave heart to the fugitives, who rallied behind them, and marched up the hill. The rebels pauſed in their purſuit, and after delivering a few ineffectual volleys withdrew, as night ſet in, and the battle was over. An hour earlier, and theſe two brigades would have turned the wavering ſcale and won a victory."

Three ſquadrons of our regiment were preſent in this engagement: the firſt, under Captain John H. Gardiner; the ſecond, under Captain Henry C. Whelan; the third, under Captain J. Henry Haſeltine—all under command of Colonel Ruſh. The regiment was drawn up in column of ſquadrons at half diſtances on the left of our line of battle, and near the Chickahominy, ſupporting artillery. We were under heavy artillery fire

all the afternoon, the men being difmounted, and ftanding to horfe. About 5 o'clock, it became evident that
we were being driven back. The roar of artillery almoft
ceafed, and increafed volleys of mufketry told of the
arrival upon the field of heavy reinforcements to the
enemy. Now the fighting was bitter and terrific. From
a rebel account of this charge I make the following
extract:

1862.
June 27th.

"Worked up to madnefs, Wilcox, Featherftone, and
Pryor, dafh forward at a run, and drive the enemy with
irrefiftible fury. On our left emerge Hood's Texan
brigade, then Whiting and Pender. Wheeling their
artillery from the front, the Federals turn part of it to
break the attack on the left and fave their retreat. The
very earth fhakes at the roar, while onward prefs our
troops, with bullet and bayonet, opening their way. It
is true one or two regiments became confufed in paffing over the deep ditch, abattis, and timber earthwork,
but thofe who went to the rear were moftly wounded
men."

The ftream of wounded men, from our front lines,
greatly increafed, came rufhing paft us to the rear; many
ftragglers, overcome with long refiftance, or fick at
heart through conftant expofure, haftened in the fame
direction. Wounded and demoralized artillerymen,
mounted on their battery horfes, with cut traces, were
flying in a diforganized and incongruous mafs from the
dreadful carnival of death. Though under fire from
artillery, we remained idle until about 6 o'clock, when
the bugles founded "attention," the command was

1862.
June 27th.

mounted, each man settled himself firmly in his saddle, and with lance at rest awaited orders. The long gray line of rebels is seen advancing over the crest of the hill in our immediate front. The 1st and 5th United States Cavalry, were ordered to charge the approaching foe, which they did in fine style, coming to close encounter, and losing heavily. They are soon driven back by superior numbers, and the long gray line comes on with the fierce yell of victory. They bear down upon our position, and we are within range of their musketry, when Captain Robinson, commanding a battery of the 3d United States Artillery, limbers up his pieces, and is moving off his guns to save them from capture. At this moment an aid from General Cook's staff, Lieutenant Wesley Merritt, 2d United States Cavalry, dashed up, and asked him to unlimber and give them another shot, to check their advance, if possible.

"Who will support me, Lieutenant?" asked the gallant captain.

"The Lancers, sir," was the reply.

"Very well: if *they* will stand by me, here goes."

In a minute the six pieces are in position, and are hurling fearful volleys of grape and canister into the advancing lines. They are checked by this unlooked for storm of death. The regiment is moved to the right of the guns with lance poised, awaiting the "charge," if necessary. The guns are hastily limbered up, and go dashing to the rear, when the rebels give us their undivided attention. Their yells are more fierce than ever, while a perfect storm of bullets warn us to retire. There is no hurry or confusion in the movements of the regiment. The lines are perfectly dressed as we move up under the cover of the fire of our own guns, which, having again taken position, are offering still further resistance to the forward march of the foe. We pass to the right of the battery, and are again faced to what is now the rear. Thus the fight rages: our weapon being unfitted for any service but the charge, we were held only to resist attacks from the enemy, and though severely exposed, had not the satisfaction of returning his fire. 1862. June 27th.

General Cook remarked, at the close of the day, that "from the first opening of the fight until its close, after 8 o'clock, the Sixth Pennsylvania Cavalry behaved like veterans."

We bivouacked that night on the battle-field. Most of the men were wearied and exhausted by hard fighting and intense excitement for two days; many being entirely without food, threw themselves at their horses' feet, and sank to sleep. Near 2 o'clock at night, orders came to form column without noise. It was with great difficulty the men could be aroused from their deep sleep. Near daylight we crossed the Chickahominy, and assisted in destroying the bridge over which we had passed to safety.

A writer on the war, speaks of a charge made by our regiment in the battle of Gaines's Mill, thus:

"Rush's regiment of Lancers did good service, not only in the fight of Friday, but in the subsequent occurrences of Savage's Station and White Oak Swamp. In the battle of Gaines's Mill, they charged, a little to the

1862.
June 27th.
south of the old mill, upon an Alabama brigade, and handled the lance with terrible effect. The scene witnessed when this fine regiment charged, may well be historical: their long lances poised, their red pennons streaming, and the riders, like so many avengers, bending forward to the charge."

This statement will be confirmed by many who saw the regiment on that day. Though not entirely correct, arises from the fact that a force of cavalry, made up of detachments from several regiments, did charge upon the foe with great success. Our regiment was called upon to furnish its proportion, and there were not more than ten or twelve lances in the force; but many supposed, from seeing this detail charging with about the force of cavalry forming a reduced regiment, that the charge was to be credited to the Lancers.

June 28th. Saturday, June 28th. Captain Whelan's squadron, composed of Company "C," his own, and Company "H," under Captain B. Lockwood, reported to General Kearney, for headquarters duty.

The right wing of our army, after crossing the Chickahominy on Friday night, at the Grapevine Bridge, fell back down the Williamsburg road toward White Oak Swamp. The left wing was attacked by Toombs, a mile east of the New Bridge Road; other troops joined him, and a vigorous attack was made upon our hastily constructed works. The attack was ably resisted, and the enemy retired, and shortly after were granted a flag of truce, to remove their dead and wounded.

At noon Keyes, who lay nearest to, crossed the White

Oak Creek, and took pofition on its oppofite bank to cover the paffage of other troops and trains. Franklin and Porter followed from the rear by the fame route, and croffed on the morning of the 29th. A rebel writer fays:

"At this time high hopes were entertained of fpeedily deftroying or capturing McClellan's army. . . . At the time of Friday's battle, he had been compelled to leave his ftrongholds on the north of the Chickahominy, and abandon the Frederickfburg and Central Railroads, and had been preffed to a pofition where he had been cut off from the principal avenues of fupply and efcape. The difpofition of our forces was fuch as to cut off all communication between McClellan and the White Houfe, on the Pamunkey River, and it was thought he would be unable to extricate his army from its perilous condition; and in the fituation of affairs on Saturday night, his efcape was thought to be impoffible."

During Sunday, the 29th, the various corps took pofition near Savage's Station. About half paft 5 o'clock, P.M., the rebel advance ftruck our lines in front of General Sumner's corps, opening fharply with artillery fupported by infantry. The action continued for about two hours with great feverity, and night clofed upon the fcene, neither party having gained any perceptible advantage. Sumner's ftand had effected its object in delaying the enemy; and before midnight, his force was on its way to White Oak Swamp, leaving behind him twenty-five hundred fick and wounded, with attendants,

1862. in the hofpital at Savage's Station, who, with all our flain heroes, fell into the hands of the enemy the following morning.

During the night all our troops fell back, and croffed White Oak Swamp, and by 5 o'clock on the morning June 30th. of the 30th, General French, with the rear guard, croffed the bridge over the creek and deftroyed it.

McClellan's whole force was now ftretched in a line ten miles long, from the Swamps to Malvern Hill and the James River. Lee's plan of battle, on this day, was to attack in column upon one point on this long line, break through it in the centre, hurl the left back upon Jackfon, operating on that flank, and attack the right in flank and rear. His plan failed, through inability to bring his force together in time to have unity of action; and inftead of the attack being made by his whole force, the action on his fide was confined to Longftreet and A. P. Hill's commands, of about eighteen thoufand men; and in place of a grand and decifive battle, there occurred a feries of combats, in which brigades only were engaged on either fide, without harmonious and united action of any large force of the enemy. The battle raged with almoft equal fury along the whole line, at different times.

This battle is known under the title of "Frazier's Farm," "Charles City Crofs-Roads," "Glendale," or "White Oak Swamp," as all thefe points were touched by our lines, and were the fcenes of defperate conteft. White Oak Creek runs through a belt of fwampy timber, and is not more than fix feet deep. It had been made paffable by haftily conftructed "corduroy" bridges.

WHITE OAK SWAMP.

General Hancock's force was, at this point, on the right of our line, where the fighting was firſt brought on. The enemy appeared from White Oak Swamp, and directly opened from ſome twenty batteries. They made deſperate efforts to croſs the creek, but were repulſed by General Smith, and kept in check until the force on their left made their ſtrong attack at Charles City Croſs-Roads, ſome four miles to the left, and about two miles from the James River.

1862.
June 30th

General McCall was ordered to take poſition on the left of the Newmarket, or Long Bridge Road, near its croſſing with the Charles City Road, in front of the Quaker Road, leading to Malvern Hill and Turkey Bridge, to protect the paſſage of our immenſe ſupply trains, now rapidly preſſing towards the James River. On the right of McCall's diviſion of Pennſylvania Reſerves, was ſtationed Kearney's diviſion, and on the left, Sumner's; ſtill further to the left, and ſlightly advanced, was General Hooker.

About half paſt 2 o'clock in the afternoon, the cavalry and infantry pickets of the "Reſerves" were driven in; and upon this diviſion, weakened by the two battles in which it had been engaged, the firſt onſet fell. Soon after the enemy opened a heavy fire of ſhell upon our centre, under cover of which they ſent forward a force to feel our lines, and ſoon after a furious attack was made by infantry; it was gallantly met and reſiſted, and the enemy driven back with great ſlaughter. The Reſerves were now ordered forward; they advanced under a ſevere fire of round ſhot and ſhell, to near Nelſon's Houſe, when they were ordered to lie down, under a

1862. flight elevation of the ground, where they awaited rein-
June 30th. forcements. The battle now raged along the whole line with terrific fury. The rebel lines being greatly ftrengthened, were again pufhed forward, and when within a few yards of us, General Seymour fhouted out, "Now, boys, up and at them!" The men leaped to their feet, and delivered one volley of well-directed mufketry, which ftaggered the enemy, when they rufhed upon them with fixed bayonets. A defperate hand to hand ftruggle followed. The two hoftile flags were furging over the mingled mafs of men, only a few feet from each other. The ftruggle was fhort, but defperate. The enemy, in overwhelming numbers, preffed in on every fide, compelling our retreat. Over the whole plain the battle raged with deftructive violence until after dark.

The rebel General A. P. Hill gives the following account, in his official report, of the condition of affairs when darknefs clofed the fcene:

"About dark, the enemy were preffing us hard along our whole line, and my laft referve, General J. R. Anderfon, was directed to advance cautioufly. Heavy reinforcements to the enemy were brought up at this time, and it feemed that a tremendous effort was being made to turn the fortunes of the battle. The volume of fire that, approaching, rolled along the line, was terrific. Seeing fome troops of Wilcox's brigade, who had rallied, they were rapidly reformed, and being directed to cheer long and loudly, moved again to the fight. This feemed to end the conteft, for in lefs than five minutes all firing ceafed, and the enemy retired."

The battle of the 30th had scarcely closed, when our forces took up the retreat to Malvern Hill.

1862.
June 30th.

On the 29th, Captain Milligan's company, "F," was ordered to report for duty to General Sumner, and was with him in the fight of that day, and the succeeding day, at White Oak Swamp. They were exposed to very heavy fire from 3½ o'clock in the afternoon until 9 in the evening. During the night, the company acted as rear guard for General Sumner's division. A day or two after this, they escorted the heavy siege artillery from Malvern Hill to Harrison's Landing, where they remained encamped and on duty for six weeks.

CHAPTER SIXTH.

Malvern Hill—Reports of McClellan and Lee—Severe Fighting—July Fourth—Congratulatory Addreſs from the General Commanding—Capture of Hoſpitals—Experience in Rebel Priſons—Harriſon's Landing—Night Shelling—Adieu to the James.

1862.
July 1ſt.

SOON after daylight on the 1ſt of July, the laſt regiment was in poſition at Malvern Hill, awaiting the developments of the day, and ready to meet the enemy if again attacked. The poſition was admirably choſen for a defenſive battle.

Malvern Hill is an elevated plateau, about a mile and a half by three-fourths of a mile in area, moſtly clear of wood, and with ſeveral converging roads croſſing it. It ſlopes gently toward the north and eaſt, down to the verge of a thick foreſt; weſtward it falls more abruptly into a ravine, which extends to the James River.

On the creſt of the hill ſeven heavy ſiege guns had been placed in poſition, and the reſerve artillery was ſo poſted, that a concentrated fire of ſixty guns could be brought to bear upon any point in front, or on the left, the direction from which the enemy muſt advance to the attack. Here the main force was maſſed. The left of the line was held by the Fifth Corps, General

MALVERN HILL.

Porter, confifting of the divifions of Sykes and Morell, and Warren's, Buchanan's, Chapman's, Griffin's, Martindale's, and Butterfield's brigades. Heintzelman's corps was on the right of Porter; Couch's divifion came next, then Kearney and Hooker; next Keyes, Sumner, and Franklin's corps, with Sedgwick and Richardfon. Next came Smith and Slocum, then the remainder of Keyes's corps, extended by a backward curve nearly to the river. Commodore Rodgers, commanding the flotilla on the James River, placed his gunboats fo as to protect our left, and to command the approaches from Richmond. There was pofted upon different parts of the field, and in fome places tier above tier, about two hundred and fifty pieces of artillery.

1862.
July 1ft.

About 10 o'clock A.M., the enemy emerged from the woods on the oppofite fide of the plain, and our pofition was diligently reconnoitred under fire from our guns.

"The Yankees," fays the rebel General Hill, "were found to be ftrongly pofted on a commanding hill, all the approaches to which could be fwept with his artillery, and were guarded by fwarms of infantry, fecurely fheltered by fences, ditches, and ravines. Tier after tier of batteries were grimly vifible, rifing in the form of an amphitheatre. We could only reach the firft line by traverfing an open fpace of from three to four hundred yards, expofed to a murderous fire of grape and canifter from the artillery, and mufketry from the infantry. If that was carried, another and another ftill more difficult remained in rear. An examination fatiffied me that an attack would be hazardous."

An ominous ftillnefs prevailed, indicating the ma-

1862.
July 1ſt.
nouvring and placing in poſition of troops. About 3 o'clock, Lee ordered the artillery attack, which he hoped would break the Union lines. "But inſtead of one or two hundred pieces, only a ſingle battery opened, and that was knocked to pieces in a few minutes." "Grimes's battery was thrown into hopeleſs diſorder by the killing of three of its horſes, and the wounding of ſeveral others, in the act of taking its ground, and never got into poſition again during the day; whereupon the Purcell battery, Captain Pegram, was ordered to replace it."

McClellan's Official Report.—"At 6 o'clock the enemy ſuddenly opened upon Couch and Porter, with the whole ſtrength of his artillery, and began at once to puſh forward his columns of attack to carry the hill. Brigade after brigade, formed under cover of the woods, ſtarted at a run to croſs the open ſpace and charge our batteries, but the heavy fire of our guns, with the cool and ſteady volleys of our infantry, in every caſe ſent them reeling back to ſhelter."

Rebel Account.—"The fire was now appalling, and to add to the horrors of the ſcene, the gunboats of the enemy in the river began to throw the moſt tremendous projectiles into the field." . . . . "A third column in the centre moved upon the Yankee guns. The dark maſs ſoon diſappeared in the cloud which enveloped all objects, and though it loſt ſtrength and ſolidity at every ſtep, it ſtill gained the ſlope where ſtood the enemy's batteries, but only to be driven back as had been their comrades before them."

Until dark, the enemy perfifted in his efforts to take the pofitions fo tenacioufly held, but all his attempts were foiled, and with heavy lofs. Long after funfet, and even until 9 o'clock at night, the artillery fire continued from both fides. With lighted fufe, the courfe of the fhells could be marked as they fped, meteor-like, through the heavens, and, as a pyrotechnical difplay, would have been regarded as very grand; but thefe were fwift-winged meffengers of death, carrying deftruction to friends and foes.

1862.
July 1ft.

During the day, our troops had but little occafion to go beyond their ftrong pofition. It was eafy to mow down the enemy with artillery and mufket-ball as they advanced. The rebels were repulfed fearfully; and had McClellan followed up his fuccefs, it would have been difaftrous to the foe.

The regiment, during thefe engagements, was conftantly expofed: ferving by detachments in all parts of the field,—fome with Sumner, one fquadron with Kearney, others with Porter, Keyes, and McCall's Pennfylvania Referves.

At Malvern Hill, the day after the battle, both armies had pickets ftationed upon the field, and the enemy were permitted to remove their wounded, but they fired upon our men when they approached for the fame purpofe. The pofition now occupied by our army, was a line of heights fome three miles long, and about two miles from the James, both flanks refting upon the river. A morafs extended between the heights and the river, from our centre to the right. At Harrifon's Landing, and on thefe heights, were collected the army ftores, fhipping, &c.

1862.
July 4th.
The anniverſary of our Nation's Birthday occurred a day or two after our arrival at Harriſon's Landing, and was duly celebrated by parades, diſplay of flags, firing ſalutes, &c., &c.

On dreſs parade, the following addreſs was read to each regiment of the army, and cauſed great rejoicing:

"HEADQUARTERS ARMY OF THE POTOMAC,
   CAMP NEAR HARRISON'S LANDING, July 4th, 1862.
"SOLDIERS OF THE ARMY OF THE POTOMAC:

"Your achievements of the laſt ten days have illuſtrated the valor and endurance of the American ſoldier. Attacked by ſuperior forces, and without hope of reinforcements, you have ſucceeded in changing your baſe of operations by a flank movement, always regarded as the moſt hazardous of military expedients. You have ſaved all your material, all your trains, and all your guns, except a few loſt in battle, taking in return guns and colors from the enemy. Upon your march, you have been aſſailed day after day with deſperate fury, by men of the ſame race and nation, ſkilfully maſſed and led. Under every diſadvantage of number, and neceſſarily of poſition, alſo, you have, in every conflict, beaten back your foes with enormous ſlaughter. Your conduct ranks you among the celebrated armies of hiſtory. No one will now queſtion that each of you may always with pride ſay, 'I BELONG TO THE ARMY OF THE POTOMAC.' You have reached the new baſe complete in organization, and unimpaired in ſpirit. The enemy may, at any moment, attack you. We are prepared to meet them. I have perſonally eſtabliſhed your lines. Let them come, and we will convert their repulſe into a final defeat. Your Government is ſtrengthening you with the reſources of a great people. On this, our Nation's Birthday, we declare to our foes, who are rebels againſt the beſt intereſts of mankind, that this army ſhall enter the capital of the ſo-called Confederacy, that our National Conſtitution ſhall prevail, and that the Union, which can alone inſure internal peace and external ſecurity to each State, 'muſt and ſhall be preſerved,' coſt what it may in time, treaſure, and blood.

"GEORGE B. MCCLELLAN."

During the ſeven days' fight, Companies "C" and "H" were on duty with General Kearney, and received great praife from him for the difficult and arduous duties performed. They formed his rear guard, covering his retreat from White Oak Swamp to Malvern Hill.

1862.
July

From the diary of private Thomas L. J. Ruffell, of Company "A," who fell into the hands of the enemy when our hofpital was captured near Cold Harbor, I make the following extracts:

"Rumors were circulated at the hofpital on the morning of the 27th of June, that our army was falling back, and that the rebels were following clofely. All patients that were able to leave the hofpital were fent away. About 10 o'clock in the morning, we were ftartled by a fierce yell of what proved to be rebel cavalry, charging upon the hofpital. They made a vaft deal of noife around the houfe, when Dr. Ellis went out and told them no refiftance could be made, as the houfe contained nothing but fick and wounded men. They then gained courage and came into the houfe, each man with his revolver in his hand. After finding nothing to oppofe them, they commenced a fearch for whifky, and found fome that had been ftored in the cellar. Several bottles of wine were buried in the garden, which were not difcovered by them. While this fearch was going on in the houfe, a party outfide affaulted the cook-houfe, carrying off all the rations that had been drawn the day previous for the hofpital, not leaving a fingle article of food of any kind. They took even the meat that was boiling for our dinners, carrying it off in a half-cooked condition. Soon the main body of the cavalry came up, under the command of General Stuart, who ordered

1862.
June.
us to be paroled, and left a guard on the hospital, when in a few minutes they passed on. In a short time the infantry of General Jackson's corps began to pass; they were very dirty, ragged, and weary. Some of them say they have been marching constantly for a week. They seemed very much worn out, and were scrutinized with wondering eyes by our prison-bound company. The rebel surgeons took the hospital by storm, taking away all the medicines they could possibly carry. There seemed to be a special demand for quinine, and Dr. Ellis had great trouble in retaining a single bottle for his own sick. About the middle of the afternoon, the roar of artillery and musketry commenced in the direction of Gaines's Mill, and towards dark, the rebel wounded were borne to the rear in great numbers, and continued to pour in all night. We remained here until the 15th of July. In the evening a train of empty wagons came up for the purpose of taking us to Richmond. We were soon ready, and moved off, leaving Dr. Ellis behind, with a few nurses, to attend to some of our men that could not bear moving. We had a beautiful night for a trip, but as our wagons were without springs, and the roads exceedingly rough, we found it very fatiguing for the sick, and painful to the wounded. We arrived in Richmond about 1 o'clock on the morning of the 16th. We were halted in front of an old tobacco warehouse, designated as Prison No. 4, where we were called in one by one, our names, regiments, place of capture, &c., recorded, and after being carefully searched, and duly robbed, were passed up stairs into an exceedingly dirty room, very confined and dif-

gufting, and at night had barely room for the men to lie down, by being packed clofe againft each other. In a day or two, all who were able to walk were ordered to prepare to go to Belle Ifland. They made up a party, and ftarted off with them; the reft of us were taken down ftairs into a back room a little cleaner than the one above. This contained a double row of tobacco preffes. A door at one end led into a courtyard, which led to another factory. The room was lighted through a row of windows opening upon this yard, but the glafs was fo obfcured by dirt, cobwebs, &c., that but little light gained admiffion. About two hundred men were confined in this room, all fick or wounded. We were fed upon what purported to be beef tea, but very little ftronger than water, and without falt, accompanied with a very fmall piece of bread, being barely enough to fuftain life.

1862. June.

"A large number of wounded arrived during the night of the 17th, and the fight prefented in the morning was moft painful. In the yard was a hydrant, furrounded by a large tub, around which were collected a great crowd of men, with every defcription of wounds, calling upon and affifting each other to wafh and drefs their wounds. No doctors vifited them or us, and nothing was adminiftered to alleviate their fufferings. Many muft die from fheer neglect of their wounds. Rebel citizens are allowed to vifit the prifon, and this morning they ftood by, with hands in their pockets, gaping on thefe poor fellows fuffering fo greatly, and with perfect unconcern and indifference. Thus are we in their power, and cannot help ourfelves.

"A young man, about twenty years of age, was led

1862.
July.

out into the yard this morning, at his requeſt, being very weak. He was aſſiſted about the crowded yard by his companions, and at length ſeated himſelf upon the ground, ſtarved, ſick, diſpirited, and exhauſted, from want of nouriſhment. After being ſeated on the ground a little while, his head fell upon his breaſt, and ſome thought he ſlept, and coming to arouſe him, found he 'ſlept the ſleep that knows no waking.' He had died there, ſurrounded by ſuffering fellow-men, with no phyſician to adminiſter anything for his relief, and no friend or mother's hand to bring him aught to revive or nouriſh him, and no loving acts or words to make his death eaſy. His name or regiment could not be aſcertained."

The men of our regiment remained here until the 24th of July, when thoſe who were then able to walk were exchanged.

The ſquadrons under Lieutenant-Colonel C. Roſs Smith, that had accompanied General Stoneman, were encamped at Yorktown the early part of July. About the 4th of the month, an alarm was created by ſome wild rumors brought to General Emory, and he hurried the little force there under his command down to Fortreſs Monroe, where they remained until the 10th, when theſe ſquadrons were ordered to rejoin the regiment. Taking tranſports in the morning, they arrived at Harriſon's Landing, and reported to the regiment about 8 o'clock in the evening.

At Harriſon's Landing, the regiment was encamped about two hundred yards from the river, on the high bluff which riſes a little back from the ſtream, and on a bare level plain. We were compelled to drink the foul water of the James River, improved a little by being filtered, by the men who would take the trouble, through the river sand. The heat was intense, and rendered less endurable to the men, from the fact that their shelters were made of black water-proof cloth. We were annoyed by swarms of stinging flies, and almost perpetual clouds of dust and sand. With these annoying circumstances attending our stay at the Landing, it is referred to with any other than pleasing recollections. The "Chickahominy Fever," as it has ever since been called, made sad work with us. Notwithstanding all our discomfort, fever, and dysentery, but few deaths occurred in the regiment, owing to the untiring efforts of the surgeons, who were unceasing in their attentions, and called to their assistance all the aid to be derived from the "Sanitary" and "Christian Commissions." These active benevolent organizations furnished many comforts and delicacies for the sick; and it affords us pleasure to bear testimony to the faithfulness of the agents at the front, and to speak with unlimited praise of the spirit inspiring the people throughout our entire land, who so heartily engaged in this great work.

While encamped at the Landing, the regiment furnished five detachments daily for guide and scout duty; with this exception, our stay here was devoid of all service, and the monotony of camp life in midsummer uninterrupted.

About the 15th of the month, General Birney took a squadron of "Lancers" on a reconnoissance and foraging expedition. They returned at night with about thirty

1862.

July 15th.

1862. milch-cows, which were diftributed among the feveral hofpitals, and their milk furnifhed the patients.

July 31ft. On the night of the 31ft of July, about half-paft 1 o'clock, our encampment was fubjected to a terrible fire of fhell and folid fhot from a rebel battery on the fouth bank of the river, having been brought there under cover of the darknefs of the night. A field battery, on this occafion, fent its miffiles on their fiery path juft over our camp; and though very many burft over us, and a great many fragments of fhell were afterward picked up in the camp, we loft but one man killed. He was found lying dead in a clear fpace in the camp, without the flighteft apparent wound or mark upon his perfon. A fpent round fhot lay near him.

Although the night was very dark, the pofition of the enemy and their guns could be difcerned; and at every difcharge from each piece, the men could be feen ftanding by it in their regular pofitions. Some of our beft gunners foon fighted their fineft pieces, and the midnight compliment of the rebels was returned "in kind." In about thirty minutes our guns filenced their fire, and the next morning a force of the Pennfylvania Referves croffed the river and deftroyed the "Coles Houfe," which had been a rendezvous for the enemy. They found three of the enemy's dead, a fhattered caiffon, and a battle flag. The immenfe fhipping in the river received no harm, though much effort was apparently made to fire the veffels.

Auguft 2d. About the 2d of Auguft, a reconnoiffance in force was made by General Hooker, commanding his divifion, and General Pleafanton, with part of the cavalry. They passed out towards Malvern Hill, drove the enemy's pickets back several miles, and on the 5th, were joined by General Sedgwick's division, when they passed beyond Malvern Hill, driving the enemy back towards Richmond. The enemy opposed our advance with infantry and artillery in about equal numbers, and it was thought the larger part of the rebel army had passed south of the James River. Colonel Averill pushed out as far as Savage's Station, and near White Oak Bridge his advance was checked by the 18th Virginia cavalry. After strong resistance on the part of the enemy, he drove them, and captured twenty-eight mounted men, whom he brought in as prisoners, leaving many killed and wounded on the field. This force returned in a few days. It was supposed that a general advance was contemplated by General McClellan at this time, and that he only changed his plans through messages received from the War Department, ordering the speedy abandonment of the Peninsula, and the James River, as a base of operations. Acquia Creek was selected as the base of offensive operations, and great activity at once prevailed in camp, hospitals, and transports. The sick were hurried away in hospital boats, and the grand army was soon on the march for Fortress Monroe, Yorktown, and other points, from which to take transports for their new field. The gunboats were on the river at proper distances to cover the march of the army. A portion of our regiment formed part of the rear guard of the army, and were the last to leave the Landing. It was melancholy enough to see the change which, in a day, had come over the scene, though we were heartily glad

1862.
August.

1862. to get away from the place. On the 13th, the enemy, anticipating an advance of our forces on Richmond, burnt the wharves at City Point.

On the 14th, Porter's corps marched by way of Charles City Court-houfe to Barrett's Ferry, near the mouth of the Chickahominy, where a fplendid pontoon bridge, of nearly a third of a mile in length, had been conftructed acrofs the river by the engineer brigade. This "*long bridge* of the Chickahominy" was protected by two gunboats, the Delaware and the Yankee, lying in the James River. Here the moft of the army bivouacked during the night. Other divifions, including McCall's Pennfylvania Referves, did not arrive at this point until near noon of the 15th. On the morning of the 18th, the rear guard croffed the river, and on the 20th, the entire army was lying near Yorktown, Fortrefs Monroe, and Newport News.

On the 8th, one fquadron was ordered to General Franklin, for provoft and efcort duty, and made the march to Fortrefs Monroe with his command, leaving Harrifon's Landing Auguft 16th.

Aug. 11th. "C" and "H" companies, being on duty at the headquarters of Major General Fitz John Porter, marched with the Fifth Corps from the Landing on the 11th, and arrived at Newport News on the 18th. This fquadron was embarked on tranfports, to accompany that corps to the affiftance, or *non-affiftance*, of General Pope, then refifting the rebel advance at Cedar Mountain. When about to fail, orders were received to rejoin the regiment; they were immediately difembarked, and found the headquarters of the command at Hamp-

ton, Virginia, and in a few days accompanied the regi- 1862.
ment to Wafhington.

On the 26th, Company "F," under command of
Captain Milligan, was attached to General Heintzelman's corps as headquarters guard, marched with that
corps to Fortrefs Monroe on the 1ft of September, and
on the 2d embarked for Wafhington, where they arrived
on the 9th, and foon after rejoined the regiment.

The headquarters of the regiment, with all the com- Sept. 3d.
panies then undetached, took tranfports on the 3d of
September for Wafhington. The paffage up the bay
was very dangerous, on account of the crowded condition of the veffels, and the prevalence of a very fevere
ftorm. The forward deck of the fteamer conveying
companies "C" and "H," was almoft entirely deftroyed
by the violence of the waves and ftorm breaking upon
it. The regiment rendezvoufed at Giefboro' Point, and
on the 6th, encamped out Seventh Street, Wafhington.

Captain Whelan's fquadron landed at Alexandria, was
ordered and marched to Falls Church, where they had
a fkirmifh with the enemy, and was foon after ordered
to the regiment on Seventh Street, Wafhington.

On the 13th of Auguft, Firft Lieutenant G. Irvine
Whitehead was appointed aide-de-camp to Major-General Keyes, commanding the Fourth corps. He remained on that duty until he was commiffioned by the
Prefident Judge Advocate of that corps, with the rank
of Major, from March 17th, 1863. This pofition he
refigned near the clofe of the year, and returned to his
regiment, and in a very fhort time was again called to
detached duty, and was appointed an Acting Affiftant In-

1862.
September.

ſpector General, on General Pleaſanton's ſtaff of the Cavalry Corps of the Army of the Potomac, which poſition he retained until failing health compelled him to reſign, July 26th, 1864.

While theſe events were tranſpiring with us, General Pope, with the "Army of Virginia," had been heavily engaged with the enemy at "Cedar," or "Slaughter Mountain," where his force, led by General Banks, advanced on the enemy on the afternoon of the 9th of Auguſt. Both ſides ſuffered ſeverely, our loſs being eſtimated at one thouſand eight hundred in killed, wounded, and priſoners. Before daylight next morning, Jackſon withdrew his rebel force, and a grand flank movement was attempted by the enemy, an effort being made to gain the heights of Centreville, in the rear of General Pope. On the 26th, the Union army marched from Warrenton towards Waſhington, in three columns. The enemy was met and fought on the 27th, by General Hooker, at Kettle Run, and by McDowell, who drove Longſtreet's corps, through Thoroughfare Gap, back over the mountains. Fighting enſued on the 29th and 30th, on the old Bull Run battle-field. On the 30th, one of the heavieſt engagements of the war occurred; but as one ſquadron only of our regiment was within range of its influence, and no caſualties occurred to the regiment, we leave others to record its misfortunes, and tell of "Pope's defeat."

CHAPTER SEVENTH.

Through Wafhington — Into Maryland — Frederick — South Mountain — Antietam — The Great Battle of the Fall of 1862 — Ordered to Frederick, Maryland.

THE army fell back through Fairfax Court-houfe, and by evening of the 2d, were all within the defences of Wafhington, fouth of the Potomac, and beyond Alexandria, except three corps on the Vienna and Chain Bridge Roads. Herculean efforts were put forth by all departments for the immediate reorganization and refitting of the army. Though much confufion exifted, ftill the work went on wonderfully night and day. Wafhington City was never in fuch a whirl of excitement. The wounded came pouring in from the front with their ftories of the battle-field, and their wounds ftill undrefled. Ambulances, carriages, and vehicles of every defcription, were rufhing in all directions: vifitors by thoufands ready to pay any price to get to the front, all anxioufly inquiring for news from the army. Long lines of lumbering wagons, carrying quartermafter's and commiffary ftores to the needy men; the conftant roll of drums and mufic of bands, leading marching troops; the fhouting of newfboys; the fpreading of rumors, however vague and unreliable; thefe, with the uncertainty

1862.
September.

1862.
September.
of the movements of the enemy, all combined to keep the city in perfect excitement, and make confusion worse confounded. The scenes on the streets, and at the hotels and depots, were beyond all description. From earliest dawn until midnight, the whole population seemed poured into the streets, while every train from the North sent its stream of humanity into this boiling sea of excitement, and increased the commotion. Thousands of visitors passed out to the battle-fields a few days since, and when there, their carriages were seized and filled with wounded men, and started back to Washington, the curiosity seekers and more worthy visitors of these scenes compelled to walk the twenty-one miles back to the city.

But in a few days the army was again in motion. About the 5th, it was ascertained that the enemy intended crossing the Upper Potomac into Maryland, and were moving towards Leesboro and Harper's Ferry. On the 6th, portions of the Army of the Potomac were on the march again, all under the direction of their favorite leader of the Peninsula. The several corps and divisions marched through the city, and were enthusiastically cheered by the vast crowds of people who, by thousands, had flocked there in the last few days. The troops moved out steadily and proudly, though with decimated ranks.

Many friends from the North entirely failed to recognize intimate acquaintances and neighbors, who had passed through the long campaigns and hard battle-fields, under the broiling sun of Virginia. Their faces were bronzed, and their clothes soiled and dusty, but they

INTO MARYLAND. 89

were proud of their military connections, and were not afhamed of clothes foiled in fuch noble fervice. The army moved through Maryland in five columns, between the Potomac River and the Baltimore and Ohio Railroad, covering both Wafhington and Baltimore, and converging near Frederick, Maryland. During the march, the work of reorganization continued rapidly, and the troops were in excellent fpirits, having great confidence in their leaders, and anxious to meet the invading foe. The advance of our army entered Frederick from the fouth, as the rear guard of the enemy were leaving from the weft and north. As foon as our column was recognized, flags were difplayed in great numbers, ladies crowded the windows, and waved their handkerchiefs, while the men came out into the ftreets, and, with great fhouting and rejoicing, we were welcomed to the city. The citizens were thoroughly difgufted with rebel rule and plunder, though the foldiers were reftrained from depredations by their commanders.

1862. September.

On the 7th of September, Major Clymer, with companies "B" and "G,"—ordered to report for duty to Major-General Franklin, then commanding the Sixth Corps,—reported to him near Rockville, Maryland. Company "I" was added to this detachment on the following day, and joined Major Clymer at Hagerftown, Maryland. Thefe companies remained with General Franklin during the Antietam campaign, and participated in the battles of Crampton Gap and Antietam, being expofed to a very heavy fire on both occafions.

On the 8th, the regiment left its encampment in Wafhington, and reported to General McClellan, and

1862. marched with the army to Frederick, over South Mountain, and participated in the engagements of this campaign.

When the regiment left Washington, Surgeon Moss remained with the sick and dismounted recruits in Camp on Seventh Street, until having passed a satisfactory examination, he was appointed Assistant Surgeon of United States Volunteers, October 4th, 1862. He resigned his position as Surgeon of the Sixth Pennsylvania Cavalry, and in December, was promoted Surgeon of United States Volunteers, and assigned to duty as Assistant Curator at the "United States Army Medical Museum," in the City of Washington, and placed on a board for the examination of candidates for position as Surgeon or Assistant Surgeon of "United States Volunteers."

On the 7th, Lieutenant Charles L. Leiper was placed in command of Company "A," which he retained until the beginning of October. On the march to Antietam,
Sept. 13th. when near Frederick, Maryland, on the 13th of September, he came upon a body of dismounted rebel cavalry in a wood. Although largely outnumbering his small force, he drove them in confusion, and made some prisoners. The enemy were armed with carbines, and though our men had only the lance and their pistols, by one determined charge they succeeded in dislodging the enemy, who fled in dismay.

Sept. 14th. On the 14th, we passed through Frederick, and to the west, over the Catoctin Mountains. This range separates the valley of the Monocacy from the Catoctin Valley. In our front was South Mountain, and along its slope we could see the smoke from the guns of the enemy, and hear the boom of their artillery. We passed on through Middletown, and saw evidences of the enemy's hatred in the destruction of the property of Union citizens.

1862. September.

General Pleasanton, with the advanced cavalry, had been skirmishing all the morning, and the enemy had at length halted, and gone into position at Turner's Gap, in the South Mountain. Here are three roads crossing the mountains, the centre one being the great National Road, leading through Boonsboro, the one to the north, the "Old Hagerstown Road," and that to the south, the "Sharpsburg Road." General Hooker was sent up on the right, while General Burnside was to pass along the road to the south, and General Reno in the centre. The enemy were here in force, under command of General Howell Cobb. Our troops being in position, a general advance of our entire line was ordered, and, with great enthusiasm, they pressed up the heights upon the enemy's guns. The attack was met with desperate resistance, but the enemy were finally forced from their position. The Pennsylvania Reserves did good service on the extreme right. In his official report, General McClellan says:

"General Meade speaks highly of General Seymour's skill in handling his brigade on the extreme right, securing, by his manœuvres, the great object of the movement, the outflanking of the enemy."

Nearly the whole of the "Cobb Legion" (*rebel*), were captured by General Newton's brigade of Franklin's

1862.
September.
corps, with their colors, on which is inscribed, "Cobb Legion—In the name of the Lord."

The stony and steep slope of the hill was strewn with the dead. The stone walls were all held by the enemy, and in driving them from these positions, we suffered severely. Especially was this the case on the left; and the road leading over the mountain at that point was called "Burnside's Stonewall Road."

As fast as possible, the wounded were conveyed to Burkittsville, where every church and private house was gladly thrown open to receive them. The Baptist Church was hastily converted into a hospital, and nearly all the rebel wounded conveyed there, where they received the same attention that was given to our own troops.

Our regiment was exposed to the artillery fire of the enemy, though suffering no loss. We marched over the field and across the mountain early the next morning, and saw hundreds of Union and rebel dead lying together in all imaginable positions. It was a painful sight, indeed, even to those accustomed to similar scenes. We passed over the mountain by the Burnside Road, following his command. Our troops crossed the mountain on Monday and Tuesday, and went streaming down into the valley beyond after the retreating foe. They passed through Boonsboro, Keedysville, and Porterstown, on towards Sharpsburg; and having crossed the Antietam, and stationed artillery on the heights beyond, prepared to meet our advancing lines. The Union forces followed by the same roads. The Antietam Creek is exceedingly irregular in its course, and at this point its banks are very high and abrupt. It is croffed by four ftone bridges, which were covered by the rebel batteries. "The enemy had the mafs of his troops concealed behind the heights, to the weft of the creek; their left and centre upon and in front of the Sharpfburg and Hagerftown Turnpike, hidden by woods and irregularities of the ground, the line extending from north to fouth."

1862.
September

The enemy's artillery was pofted on every favorable point, and their fupports and referves concealed in the ravines near their line of battle. The face of the country being very rolling, their troops could manœuvre without being obferved.

Burnfide's men having turned to the fouth from the foot of the mountain, came up to the creek, forming the left of our forces in line of battle. Porter had a commanding pofition to his right; Sumner joined him; and on the extreme right, General Hooker's forces extended into the woods towards the road to Williamfport, on the Potomac. The line thus covered was nearly five miles in extent. The rebel lines ran nearly parallel with our own, bending backward on their left to the Potomac; their line extending from the Antietam Creek to the Potomac River, thus having their flanks and rear covered by thefe ftreams.

About daylight of the 16th, the enemy opened fire from their artillery on our forces getting into pofition. They were promptly anfwered by our guns. The firing continued for a fhort time, and was renewed at intervals through the entire day. Some of our batteries continued firing until after 9 o'clock at night, and occafional fhots were exchanged all through the night by

1862. the advance pickets, who were within a very short dis-
Sept. 17th. tance of each other. Some of our advance declared they
slept among the rebels. About 2 o'clock on the morning of the 17th, the regiment of Reserves, known as the "Bucktails," opened a brisk fire, which was continued until they exhausted their ammunition, and were relieved by the 2d Pennsylvania Reserves at daylight. Shortly after daylight, the entire corps became heavily engaged, and General Hooker then ordered up General Mansfield's corps. Thus was the battle of Antietam opened.

The contest soon became very severe, as the enemy threw in heavy reinforcements, and Generals Ricketts, Meade, Williams, Green, Crawford, and King, with their divisions, were heavily engaged.

Hooker pushed forward his line immediately, directed by General Mansfield, who fell mortally wounded while leading his men, and the command of his corps devolved upon General Williams. The 124th and 127th Pennsylvania regiments were placed on the turnpike, and extended into the woods on the right, and beyond J. Miller's house. These were new regiments, and this their first engagement, and they behaved most gallantly. The attack on our part was opened by Knapp's and Hampton's Pennsylvania, and Cochran's New York batteries. Our line advanced over an open field to a stone fence, continued by breastwork and rail fence, beyond which was a cornfield. Behind and to the right of this field of high corn, was a dense woods, in the edge of which, on the turnpike road, stood a small white Dunkard church. The tide of battle rolled and surged over thefe fields. The rebels were driven from their 1862. ftrong pofition behind the ftone wall, through the corn- Sept. 17th. field into the woods beyond, when our men firft charged them. In the woods they rallied, and with ftrong reinforcements, our troops were hurled back to their firft pofition. Our batteries opened deftructively upon the advancing foe, when the Union forces again advanced, driving everything before them, until the woods were reached again, when they were driven back again in turn. Thus the tide ebbed and flowed, until the ftone wall was trampled down, the fence fcattered, the ftanding corn lay level with the ground, and hundreds of Union and rebel foldiers covered the field. Four times were our gallant men driven from the field; and it was occupied by the enemy, only to be driven back to their fhelter of the woods at laft, while we were left in poffeffion of the field. About 9 o'clock, General Sedgwick's divifion came up to the fupport of thefe worn and exhaufted heroes. After fevere fighting for fome time, the line became very much broken, and a heavy column of the enemy fucceeded in forcing back the troops of General Green's divifion, and appeared in the rear of Sedgwick's left. General Howard faced the third line to the rear preparatory to a change of front, to meet the advancing column, but this line fuffered feverely, and gave way towards the right and rear, and was followed by the firft and fecond lines. General Gorman's brigade, and one of General Dana's, rallied and checked the advance of the enemy. The other lines now formed on Gorman's left, and poured a deftructive fire upon the foe. At this time our lines were ftrengthened by the arrival

1862.
Sept. 17th.
of Sedgwick's divifion, led by General Sumner. The enemy made a very defperate attempt to turn the left of this command, which was unprotected on that flank, in confequence of the confufion on the line that, for a fhort time, fucceeded the killing of General Mansfield.

In his report before the "Committee on the Conduct of the War," General Sumner fays:

"My right divifion faced from the fevere fire of the enemy, and marched at leaft a third of a mile before I could ftop them. They did not break, but marched off in columns from the fire. They were then halted, and placed in a pofition which was held. My other two divifions, under Generals French and Richardfon, drove the enemy a confiderable diftance, and never retreated an inch."

From General Franklin's Report.—"We remained in Pleafant Valley until the morning of Wednefday, when, by direction of General McClellan, I marched to report to him, at the battle-field of Antietam. The advance of my command arrived there about 10 o'clock; and as the right of our army was then in a critical condition, General McClellan ordered me to report at once to General Sumner. General Smith had the advance, and one of his brigades was placed in fupport of fome batteries on the right, which were only faved from capture by the timely arrival of this brigade. The fecond brigade of General Smith went to affift General French, of Sumner's divifion; the third brigade was placed near the Dunkard church. The enemy advanced, and were

ANTIETAM. 97

charged by General Smith, and a severe musketry fight, 1862.
of fifteen or twenty minutes, drove them back into the Sept. 17th.
woods.

"While this charge was being made, General Slocum arrived upon the field. Two brigades were formed in line of battle, in front of the Dunkard church, with the intention of making an attack upon the enemy, now driven to the woods. General Sumner advised me not to make the attack, for if it failed, the right would be entirely destroyed. I informed him that I thought it a very necessary action, and would make the attack, unless he assumed the responsibility of forbidding it. He assumed the responsibility, and ordered me not to make it. My whole command remained during the remainder of the day in the position I have stated, under a severe artillery fire."

Companies "B," "G," and "I," of our regiment, were with General Franklin on this part of the field, and were greatly exposed during all the afternoon.

About the time of General Sedgwick's advance, General Hooker was severely wounded while leading his command. He was taken to the rear, and General Meade assumed command of the corps.

Towards the middle of the afternoon, General McClellan found that Sumner, Meade, and Mansfield, had met with serious losses, and several general officers had been carried from the field, wounded or killed, and orders were given to reinforce this portion of the line with brigades from Porter's corps, and renew the attack; but General Sumner expressed the most decided opinion

1862. against another attack that day, and the advance was
Sept. 17th. abandoned.

The cavalry, under General Pleasanton, were posted in the centre to the rear, from which position they could descend quickly to any part of the field. Four batteries of horse artillery were stationed with the cavalry, and were commanded by Captains Robertson, Tidball, Gibson, and Lieutenant Haines. On a high hill to their rear, and overlooking nearly the entire field, General McClellan established his headquarters.

General Burnside's corps held the left of the line, opposite the bridge, on the Rohrersville and Sharpsburg Road. On the opposite side of the creek, the bluffs were very abrupt, and the high hills afforded splendid positions for artillery. The best position of the enemy was on this part of the field, and the most desperate and determined fighting could alone secure us any advantage. General Burnside thus describes the action on this part of the field:

"About 10 o'clock, I received an order from General McClellan to make the attack on the bridge, and accordingly directed General Cook's brigade of Cox's division, to make a direct attack upon the bridge, and supported him by the divisions of Generals Sturgis and Wilcox. I ordered General Rodman to endeavor to effect a crossing at the ford below with his division, supported by Colonel Scammon's brigade of General Cox's division. General Cook soon discovered, from his position, that it would be impossible for him to carry the bridge, and so reported. I then ordered General Sturgis to carry it with his division. He ordered one of his brigades to make the attack, but after two gallant assaults they were driven back. I then ordered General Sturgis to put in another brigade, which brigade carried the bridge at once by assault; about the same time, Rodman carried the ford below. General Cook succeeded in finding a crossing-place above the bridge. The bridge was carried about half past 10 o'clock. Before 4 o'clock, the whole command had crossed with the batteries, and taken position on the heights just above the bridge. This whole movement, even after the bridge was carried, had to be performed under a very heavy artillery fire from the enemy. Soon after the command was formed there, I received instructions to make an attack upon the high ground surrounding the town of Sharpsburg. General Sturgis was placed in reserve, and I ordered the attack, having General Wilson's division on the extreme right, General Rodman on the extreme left, and General Cox's division acting as support to these two. The attacks were made, and the heights, which would enable us to hold the town of Sharpsburg, carried. But by this time the enemy had brought away from the extreme left of their line, portions of their force, and concentrated them against us. At the same time, the light division of A. P. Hill came up opposite my extreme left, and forced it to fall back. I immediately ordered General Sturgis's division, though nearly out of ammunition, up to its support, and they held their position until nightfall. In the mean time I had sent to General McClellan for reinforcements, but received a message from him that he could not give me any, at the same

1862.
Sept. 17th.

1862.
Sept. 17th.
time directing me to hold the bridge at all hazards. The troops accordingly fell back to the firſt poſition they had occupied after croſſing the bridge, our ſkirmiſhers being well up to our advanced poſition. This poſition was held by us during the night."

On the advance of the cavalry, the 6th Pennſylvania was ſent acroſs the bridge on the Keedyſville and Sharpſburg road, on the left of our poſition. Colonel Childs, of the 2d Pennſylvania, commanded the brigade, compoſed of his regiment, which had the advance, the 4th Indiana, and the 6th Pennſylvania cavalry. The croſſing of the ſtone bridge over the Antietam Creek was exceedingly hazardous, as it was perfectly enfiladed by the rebel artillery, which had reſiſted the croſſing of infantry for ſome hours. We daſhed acroſs at full gallop through a terrible fire, and, aſſiſted by Captain Tidball's battery, drove the rebel batteries from their poſition. Colonel Childs was killed, and twenty men of the command. Our regiment fortunately eſcaped with ſome ſlightly wounded, and ſeveral horſes ſhot on the bridge. We took up poſition on the weſt bank of the ſtream, under the ſhelter of the hill to the left of the road, having a ſtone barn and mill on our right. Here we remained moſt of the day, being held in reſerve, and guarding the bridge. At night we bivouacked on the battle-field.

The engagement cloſed at night, when both armies were thoroughly exhauſted. The poſition of the enemy had been ſelected with great care, and in natural advantages was everything that could be deſired by them.

ANTIETAM.

This strong position was attacked by our troops early in the day, and for fourteen hours the battle raged with but slight intermission. Nearly two hundred thousand men and five hundred pieces of artillery were engaged. Our loss was two thousand and ten killed, nine thousand four hundred and sixteen wounded, and one thousand and forty-three missing: making a total loss to the army of twelve thousand four hundred and sixty-nine.

1862.
Sept. 17th

Major Davis, Assistant Inspector-General, who superintended the burial of the dead, reports three thousand rebel dead buried upon the field by our own troops. Previous to this, the enemy had buried many of their own men upon the distant portion of the field which they occupied after the fight, probably at least five hundred more. Some three thousand five hundred prisoners fell into our hands. From these known facts, we suppose the rebel loss could not be less than twenty-two thousand.

"It may safely be concluded," says General McClellan, "that the rebel army lost at least thirty thousand of their best troops during their brief campaign in Maryland." "From the time our troops first encountered the enemy in Maryland, until he was driven back into Virginia, we captured thirteen guns, seven caissons, nine limbers, two forges, two caisson bodies, thirty-nine colors, and one signal flag. We have not lost a single gun or color. On the battle-field of Antietam we collected fourteen thousand small arms, and hundreds were carried away by citizens, or distributed to unarmed recruits arriving immediately after the battle."

1862.
Sept. 18th.
On the 18th the attack was not renewed, as our troops were greatly exhaufted from recent long and rapid marches, and the fevere and protracted battle of the day previous. General McClellan gives the following as his reafon for not attacking on the 18th:

"I found that our lofs had been fo great, and that there was fo much diforganization in fome of the commands, that I did not confider it proper to renew the attack that day, efpecially as I was fure of the arrival that day of two frefh divifions, amounting to about fifteen thoufand men. As an inftance of the condition of the troops that morning, I happen to recollect the returns of the Firft Corps (General Hooker's), made that morning, by which there were three thoufand five hundred men reported prefent for duty; four days after that the return of the fame corps fhowed thirteen thoufand five hundred. I had arranged, however, to renew the attack on the 19th, but I learned fome time during the night, or early in the morning, that the enemy had abandoned his pofition. He moved with great rapidity, and not being encumbered with wagons, was enabled to get his troops acrofs the river before we could do him any ferious injury. I think that, taking into confideration what the troops had gone through, we got as much out of them in this Antietam campaign as human endurance could bear."

The wounded were collected in and around the neighboring farm-houfes, barns, fheds, &c., and as rapidly as poffible, conveyed to Hagerftown, Frederick, and other towns in the vicinity, where hospitals had been established in all public halls, churches, &c.

1862.
Sept. 19th.

On the 19th, General Griffin, with a portion of the Fifth Corps, crossed the river in the evening, and carried the enemy's batteries under a heavy fire. He captured several guns, caissons, &c., and drove back the force there stationed to cover the retreat of the army.

On the same day, our regiment removed to the little town of Fair Play, where we encamped for ten days, doing picket duty at Dam No. 4, on the Potomac River. The regiment was marched from Fair Play to Frederick, Maryland, where we were ordered to refit, and recruit the regiment to twelve companies.

On the morning of the 20th, a reconnoissance was sent out under General Porter, who crossed the river, and was led into ambush about one and a half miles beyond, and suffered severely, being driven back to the river in great confusion. It was in this reconnoissance that the "Corn Exchange Regiment" (118th Pennsylvania Volunteers), Colonel Prevost, one of our own Philadelphia regiments, recently brought into active service, was so badly cut up.

CHAPTER EIGHTH.

Position of the Army of the Potomac—Stuart's Raid into Pennsylvania—The Sixth Pennsylvania sent out to Picket the Roads to the North—Scouting Duty—The Rebel Column at Emmettsburg—Report of Colonel Rush—Captain Cadwalader and his Company near being Captured—Rebels Escape—Army moves into Virginia—Several Companies rejoin the Army—Fredericksburg.

1862.
Sept. 21st.

ON the 21st of September, Franklin's corps marched to Williamsport, to reinforce General Couch. They occupied the town, the enemy retiring on their approach. General Williams's (Banks's) corps occupied Maryland Heights; Sumner's corps marched to the same point soon after. Burnside's, Porter's, and Meade's corps lay along the Potomac, the headquarters of the army being near Shepardstown. On the 23d, Sumner's and Williams's corps occupied Harper's Ferry.

The army continued in this vicinity, refitting and reorganizing, until the 8th of October, when the headquarters of the army were removed to Harper's Ferry, and an advance determined upon, the enemy lying near Winchester, Virginia.

On the 10th, the rebel cavalry, under General J. E. B. Stuart, started on a raid, to the rear of our army, into

Pennſylvania. He croſſed his force, four regiments of cavalry, with four guns, in all about three thouſand men, at McCoy's Ferry, on the Upper Potomac, where he captured our pickets, and was ſeveral hours on his march before intelligence reached General McClellan of his croſſing. All the cavalry that could be collected to purſue him only amounted to about one thouſand men, in conſequence of the abſence of moſt of the cavalry near Cumberland, in purſuit of another rebel cavalry force which had made its appearance at the Little Cacapon, and other points.

1862.

General Pleaſanton was ſent with the remaining ſmall force, and a horſe battery, in purſuit. He marched ſeventy-eight miles in the next twenty-four hours, and did not come up with Stuart until he had reached the Potomac, at the mouth of the Monocacy, where he was then croſſing, having made a forced march of ninety miles in twenty-four hours.

About 10 o'clock on the morning of the 10th, a diſpatch was received by Colonel Ruſh, at our camp near Frederick, from General John Buford, informing us of the approach of Stuart, then near Chamberſburg, and ordering him to ſend out patrols on all roads to the north, and report promptly. All the approaches from Gettyſburg and the northweſt were carefully watched by forces ſent from our camp. Four ſmall companies, of about one hundred and fifty men in all, were ſent out towards Emmettſburg. They received no information of the enemy between their camp and Emmettſburg, where they arrived near 4 o'clock in the afternoon. They then puſhed on towards Gettyſburg, ſcouting well

Oct. 10th.

1862.
October.
to their left. An hour after paſſing Emmettſburg, they received information that the advance-guard of the rebels, about four hundred ſtrong, had charged into that place, and held the town. The rebels threw out pickets covering all the roads paſſing through or near Emmettſburg, thus cutting off all communication with Frederick.

Colonel Ruſh thus ſtates, in his report to General Buford of this ſcout:

"All the couriers ſent to me by my force, to appriſe me of the preſence of the rebels, were captured or turned back until after midnight. At 3 P.M. on the 11th, I received a telegraphic order from General Marcy, to ſend one ſquadron at once to Middletown, to picket and ſcout the valley northward. This was at once done, but no important information was received from them. At 6.30 P.M., your note of 2.30 P.M., of the ſame date, was received, as follows:

"'Your diſpatch has juſt arrived. You are doing admirably. Extend your reconnoiſſance farther towards Gettyſburg, to gain information, and tranſmit all information to General Pleaſanton, at Mechanicſtown. Stuart's cavalry left Gettyſburg this morning at 9 o'clock. General Pleaſanton is to follow to intercept Stuart. If you can uſe any of the 1ſt Maine cavalry, do ſo. Make them picket eaſt of Frederick.

(Signed)   JOHN BUFORD,
Chief of Cavalry.'

"Rumors from Frederick reached me that the rebels were reported at Emmettſburg; and knowing that General Pleaſanton would come the turnpike road through Mechanicſtown, I at once called on Colonel Allen, of the 1st Maine cavalry, for one company, and sent my only remaining company. These two companies were ordered to proceed, one towards Woodsborough and one by Johnsville, with instructions to cover the line of country with scouts from the vicinity of Cregersville, Woodsborough, New Windsor, and Westminster, and to communicate any information to General Pleasanton and myself. As my company, ordered to Woodsborough, entered the town at 10½ P.M., they found the head of the rebel column just passing through, and taking the road to Liberty. This information was communicated to me at 12 o'clock, midnight, and that it had been sent to General Pleasanton, at Mechanicstown. It was soon confirmed that all the force of Stuart was passing towards Liberty. I at once sent a message and dispatch to General Marcy and yourself. A large portion of the rebel column halted near Woodsborough and Liberty, to feed and get information of our forces. Their rear-guard did not leave Liberty until about 7 A.M. on the 12th. I had no force whatever left me to follow their rear, or to in any way harass their march.

"I regret that I could not do more to check this unfortunate raid. My scouts captured one prisoner from the 1st Virginia cavalry. He tells me that the rebel force consisted of the 1st, 3d, 4th, 5th, 9th, and 10th Virginia cavalry; the 7th and 9th North Carolina cavalry; the 'Cobb Legion,' and 'Jeff. Davis Legion,' and was between four and five thousand strong, and that they had captured and carried off with them at least fifteen hundred horses from Pennsylvania.

"I have no casualties to report in my regiment. I

1862.
Oct. 12th.
would specially commend to your notice Corporal John Anderson, of Company 'D,' regiment of Lancers, for gallantry on the scout at Woodsborough. He dismounted, and entered the town on foot, in disguise. Whilst the rebel column was passing, he talked freely with their men; was suspected and detained, but afterwards escaped, and rejoined me soon after daylight, bringing most valuable information. I would also mention private Joseph Dougherty, of the same company and regiment, for gallantry in dashing through Emmettsburg while it was occupied by the enemy, in order to carry a message from me to my companies near Gettysburg."

About 9 o'clock on the morning of the 12th, the raiders reached the Potomac, near the mouth of the Monocacy. They were there attacked by General Pleasanton with his small force. After getting his guns in position, and opening fire upon them, they retreated to the ford three miles below, where they covered their crossing with the guns they had with them, and some that had been placed in position for them. A regiment of cavalry, and some infantry, were sent down the towpath to intercept their crossing, and every exertion used to get the guns with the main column on a hill, into suitable position to reach them. Our battery horses were so exhausted that they could not draw these guns into position, and men had to be substituted for them. This allowed time for the rebels to escape. We had no artillery at this point, and with the exception of a few infantry companies, our small cavalry force had no assistance.

General McClellan, in his official report, says: 1862.
Oct. 12th.

"The rapid movement of the enemy precluded the possibility of marching our infantry from any point of our lines with a possibility of intercepting them. Cavalry is the only description of force that can prevent these raids. Our cavalry had been constantly occupied in scouting and reconnoissances, and this severe labor has worked down the horses, and rendered many of them unserviceable, so that at this time no more than one half of our cavalry are fit for active service in the field. The enemy is well provided with cavalry, while our cavalry force, even with every man well mounted, would be inadequate to the requirements of the service."

Captain Cadwalader, with his company of "Lancers," came near being captured at Emmettsburg on the night of the 11th. He arrived near the town, and did not know that the rebels were within many miles. He thought it would be well to investigate the state of affairs before making a demonstration, and accordingly halted his command in a lane, and, with a sergeant, moved forward a short distance, when he came upon a column of cavalry halted in the main street of the town. Seeing that they wore blue uniforms, he supposed them to be some of our own cavalry. Riding along the column, he asked "What regiment is this?" "Stuart's Cavalry," was the reply. Here was a dilemma. He had stumbled on the main column of the raiders, and at once concluded that he and his little company had a very fair prospect of a trip to Richmond as prisoners.

1862. He replied, in a carelefs tone, "I know that, but what regiment are you?" The man anfwered, but his fufpicions were aroufed, and he eyed the captain fharply. Fortunately the night was dark, and objects could not be examined minutely. As the captain was about to move on, the rebel called after him, "Hallo! you're a Yankee foldier, ain't you?" The captain turned his head, and replied promptly, "What in —— are you talking about? Don't you know the difference between a Yankee and a Confederate foldier?" Thus reaffured, the foldier returned to his place, after again giving his regiment and company. The captain moved off, and the rebel column was juft then ordered forward. As foon as poffible, he drew off from the road to the lane in which he had left his own company. They remained concealed until the rebel column had paffed. Intelligence was immediately fent to General Pleafanton and Colonel Rufh, of the prefence and force of the enemy.

Oct. 13th. The feveral parties of our regiment engaged on this fcout returned to camp on the evening of the 13th. We were here encamped about one and a half miles out of the city. Active efforts were made to refit the command, and while doing fo, the regiment performed daily patrol duty in Frederick City.

Oct. 14th. On the 14th, Lieutenant Leiper, with a number of non-commiffioned officers and privates, were placed on recruiting duty, and ordered to Philadelphia, where a recruiting office was opened at the fouthweft corner of Eighth and Cheftnut Streets. This was done in compliance with an order from the War Department, that all regiments of cavalry fhould confift of not lefs than twelve companies. Companies "L" and "M" were 1862. rapidly filled up, and commanded by Captains Leiper and Clark.

From October 26th to November 2d, the army moved again into Virginia. At the latter date, our advance was near Upperville. On the 5th of November, our troops were on the line of the railroad from Piedmont to Salem, and the cavalry in the vicinity of Chester Gap. On the 7th, the whole force was concentrated near Warrenton.

On the 2d of November, Major Clymer, with Com- Nov. 2d. panies "B" and "G," and Captain Starr, with Company "I," were relieved from duty with General Franklin, then commanding the Sixth Corps, by Major Hazeltine's squadron, compofed of Companies "E" and "F," and Captain Newhall's Company "K." The laftnamed companies joined General Franklin, near New Berlin, Maryland, and croffed the Potomac with him, while the relieved companies joined the regiment near Frederick.

When the army was organized into grand divifions a few days later, General Smith affumed command of the Sixth Corps, and Franklin of the left grand divifion. Captain Newhall was appointed on detached duty as Provoft Marfhal of the Sixth Corps, and reported for that duty, ufing his company as was required by that office. This pofition he retained during the Frederickfburg campaign, and until the 24th of February, 1863.

On the 5th of November, Major-General McClellan Nov. 5th. was relieved from command of the Army of the Potomac, and Major-General A. E. Burnfide appointed to

1862. the command of that army. This order was received in the army on the 8th. General Burnſide decided to move the army on Richmond by way of Frederickſburg, and requeſted pontoon bridges to be ſent to that point of the Rappahannock at once. This part of the plan, that had to be attended to in Waſhington, was, by ſome unaccountable means, neglected for ſeveral days, and they were not ſtarted from there until the 19th, and on that day it commenced raining, which delayed them ſo much, and the roads became ſo bad, that when they got to Dumfries, they floated the pontoons off the wagons, ſent to Waſhington for a ſteamer, and carried them down to Acquia Creek by water, ſending the wagons around by land. They did not arrive at Frederickſburg until the 22d or 23d of November. The army having arrived there on the 19th, awaited anxiouſly the arrival of the bridges, as the river had become ſo ſwollen that it was impoſſible to ford it, and ſupply the army, had it marched to the fords above. This unfortunate delay robbed us of a great ſucceſs in this expedition.

Nov. 29th. Companies "A," "D," "C," "H," and "I," under Lieutenant-Colonel C. Roſs Smith, marched from Frederick to rejoin the army on the Rappahannock. Reveille ſounded at 5 o'clock, and by 7, they were in line on the road. Paſſed through Frederick, and marched ſteadily until near midnight, when they halted at Rockville, and encamped on the Fair Grounds.

On the following day they marched at ſunriſe, and at noon arrived at Meridian Hill, Waſhington, and encamped.

Dec. 2d. On the 2d of December, left camp at noon, croſſed the Long Bridge, and encamped at night three miles beyond Alexandria, Virginia: moved the next morning, marched twenty miles, and encamped for the night in denſe woods. On the 4th, marched to Brooks's Station, on the Acquia Creek Railroad, where they arrived near midnight. On the 7th, marched ſome eight miles to General Franklin's headquarters, near White Oak Church, about three miles from Falmouth, and about one mile back from the Rappahannock. On the 11th, Company "A," under Lieutenant Neill, was ſent on picket duty along the river. They were relieved at midnight by infantry, and got into camp again at 2 o'clock on the morning of the 12th. At $4\frac{1}{2}$ o'clock, the command was in the ſaddle, and moved down toward the river. Heavy artillery firing was heard on the right of our line near Frederickſburg. We moved with the left grand diviſion to the lower bridge, about two miles below the city, where we were diſmounted, and "ſtood to horſe" until 5 P.M., when we unſaddled and bivouacked for the night. General Franklin's grand diviſion croſſed the river to-day, under cover of heavy fog, and early the following morning became engaged. Our regiment was in the ſaddle by daylight, and croſſed the river about 9 o'clock, and were placed in charge of the bridge, aƈting as provoſt guard, to whom all priſoners on the left were confided. Though expoſed to artillery fire all day, we were not engaged.

1862.

Dec. 7th.

Dec. 13th.

Three bridges were thrown acroſs the river oppoſite Frederickſburg, and two below. Sumner and Hooker croſſed on the upper bridges, while Franklin was croſſing below. The army was divided, to make two attacks upon the enemy. On the right Generals Hooker and

1862. Sumner advanced acrofs the open plain, ftretching to
December. the heights to the rear of the town, and ftormed the
enemy's works. The attack failed, owing to the enemy's fortifications being much more formidable than they were fuppofed to be.

General Sumner defcribes thefe fortifications as "rifing tier above tier; and had we carried the firft we could not have held it, becaufe their next tier was a much more formidable row of fortifications, only a mile diftant, and on a higher pofition ftill, while heavy maffes of infantry were between the two crefts. Repeated affaults were made, but the troops were driven back in fpite of all their efforts. The principal obftacle they found was a large ftone wall, which was the outwork of the enemy. This wall was fome four or five hundred yards in length, and the enemy's artillery enfiladed the wall on both fides. They held their fire until our troops arrived at a certain point, when they arofe, and poured volley after volley upon us from the ftone wall, while their artillery perfectly enfiladed our lines. No troops could ftand fuch a fire as that."

CHAPTER NINTH.

Battle of Fredericksburg—General Hooker's Account—General Franklin's Left Grand Division—General Franklin and Meade's Reports—The Sixth as Provost Guard of the Left Grand Division—Recrossing the Rappahannock—Details from the Regiment—Colonel Rush, with Companies " B" and " G," Rejoin—They march from Washington, and have a Skirmish at Occoquan.

THE engagement on the 13th was extremely heavy on all parts of the field all day, and our loss was very great. One advance made by General Hooker is thus described by him, and confirms the severity of the fighting:

1862.
Dec. 13th

"When the word was given, the men moved forward with great impetuosity: they ran and hurrahed, and I was encouraged by the great good-feeling that pervaded them. The head of the column advanced to within about fifteen or twenty yards of the stone wall, which was the advanced position held by the rebels, when they were thrown back as quickly as they had advanced. Probably the whole of the advance did not occupy fifteen minutes. Out of about four thousand, they left behind them, on the field, seventeen hundred and sixty

1862.
Dec. 13th.
of their number killed or wounded. The enemy held thefe pofitions with about thirty thoufand men. In addition to the mufketry fire to which my men were expofed, the crefts of the hills furrounding Frederickfburg formed almoft a femicircle, and thefe were filled with artillery, and the focus was the column that moved up to the affault, and was within good canifter range."

Repeated charges were made upon thefe formidable works. On the left, General Franklin was directed "to hold his whole command in pofition for a rapid movement down the old Richmond road, and to fend out one divifion below Smithfield, to feize the heights," &c. In his teftimony before the Committee on the Conduct of the War, he fays:

"I confulted with my Corps commanders about this order, as it was not what we expected, and concluded that it meant that there fhould be what is termed an armed reconnoiffance, or an obfervation in force made of the enemy's lines with one divifion, and that I fhould keep it well fupported, and keep the command in readinefs for a rapid movement along the Richmond road."

In confequence of a mifunderftanding between Generals Burnfide and Franklin, the left grand divifion, though heavily engaged, was not exerting its energy in the direction defired. General Meade became engaged about 11 o'clock, and foon after Generals Doubleday, Gibbon, Birney, Sickles, and Newton, numbering about forty thoufand. About 3 o'clock, the rebels were driven back into the woods on the left, and though the attacking troops suffered severely, everything indicated that a strong effort made just then would have been crowned with great success. We here captured some four hundred prisoners. Darkness came on about 5 o'clock, and the engagement ceased.

1862.
Dec. 13th.

General Franklin has received great censure for not vigorously supporting General Meade's charge, and pushing back the enemy's right, as it is claimed could have been done: this would have enabled us to have flanked their stronger position on our centre and right. He was evidently fighting the enemy on his weak side.

General Meade, in his testimony, says:

"The left grand division was composed of about forty thousand men of his own command, and additional troops, numbering fifteen or twenty thousand, sent to him from the right, to which great objection was made by officers on that part of the field. In all, he had not less than sixty thousand men under his command. The actual attack on our left was made by about ten thousand men. My division succeeded in driving the enemy from all their advanced works, breaking through their lines, and occupying the heights: piercing their lines, and getting into the presence of their reserves. I had penetrated their lines so far, that I had no support on either flank. The enemy concentrated their forces, and attacked me on my front and both flanks, and I was forced to fall back."

General Meade believes if we had held that position,

1862. we would have been able to break the enemy's lines, and compel an evacuation of their line of works to the rear of Frederickſburg. He thinks the failure here owing entirely to the want of a large force in this attack.

Dec. 15th. No movement was made by the army during Sunday, nor on Monday, until late in the night, when, under cover of the darkneſs, the army was withdrawn to the north bank of the river, and went into camp, and very ſoon after into winter quarters.

Dec. 18th. On the 18th, part of Company "A" was detailed for duty with Profeſſor Bache, Chief Engineer on the ſtaff of General Franklin. About this time one company was placed on ſafeguard duty along the river, a corporal's guard being ſtationed at each houſe below Falmouth for four miles. One ſquadron was ſent to "Army Head-quarters;" two companies were ſent to General Reynolds; one to General Newton; three remained with General Franklin; while the balance went into camp near White Oak Church.

Colonel Ruſh, with Companies "B" and "G," having marched from Frederick, Maryland, joined the balance of the regiment on the 24th of December.

Lieutenant-Colonel Smith, being detached as Provoſt Marſhal of the left grand diviſion, received authority to uſe the regiment in provoſt duty.

In the Philadelphia Inquirer of January 8th, 1863, appears an account of the march of Colonel Ruſh, with theſe two companies, from Waſhington, with the following incident of the march:

"At the town of Occoquan, there is a ferry acroſs

the Occoquan Creek, now much used for the crossing of army trains, sutlers' wagons, &c. On Thursday, the 18th instant, the rebels captured a train of army wagons at that point, and partly destroyed the boat, but did not move the remainder of the train from there until Friday, the 19th. On the morning of that day, one small squadron of 'Rush's Lancers' were marching under orders from General Heintzelman, in company with the 17th Pennsylvania Cavalry (a recruit regiment, and perfectly green), to join the Army of the Potomac. The road being picketed from Alexandria to the Occoquan, and the pickets reporting to us that there was no enemy about, the march was made without anticipation of attack. On reaching the river, and when opposite the town of Occoquan, the head of our column was attacked by carbineers, dismounted, in a wood. Colonel Rush, by reference to his map, found that we could cross the stream at Snyder's Ford, two and a half miles above Occoquan; so one battalion of the 17th was posted to hold the enemy at the ferry, and the squadron of Lancers immediately started for the ford, with a view of crossing and capturing the rebels by getting to their rear. On arriving at the ford, we discovered another body of the enemy, one hundred and forty strong, drawn up in line on the opposite shore, being stationed there to hold the ford. The advance of Lancers was supported by the 17th Pennsylvania, and pushed over the river under fire, when a brisk skirmish occurred. It lasted only for a few minutes, when the enemy fled, leaving two of their wounded, who were captured. In their flight, the enemy threw away their arms, many of which were

1862.

Dec. 18th.

1862. picked up by our men. We purſued them to Occoquan
Dec. 19th. ſo quickly, that twelve of the wagons they had captured
the evening before, with horſes and harneſs complete,
were retaken by us, and brought ſafely to the Army
Headquarters. Colonel Ruſh ſent ſcouting parties in
all directions, ſome of whom preſſed the enemy ſo cloſely,
that they fired the portion of the train yet in their poſſeſſion and eſcaped."

The following is a liſt of changes, promotions, &c.,
made in the Staff and Line to this date:

Captain George W. Clymer, Company "G," was
promoted and muſtered as Major, to date from March
29th, 1862.

Lieutenant Auguſtus F. Bertolett reſigned April 15th,
1862, in conſequence of preſſing buſineſs engagements.

Sergeant A. D. Price appointed Second Lieutenant,
and muſtered as ſuch from April 22d, 1862.

Sergeant-Major A. P. Morrow, appointed Second
Lieutenant Company "B," March 1ſt, 1862; captured
by the rebel General Stuart, June 17th, 1862; taken to
Richmond, and confined in Libby priſon, where he remained until Auguſt 28th, when exchanged. He was
promoted Firſt Lieutenant Company "C" at Frederick,
Maryland, November 9th, 1862.

Chaplain Waſhington B. Erben reſigned July 18th,
1862, while the regiment was lying at Harriſon's Landing, in conſequence of diſeaſe contracted in the ſwamps
of the Chickahominy. He had been faithful in his ſervice, had held religious meetings whenever the exigen-

cies of the service would permit, and distributed many tracts and religious papers. At the formation of the regiment, every man was presented with a pocket copy of the New Testament, furnished by the Philadelphia Bible Society. A small soldier's library, the gift of St. Andrew's Episcopal Church, of which Colonel Rush was a member, was also distributed by the Chaplain. The general experience of the Chaplain was, " That so long as the regiment was in camp, he was able to hold religious services with some degree of regularity, and to maintain a satisfactory personal intercourse with the men; but after the regiment took the field, the cavalry was kept in such constant motion, the squadrons were so often on detached duty, and the men were worked so hard, and so excited, that his opportunities for religious instruction or intercourse with the soldiers became very irregular. These hindrances to a proper religious influence upon the men, together with sickness, led to his resignation."

1862. December.

Captain Joseph Wright died May 18th, 1862, at Wilkesbarre, Pennsylvania.

George W. Pepper was commissioned Second Lieutenant of Company "H," in October, 1862. He served with the regiment during the Fredericksburg campaign, and participated in Stoneman's raid in the spring of 1863. In consequence of an injury received by falling with his horse, he was compelled to resign, and was discharged on surgeon's certificate of disability, May 22d, 1863.

Sergeant E. P. Bertrand was commissioned and mustered as Second Lieutenant of Company "A," November 1st, 1862.

1862.   Second Lieutenant Edwin L. Teirs, promoted Firſt
December. Lieutenant of Company "L," November 1ſt, 1862. On the 15th of January, 1863, he received a ſevere injury by his horſe falling with him, was allowed ſick leave, and after ſix months' abſence under medical treatment, went to Baltimore for examination before a Medical Board. As a long time muſt elapſe before he would be fit for duty, the Board recommended his honorable diſcharge from the ſervice.

Charles B. Coxe, commiſſioned and muſtered Second Lieutenant Company "M," November, 1862.

CHAPTER TENTH.

A General Advance—Winter Campaign—" Burnſide's Mud March"—Burnſide's Farewell Addreſs to the Army—Belle Plain—The Cavalry Reviewed by Preſident Lincoln— Opening of the Spring Campaign—Colonel Ruſh leaves the Regiment and Field Service—Major Robert Morris, Jr.

D URING the early part of January, a part of the regiment was placed on ſafeguard duty along the Rappahannock, below Falmouth. On the 11th, Companies "A" and "D" were ordered to report to General Reynolds, commanding the First Corps, for provoſt duty, Captain Treichel being appointed Provoſt Marſhal of the corps.

1863.

Jan. 11th

The rebels can be ſeen daily at work, fortifying at every point available for croſſing, by throwing up earthworks, and digging rifle pits, near the ſeveral fords of the river. They have alſo eſtabliſhed a double line of pickets, and a corps of obſervation, from the upper fords of the Rappahannock to Port Royal, nearly twenty-five miles below Frederickſburg.

An advance movement was determined upon by General Burnſide late in December, the croſſing to be effected at the Sedden Houſe, a ſhort diſtance below Hayfield; while two thouſand five hundred cavalry, with

1863. a battery of artillery, were to crofs the river above at Kelley's Ford, march to the rear of the rebel army, deftroy the feveral railroads leading to Richmond, and paffing beyond the rebel capital, join General Peck at Suffolk. This plan was abandoned after orders had been iffued for the movement, and the cavalry had already marched to Kelley's Ford, in confequence of the following telegram, received by General Burnfide, from the Prefident:

"I have good reafon for faying that you muft not make a general movement without letting me know of it."

General Burnfide went to Wafhington, and there learned that the Prefident had been called upon by fome general officers of the Army of the Potomac, who were diffatisfied with the movement contemplated, and feared difafter. General Burnfide then ftated his plan to the Prefident, General Halleck, and Secretary Stanton, and an advance was decided upon in accordance with his propofitions.

On his return to the army, General Burnfide became fatisfied that by this time his contemplated movement had been communicated to the enemy, and a different plan of advance was decided upon. It was determined to crofs the army at Banks's and United States Fords.

Jan. 19th. A general order was iffued, announcing that the Army of the Potomac was "about to meet the enemy once more," and that the "aufpicious moment had arrived to ftrike a great and mortal blow to the rebellion, and to gain that decided victory which is due to the country."

Jan. 20th. Early on Monday the troops were fet in motion,—

General Hooker's command moving in column by one road, General Franklin's grand divifion by another,— and marched to the feveral fords of the Upper Rappahannock. We were permitted to remain undifturbed in camp, with orders to move at daylight on the 21ft. During the afternoon, the indications of rain became very decided, and before midnight a heavy ftorm was raging. With great difappointment at the probable delay that might be occafioned by a fevere rain, we waited anxioufly for the morrow, hoping for more favorable weather.

1863.

Wednefday morning the ftorm continued with great violence. Tents were ftruck about 6 o'clock; at 9, the bugles founded "to horfe," and we moved flowly out of the woods on to the road, which was by this time in an indefcribably bad condition. Mud was in the afcendency, and the great army defeated by impaffable roads. Guns, caiffons, pontoons, wagons, all find it impoffible to move with their ufual horfe-power; teams are doubled, and even tripled, while men are at the wheels of the gun-carriages, ftraining every mufcle to move them forward. The utmoft effort was put forth to get pontoons enough into pofition to conftruct a bridge; heavy double teams were harneffed to each pontoon boat, but every effort was futile. Long ropes were then attached, and a hundred and fifty men added their united effort, with but little more fuccefs; they would flounder through the mire for a few feet, and then give up exhaufted. Night came on, but no pontoons had reached the river. The rebels had difcovered what was going on, and the pickets on the oppofite bank called over to ours, that they

Jan. 21ft.

1863.
January.
"would come over in the morning, and help us build that bridge." Horses, wagons, and troops, wear one universal coat of mud. Men march in it to their knees, and are splashed with it to their heads. The mounted troops, marching in column, present even a worse appearance than the infantry; horses, riders, and their accoutrements, are all spattered with mud by their companions as the column moves on.

On reaching a point near Banks's Ford, we were drawn off the road into a woods, where we bivouacked for the night. The cold storm of snow and rain continued all the night through, while the soft spongy soil was thoroughly saturated by the two days' rain. The wind howled dismally through the trees; and we found that a cold, blustery, stormy night in midwinter, was not one of the most inviting occasions on which to spend a night in a bleak forest, with but slight shelter or food. Many of the men had brought their shelter tents, and making a flooring of hemlock, spruce, or pine boughs, are soon settled for the night, weariness of body rendering their beds inviting. Huge fires are kindled by others, who, less fortunate or thoughtful in reference to shelter tents, are now driven to the necessity of keeping up a good fire. Rails, logs, &c., are gathered in great quantities, and are piled near the fires ready for use. Around each fire is gathered a circle of men, who are either seated near it, smoking their pipes as a sort of solace in their extremity; or, wrapped in their blankets, with a friendly stone or log for a pillow, are lying with feet to the fire, in total forgetfulness of snow, rain, or cold, in deep sleep, the pelting rain upon their gum blankets not disturbing them in the least. With many, the night was one of restless, weary, waiting for the dawn.

1863.

Thursday morning came with unabated storm of rain and snow. Over the most smoky fires imaginable, from green wood and eddying winds, we prepared our cups of coffee, and partook of breakfast, so called; after which, with stamping around the fires in wet boots, and unsuccessful efforts to keep near the fire and yet escape the smoke, which seemed this day more than ever determined to defeat our plans; with counter smoking from a multitude of friendly pipes, and cheerful chatting and speculating as to movements, the time wore on until noon, when we were rejoiced to receive an order to return to our camp, near White Oak Church, which we promptly prepared to do. It was no longer a question by what lines the army should advance, but by what possible means it could return to its base of supplies, as provisions could not be conveyed through these all but bottomless roads, to the troops. A writer in the New York Times says:

Jan. 22d.

"It was a curious sight presented by the army, as we rode over the ground occupied by it. One might fancy some new geologic cataclysm had overtaken the world, and that he saw around him the elemental wrecks left by another deluge. An indescribable chaos of pontoons, wagons, and artillery, incumbered the roads; supply wagons upset by the roadside; artillery stalled in the mud; ammunition trains mired by the way. Horses and mules dropped down dead, exhausted with the effort to move their loads through the hideous medium. A

1863. hundred and fifty dead animals, many of them buried in the liquid muck, were counted in the courfe of a morning's ride."

We plodded our weary nine miles back again to the friendly grove called our camp, where we arrived near nightfall. Tents were hurriedly put up, and though the ground, tents, clothing, and everything about us were as wet and uncomfortable as could be, we flept foundly.

Thus ended a campaign which prefented, at its opening, every human promife of fuccefs. The odd experiences of "Burnfide's Mud March" will never be forgotten by thofe who participated in it.

Jan. 26th On the 26th, General Burnfide was relieved of the command of the Army of the Potomac, at his own requeft, and was fucceeded by Major-General Hooker. Major-Generals W. B. Franklin and E. V. Sumner were likewife relieved of command. There was much about General Burnfide to make him beloved and honored. He poffeffed fuch high fenfe of honor, fo much felf-facrificing magnanimity, and fo much bravery, that he will always be remembered with affection and efteem. His farewell to the army was made in General Orders, No. 9, viz.:

"By direction of the Prefident of the United States, the Commanding General this day transfers the command of this army to Major-General Jofeph Hooker. The fhort time that he has directed your movements has not been fruitful of victory, or any confiderable advancement of our lines, but it has again demonftrated an amount of courage, patience, and endurance that, under more favorable circumſtances, would have accompliſhed great reſults. Continue to exerciſe theſe virtues; be true in your devotion to your country, and the principles you have ſworn to maintain; give to the brave and ſkilful General, who has long been identified with your organization, and who is now to command you, your full and cordial ſupport, and you will deſerve ſucceſs. His prayers are that God may be with you, and grant you continued ſucceſs, until the rebellion is cruſhed."

1863.

The army went again into winter quarters, in the valleys and on the ſouthern ſlopes of the hills along the railroad, from Acquia Creek to Falmouth; northweſt from Falmouth along the river, and back to Stafford Court-houſe; ſouth and eaſt to White Oak Church and Belle Plain Landing on the Potomac.

February.

On the 1ſt of March, we changed camp from White Oak Church to Belle Plain Landing. Here a large camp was laid out, in a denſe woods, fitted up in the moſt beautiful camp ſtyle. The company ſtreets were each a hundred feet in width, with officers' quarters at the head of each, and about thirty feet from the firſt company quarters. Huts were built of hewn logs, the roof being formed of ſhelter tents. They were very comfortable, and attractive in appearance. No troops were encamped within a mile or two of us, which ſaved us from much annoyance, and allowed us to occupy all the ground we deſired. This camp was facetiouſly called by ſome, the "Camp of Magnificent Diſtances."

March 1ſt.

1863. While encamped here, Companies "I" and "E," under Captains Starr and Carpenter, were fent to general headquarters, as efcort to Major-General Hooker.

Mar. 5th. On the 5th of March, Companies "L" and "M," in charge of Major Robert Morris, Jr., ftarted from Frederick, Maryland, and marched to Wafhington, D. C., where they took tranfports for Belle Plain Landing.

Mar. 17th. On the 17th of March, the firft real cavalry battle of the war was fought at Kelley's Ford, by troops under General Averill. The regiments engaged were the 1ft and 5th United States, under Captains Reno and Leib; the 3d and 16th Pennfylvania cavalry, under Colonel McIntofh; the 1ft Rhode Ifland, 4th New York, and 6th Ohio, Colonel Duffie; and the 6th New York horfe artillery, of fix guns. The 5th regulars behaved with fpecial gallantry. Led by Captain Leib, they charged upon the enemy in fine ftyle, broke their line, and fcattered the force in their front. Captain Hunt, with three fquadrons 1ft United States, did good fervice in fupporting the battery. The 3d and 16th Pennfylvania alfo drove the enemy by a determined charge. Our forces held the field at the clofe of the day. The 6th Pennfylvania was not on this expedition, being encamped at Belle Plain.

April 2d. Private Howard Haines, Company "F," was buried to-day with military honors.

April 6th. On the 6th, the cavalry corps was reviewed by Prefident Lincoln. The Philadelphia Inquirer contained the following report:

"The fineft cavalry difplay ever witneffed in the

United States, was that of the review of the cavalry of this army to-day by the Prefident. Every regiment turned out in its largeft poffible numbers, and the difplay was moft impofing."

After an account of the infpection by the Prefident, and the paffing in review of the troops before him, occurs this allufion to the Sixth Pennfylvania Cavalry:

"One of the moft beautiful movements of the whole day, was that near the clofe of the review, when the Sixth Pennfylvania Cavalry, familiarly known as 'Rufh's Lancers,' were brought around the houfe, into the field, at full gallop, with company fronts, and at that gait executed moft perfectly one of the moft difficult cavalry movements, that of wheeling by companies into regimental line, facing the immenfe company of military authorities there gathered, and forming a moft perfectly dreffed line on the inftant, every horfe fteady, and halted juft in his right place, the men looking proud that they were able to accomplifh fo eafily this moft difficult manœuvre while at full gallop, the diftances between the feveral fquadrons being moft accurately preferved. I have really heard more praife given to this regiment in this fingle movement, than of any other occurrence of the day. It certainly exhibited the great proficiency of drill that has been attained by one of the beft of Philadelphia regiments."

On Saturday, April 12th, orders were received for the regiment to prepare for the fpring campaign, and to

1863.
April 11th.
be in readiness to abandon their winter quarters, and move on Monday. This order was conveyed in the following circular:

> "HEADQUARTERS CAVALRY CORPS, ARMY OF THE POTOMAC,
> April 11th, 1863.
>
> "*First.* The effective force of this corps will be in readiness to move at daylight on Monday, April 13th.
>
> "*Second.* Each trooper will carry on his horse not less than three days' rations for himself and horse, and as much more as shall be judged practicable for him to take on short marches; and he will carry as much ammunition for the arms he bears as he can conveniently on his person, the amount not to be less in any case than forty rounds of carbine, and twenty rounds of pistol cartridge.
>
> "*Third.* The pack trains will be loaded with five days' rations for the men. The supply trains will be loaded with rations of grain and subsistence in such proportion, that men and animals will be supplied to the same date.
>
> "*Fourth.* Some convenient point will be selected in each division and Buford's brigade, at which camp and garrison equipage, quartermaster's and subsistence stores, with private property, will be left in charge of an officer and the dismounted men, who will constitute the depot guards for this property. All superfluous articles of clothing, camp and garrison equipage, and, in fact, of every kind, will be left with the regimental baggage at these depots.
>
> "*Fifth.* The sick of each division will be assembled at the division hospitals. Rush's Lancers will send their sick to the hospital of Gregg's division, &c.
>
> "*Sixth.* The headquarters of the corps will be designated at night, during the campaign, either in bivouac or on the march, by a red lantern.
>
> "By command of
> "MAJOR-GENERAL STONEMAN."

The remainder of the day, and the Sabbath following, were spent in preparations for active service. Early on the morning of the 13th, the familiar notes of the "general" sounded through the camp; it was followed

SPRING CAMPAIGN. 133

by "boots and faddle," and we were foon mounted, and 1863.
on the line of march.

A farewell cheer was given to our old camping-ground April 13th
as the regiment moved out. The entire corps rendezvoufed at General Stoneman's headquarters, and ftarted
from there about 10 o'clock, being divided into three
divifions, under Generals Buford, Gregg, and Averill,
with the 6th Pennfylvania, Colonel Rufh, forming an
independent command, all under General Stoneman.
We marched all day to the northweft, and bivouacked
at night near the "Spotted Tavern," and Hartwood
Church.

Our breakfaft was eaten haftily on the following morn- April 14th.
ing, and at an early hour we were again in the faddle.
Marched flowly all day, and by a circuitous route reached
Bealton Station, on the Orange and Alexandria Railroad early in the evening, where we bivouacked for the
night on low ground in the edge of a wood. The
evening was magnificent, and all were in fine fpirits.
Our regiment had been felected for fpecial duty, on
which it was to ftart early the next morning. After
croffing the Rappahannock with the main command, we
were to proceed rapidly to the vicinity of Richmond,
deftroy railroads, canals, telegraph lines, and by forced
march, to join our forces either at Suffolk or Fortrefs
Monroe. With minds ftirred at the refponfibility and
honor of this felection, we were wakeful, and fat around
our camp fires until after midnight, difcuffing the important work before us, its dangers and rewards.

A little after 2 o'clock in the morning, a heavy ftorm
fet in, and the rain fell in torrents. Morning found us

1863. in a great swamp, with several inches of water over all the ground. We were marched towards the river, but on examination, it was found to be so swollen that it was impossible to cross it at the usual fords. After being in the saddle some four hours, we returned, and again went into camp, in the same swampy field we had left in the morning. The remainder of the day, until dark, was spent in collecting rails, and making arrangements for the night. Rails were placed together on the ground, and covered with boughs, by which comparatively dry though very angular beds were secured.

April 20th. We remained in this vicinity from the 15th to the 20th, changing camp twice. Heavy rains continued nearly every day, and we had very limited protection from the storm, and scanty allowance of food.

We left camp on the morning of the 20th, and marched all day through wretched roads, and heavy showers, and halted at night two miles southeast of Warrenton, tired, wet, and hungry. Captain Treichel, with Company "A," was sent on a reconnoissance to Warrenton. He made a dash into the town, which was reported as being occupied by a small force of the enemy, but meeting none, he stationed his pickets on the roads approaching the town, and remained in charge of the April 22d. place until the morning of the 22d, when he joined the regiment as we passed through, and marched to Warrenton Junction, on the Orange and Alexandria Railroad. At night we were again exposed to a very heavy rain, which continued for three days, much to our discomfort.

April 27th. On the 27th, the rain abated, the sun shone out clear and warm, the streams were falling, roads improving, and an early movement expected.

1863. April.

At dress parade this evening, Colonel Rush, in an affecting speech, took leave of the regiment, deeming it very doubtful that he should be able to rejoin the command this campaign. He expressed great regret at being compelled to leave just at this juncture, but the severe exposure of the last three weeks had revived a chronic disease contracted while serving in Mexico. On the earnest recommendation of Surgeon Coover, he applied for, and received, a sick-leave on surgeon's certificate of disability, and on the following morning left for Washington. The honorable position attained by the regiment in its later campaigns, is doubtless due to the military skill and knowledge, and the superior qualities of Colonel Rush as an organizer and disciplinarian.

The command of the regiment now devolved on Major Robert Morris Jr., Lieutenant-Colonel C. Ross Smith being on detached duty on the staff of General Stoneman.

CHAPTER ELEVENTH.

Stoneman's Raid—Croſſing the Rappahannock—Orange Springs—Louiſa Court-Houſe—A Skirmiſh—Colonel Percy Wyndham—Columbia on the James—General Gregg's Expedition—Captain Lord and the Firſt United States—The Fifth United States Cavalry—Thompſon's Croſs-Roads—The Return—Diſmal Night Rides.

1863.
April 28th.   ABOUT 5 o'clock in the evening of the 28th, five days' rations and three days' forage were iſſued, and orders to hold the regiment in readineſs to move at a moment's notice. Tents were immediately ſtruck, wagons loaded, horſes ſaddled, and the whole command ordered to ſtand to horſe, and await orders. Hour after hour paſſed, finding us in the ſame poſition: midnight, and we are ſtill impatiently waiting, and wondering why we do not move. Near midnight rain began to fall, and continued with increaſed ſeverity as the day dawned.

April 29th.   On the 29th, we marched to Kelley's Ford, on the Rappahannock, where we forded the ſtream about 3 o'clock, P.M. The croſſing was quite hazardous, in conſequence of the river being high and running very ſwiftly. The Fifth, Eleventh, and Twelfth Corps, croſſed on pontoons at the ſame time, a ſhort diſtance below the ford.

Soon after we had effected the crossing, artillery firing was heard towards the right, and we were hurried off in that direction. It proved to be from a small force of the enemy, who opposed the crossing of Colonel Averill near the railroad bridge, the enemy retreating after a short skirmish. General Buford went to the left, and exchanged a few shots with a force found there. They scattered before our advancing column, and we moved forward to near Fleshman's River, where we halted in a newly ploughed field, and without fire, or shelter from a cold merciless storm, we spent the night. *1863. April 29th*

It was dark and dreary in the extreme: no bugle calls were sounded, and strict silence was observed, as we were supposed to be in proximity to the rebels. The vivid flashes of lightning alone illuminated the scene. Our pickets were charged during the night by straggling bands of rebel cavalry, but the troops were not generally alarmed.

Up to this time no one but the generals in command were aware of our destination; but at 12 o'clock that night, the commanders of the several regiments were assembled, and informed by General Stoneman of his plans and instructions. They were ordered to send to the rear every description of wagon, the pack mules, led horses, and all animals that would not be able to march fifty miles a day; to provide themselves with eight days' rations, and as much grain as each man could carry upon his horse, and to be in readiness to move at 4 o'clock in the morning.

At 2 o'clock, all were busily engaged in these preparations, and the hours until daylight consumed in draw

1863. ing and diftributing rations, and fpeculations upon the probable refult of the expedition. Nearly all were jubilant at the profpect before them, while vifions of Libby prifon, or Belle Ifle, weakened the nerves of fome. It was daylight when the train to the rear was in readinefs to move, and the laft mule with extra baggage was difpatched, and our forward march was refumed. We were obliged to move cautioufly, being ignorant of the exact locality of the enemy; and it was 11 o'clock before we reached the Rapidan.

April 30th. The advance of General Buford's column arrived at Morton's Ford, on the Rapidan, about noon, and Captain Leiper was fent acrofs on a reconnoiffance. He came upon and fcattered a rebel force, charging them with the lance, and returned with eleven prifoners, having loft Lieutenant Lennig, captured by the enemy. The prifoners brought in all belonged to the Fauquier County Artillery, and formed part of a force fome fixteen hundred ftrong, commanded by General W. H. Lee, that had been encamped between this and Raccoon Ford the night previous. The condition of the country was reported to General Buford, and his command croffed as rapidly as the fwollen condition of the ftream would permit, and marched to Raccoon Ford, where the balance of the force was croffing. We there bivouacked for the night. Hungry, wet, and fatigued, we were illy prepared to fpend a night in ftanding to horfe, but fuch were our orders; and without unfaddling, the regiment was drawn up in clofe column of companies, the men difmounted, and ordered to ftand at their horfes' heads all night. No fires could be kindled;

and as a denfe fog fettled down in the valley during the night, it became very cold, and our clothing being wet, we fuffered greatly before morning. Many fank exhaufted at their horfes' heads, and with reins faftened to wrift, flept for hours defpite the difcomfort.

1863.

Our courfe the next day was in a foutheafterly direction, General Buford marching towards Orange Courthoufe, while General Gregg paffed on to Orange Springs. The advance, under Major Beaumont, of the 1ft New Jerfey Cavalry, reached Orange Springs at 1 o'clock in the afternoon, where they encountered a fmall force of the enemy. The major at once charged them, capturing a major and feveral men, and difperfing the reft. He was informed that a large fupply train paffed there in the morning in great hafte, throwing away large quantities of forage and provifions; and that the rebels were falling back from Culpepper towards Spottfylvania Court-houfe, taking with them as much of their movable effects as poffible, and driving a great number of negroes before them. In hopes of overhauling this company, General Gregg fent Colonel Wyndham, who commanded the fecond brigade of his divifion, after them, with inftructions to follow them for five miles, and if he faw nothing of them, to return, as time was too valuable to wafte in further purfuit. The Colonel went the five miles on a trot, but faw nothing of the enemy. In the mean time our men, to amufe themfelves, inftituted a fearch through the different houfes in the vicinity, and fucceeded in bringing to light a great quantity of contraband goods. In one houfe they found feveral dozen pairs of valuable high top-boots and fol-

May 1ft.

1863. diers' shoes, evidently of Northern manufacture. In almost every house they found muskets, rifles, and shot guns; and in one house a fine gray uniform belonging to a field officer.

There was considerable straggling to-day, as the men were without rations. Every smokehouse and farmyard near the line of our march, was made to contribute to our comfort. Chickens, ducks, and hams, in great numbers, were secured. During the morning the clouds broke away, and under the genial influence of the bright sunshine, fresh spirit seemed to possess the men. The evening being pleasant, and the moon shining brightly, we marched until 3 o'clock in the morning, when we forded the North Anna, and halted until daylight. Our horses were unsaddled, and we were allowed fires for the first time since leaving Warrenton Junction. A good meal of warm coffee, chicken, and corn pone, was enjoyed greatly. We here rested for about three hours, and moved at 7 o'clock on the morning of

May 2d. the 2d, and about noon came to Louisa Court-house. This place we expected to find defended, as the Virginia Central Railroad, connecting Fredericksburg with Gordonsville, passes through it. We halted about a mile from the town, when Colonel Kilpatrick, with the 7th New York Cavalry (the "Harris Light"), charged through the town, his boys yelling like demons. They secured a few prisoners, but met no regular force of the enemy. The inhabitants were much terrified at such unusual proceedings, doubtless expecting that the Yankees were about to murder them all, and were greatly surprised when they saw the post-office and public buildings alone disturbed. The telegraph office was taken possession of, and an operator seated, who received telegrams from the rebel capital. We thus obtained information of the successful operations of General Hooker, on the south of the Rappahannock, up to that time. For nearly an hour we received rebel intelligence. When the discovery was made in Richmond that the "Yankees" held the line, some very decided remarks of disapprobation came over the wires, when they ceased to communicate.

1863.
May 2d

One squadron of the 10th New York, under Colonel Irwin, was sent five miles above the town, and another, under Major Avery, of the same regiment, five miles below, when the work of destruction began. The track was torn up, bridges and culverts destroyed, and stations and water tanks burned.

While halting in Louisa Court-house, intelligence was received that a large force of rebel cavalry was approaching on the Gordonsville Road, and was distant only about an hour's march. General Gregg passed through the town, and found Colonel Wyndham's brigade in line of battle on the brow of a hill, a short distance beyond the town. After waiting there for an hour or more for the approach of the enemy, he returned, when the march was resumed, leaving as a rear-guard a portion of the 1st Maine Cavalry. Shortly after our departure, the enemy came in sight, and attacking our small force, compelled it to fall back. The 2d New York was immediately sent to their support, and after a sharp skirmish the enemy withdrew. At 3 o'clock, we were again in line of march on the road. We moved steadily forward

1863.

May 3d.

until half-past 11 o'clock, passing through a beautiful district of country, and having a clear moonlight night for the march. We halted at "Thompson's Cross-Roads," or "Four Corners," near midnight.

General Stoneman immediately called his commanders together, and explained his general plan of operations, and by half-past 2 o'clock on the morning of the 3d, the several expeditions had been started on their perilous and important work. On the march thus far, General Buford's command had captured a train of twenty-six wagons, with four-mule teams to each. We were now in the very heart of the enemy's country, and what was to be done must be done quickly, as the enemy were known to be concentrating all the force they could get together to prevent the accomplishment of our designs.

Colonel Percy Wyndham, of the 1st New Jersey Cavalry, with his own and the 1st Maine regiment, in all about six hundred men, took a southerly direction, crossing Owen's Creek, Licking Hole Creek, and several other small streams, and reached Columbia, on the James River, at about 8 A.M. on the 3d.

The country through which we passed was inhabited mostly by wealthy farmers, who had never before had the pleasure of seeing any of the detested Yankee army; and as they were totally ignorant of our presence in that vicinity, their looks of wonderment and surprise can be better imagined than described. As many of our horses had given out, and the best of them were in worn condition, the colonel detailed a squad of men to scour the country, and take every horse fit for service. Very

COLUMBIA ON THE JAMES. 143

many valuable horses were obtained in this way. We arrived in the vicinity of Columbia at 9 o'clock. As we approached the town, horsemen were seen hovering about, watching our movements, and one of our videttes reported a large force of cavalry about a mile ahead. Captain W. R. Robbins, of the 1st New Jersey, was sent out with six men to ascertain the facts of the case. He scoured the country for a distance of some five or six miles, capturing some prisoners, but discovered no enemy in force.

1863.
May 3d.

Colonel Wyndham now made a disposition of his forces. He stationed the 1st Maryland outside of the town, and charged through it with the 1st New Jersey, under Lieutenant-Colonel Broderick. As we entered the town, the rebels were seen to leave on the opposite side, in great haste. Chase was immediately given them by Captains Kester, Lucas, Gray, Boyd, and others, who succeeded in making a few prisoners.

Parties were at once detailed to cut the canal, destroy the locks, burn the bridges, tow-boats, canal-boats, &c. In ten minutes from the time we entered the town, flames were issuing from five bridges, and several canal-boats loaded with forage and commissary stores; while two parties, under the supervision of Major Russell, of the 1st Maryland, and Lieutenant-Colonel Broderick, were engaged in cutting down the bank of the canal, and destroying the locks; and another party, under Captains Thomas and Hicks, of Colonel Wyndham's staff, were in the town, destroying an immense storehouse filled with supplies of every description for the rebel army.

1863.
May.
A large quantity of whiskey, nicely bottled, labelled, and boxed, for the medical purveyor's office, Richmond, was carried off or destroyed.

The inhabitants were much terrified at our presence; and one lady came running out of her house, as we passed up the street, and asked if we would be kind enough not to murder the women and children. She was assured that the only object of the expedition was to destroy government property. No house was entered, or citizen insulted, or molested in any way; and the object of the expedition having been accomplished, the troops quietly left the town. The only part of the expedition which they were unable to accomplish, was the destruction of the aqueduct, where the canal crosses the Rivanna River. This is built of solid masonry, and is of immense strength, and we had no means of destroying it. After leaving the town, Major Beaumont volunteered to return with a company, and again attempt its destruction, and was permitted to do so by Colonel Wyndham. He succeeded in finding powder and fuse in Columbia, but in consequence of the short time he had to work, was unable to accomplish its destruction.

This canal runs along the James River from Lynchburg to Richmond, and nearly one half of their supplies for the army were transported over it. Sufficient damage was done to render it useless for at least three weeks. This command returned to Stoneman's headquarters in safety about dusk, having marched over sixty miles.

General Gregg's command moved upon the Fredericksburg and Richmond Railroad to Ashland. On 1863. the way there a long bridge, over the South Anna River, May 3d. was burned, and a detachment was sent to destroy the Ground-squirrel Bridge. The column then marched on the Richmond and Gordonsville Pike to within eight miles of Ashland, where they bivouacked Monday night. On the following morning they entered Ashland, where a train of cars, filled with troops, many of whom were sick, was captured; the train was destroyed, and the prisoners paroled. In the rebel government stables a large number of public horses and mules were found, with twenty wagons and complete sets of harness. The animals were brought away, but the stables, storehouses, wagons and harness, were burned. Just outside of the town, eighteen more wagons, each drawn by six mules, were also captured. They struck the Virginia Central Railroad, at Hanover Station, at about 8 o'clock, P.M. Here they captured and paroled thirty officers and men, burnt a trestle-work bridge, the railroad depot, storehouses, stables and cars, all belonging to, or in use by, the rebel government. Over a thousand sacks of flour were destroyed, and a large quantity of clothing, camp, and garrison equipage. A portion of this command was here detached, under Colonels Kilpatrick and Davis, who forced their way through to Yorktown, and there again entered the Union lines.

General Gregg returned to Thompson's Cross-roads on the 5th, having accomplished more than was expected from his expedition.

While this was in progress, another force, under Captain R. S. C. Lord, commanding the 1st United States

1863.
May 3d.
Cavalry, was sent to Tolersville, to destroy the Virginia Central Railroad at that point. Tolersville is situated about six miles from Louisa Court-house. They tore up the track for miles, burned the ties, destroyed switches, bridges, culverts, &c., rendering the road impassable for weeks. A portion of the command, under Captain Eugene Baker, then went six miles further to Frederick Hall, and cut the railroad at that point. They also destroyed the telegraph instruments, wires, and a great amount of government property. At sunset, Captain John Feelner, of the same regiment, with thirty men, proceeded on the road towards Fredericksburg, some six miles, where a bridge, over two hundred feet long, crosses the North Anna River. The bridge was guarded by rebel infantry. The captain charged across it, driving the enemy from it, and succeeded in burning it, without the loss of a man, and captured five prisoners.

The length of time the regiment was absent caused much uneasiness at headquarters; and General Stoneman, fearing they were in trouble, sent out a squadron of the 6th Regulars, under Captain Claflin, to communicate with them, which he did, and returned with the command.

Captain Lord was highly complimented, by both Generals Stoneman and Buford, on the success of the expedition, as it was considered by them one of the most hazardous and important of the whole expedition.

Captain Harrison, commanding the 5th Regulars, was sent with the regiment to destroy a bridge over the James River, at Cartersville, some twelve miles south of Columbia. He started late on Sunday night, and arrived at "Shannon's," or, as it is here called, "Flemming's," Crofs-roads at 2 o'clock, and bivouacked till daylight. Two hundred picked men were then felected and placed under Captain Drummond, with inftructions to proceed to Carterfville, and deftroy the bridge at all hazards. Captain Harrifon, with the balance of the command, remained at "Flemming's," to protect him from attack from that direction. Shortly after funrife, Lieutenant Haftings, with fifteen men, was patrolling the road in the direction of Gordonfville, when he difcovered the approach of a large body of rebel cavalry. He at once perceived that the fafety of Captain Harrifon depended upon his prompt action. He immediately charged the advance guard, driving them back upon the main column. Lieutenant Haftings only had thirty men, all told, the remainder being ftationed on the feveral roads as pickets. He drew these up in line acrofs the road, and prepared to refift the advance of the enemy as long as poffible. He refifted a charge made by double his number, and efcaped with nearly all his men. The enemy captured fome of the pickets of the 5th Cavalry, including Captain Owen and Lieutenant Buford. Word was at once fent to General Stoneman of the proximity of the rebels, and he came down with General Buford's command and the Lancers at a trot, but they did not arrive in time to meet the enemy. While thefe expeditions were out, our regiment was retained as a provoft and headquarters guard to General Stoneman.

1863. May 4th.

Early on Sunday morning we were drawn up in line of battle, fupporting a fection of artillery, at Thompfon's

1863. Cross-roads, and remained in this position all day. Nearly the entire command of General Buford was stationed near Shannon Hill. A detachment of the 5th United States Cavalry, under Captain T. Drummond, sent to destroy the canal and bridge near Cedar Point, most effectually accomplished their work. During the night of the 3d, it is believed both Hampton's and Lee's brigades were encamped within two miles of our position. On the morning of the 4th, a picket consisting of sixty men, commanded by Lieutenant Stoddard, of the 5th United States, was attacked, and fifteen of the number captured; on the alarm being given, reinforcements were dispatched, when the rebels were driven off, and the remainder of the day was spent in quiet watching.

The work of the expedition had been accomplished satisfactorily, and as we had no intelligence from General Hooker,—our communication having entirely ceased through failures on the part of General Averill,—General Stoneman called a council of his officers, when it was determined to return by the same route over which we had marched in coming out.

May 5th. On the morning of the 5th, the entire force was concentrated at Yanceville, and in the afternoon we started on our return trip. The Sixth marched with General Buford's command, and when near Louisa Court-house, we made a circuit, taking us near Gordonsville. At Trevillian Station, a large water tank and depot were destroyed. Here we halted for an hour, scouting for several miles. A rebel battery was discovered on the road towards Gordonsville, but as we were instructed not to bring on any engagement with the enemy if it could be avoided, no attack was made. When our main column had all paſſed on, we were ordered to follow, forming the rear-guard for the entire force.

1863.
May 5th.

Early in the evening rain began to fall, and increaſed in violence until midnight. We were in a ſtrange country, and the roads bad beyond deſcription. Many of our horſes mired, and were left floundering in the mud, while the diſmounted trooper, with "traps" upon his back, trudged on as faſt as poſſible, until a friendly ſtable would furniſh him a remount; or if not ſo fortunate, or more thoroughly exhauſted, he would wrap himſelf in his horſe-blanket, and ſleep by the roadſide until morning. Many of our men thus dropping out by the way, were captured by the enemy.

The night was very dark, and much of the way led us through denſe woods, intenſifying the darkneſs; and for ſeveral hours it was utterly impoſſible for one to ſee the perſon riding immediately in advance, or even the head of the animal upon which he was himſelf mounted. We marched all night, wet, hungry, and tired, and about 2 o'clock on the morning of the 6th, forded the North Anna. The water was very high, and running very rapidly. Our animals being exhauſted by hard marching, great difficulty was found in croſſing, ſeveral of our horſes being carried down by the violence of the ſtream. After croſſing, we marched until 4 o'clock, when we halted in a denſe wood until daylight. Fires were ſoon ſtarted, coffee prepared, and after a light lunch, we wrapped ourſelves in wet blankets and were ſoon aſleep.

During the night, Captain Treichel's ſquadron became ſeparated from the column, and after marching ſeveral

1863. miles on a by-road, and experiencing great difficulty in crossing swollen streams, halted until daylight, and by hard marching rejoined the column the next afternoon.

May 6th. At 7 o'clock on the morning of the 6th, we were aroused to cold, rain, and hunger. The rain continued all day and the succeeding night.

Our march to-day was made very cautiously. Halts were ordered every few miles, while the country in our front and flanks was diligently patrolled. Up to this time we were without intelligence from General Hooker, and were in blissful ignorance of the disaster at Chancellorsville. Night closed upon us early. Being without rations, we had no good meal during the day, and at night, wet, hungry, and exhausted, we settled ourselves again in the saddle for an all-night's march. It was darker, if possible, than the night previous. To guide one's horse was simply impossible, and our only assurance of keeping with the column, was found in trusting to the more reliable instincts of our animals.

The mud was deep, and worked into a very soft condition. From the unceasing splash of liquid mud, one would suppose we were marching in a stream of water to our horses' knees. Our clothing being thoroughly saturated for more than two days, and a keen wind and cold driving rain in our faces, rendered this night's ride anything but pleasant. We were so thoroughly exhausted, that many slept for hours while their faithful horses moved on with the column; while occasionally a weary rider and jaded beast were passed on the roadside, having marched to the point of possible endurance for that night.

The long, weary, stormy night wore on, and near daylight on the morning of the 7th, we forded the Rapidan at Raccoon Ford. We here halted until 10 o'clock, when the rear of the column crossed. The country was patrolled to Kelley's Ford, and reported free of the enemy. We marched slowly all the afternoon, and about 9 o'clock P.M., we arrived at Kelley's Ford, but the night being too dark to effect a crossing in safety, we bivouacked in a low wet field until daylight, every man serving as hitching-post for his own horse. At daylight we moved down to the ford, and as rapidly as possible crossed to the north bank of the Rappahannock. Great difficulty was experienced in crossing, as the river was very high, and running with great violence. Our horses, being thoroughly exhausted, were scarcely able to stem the swift current of the stream, and in several cases both horse and rider were carried down the river. The banks at this point are quite high and abrupt, and for several hundred yards below the ford, the ascent from the river to the level country above is impossible, and but very little assistance could be rendered those who failed in the crossing. Out of the many thus carried down by the river, all were rescued but two, who, despite all efforts to save them, were drowned.

1863.
May 7th.

The Sixth crossed early in the morning, and bivouacked on the north bank while the entire force crossed. We were allowed large fires, and though the day was damp and our clothing very wet, we ate heartily, and slept soundly until near night, when we were marched to Rappahannock Station, on the Orange and Alexandria Railroad. We there bivouacked on high

1863. ground, and collecting great quantities of rails from the fences near by, kept up large fires all night, and enjoyed positive rest, seasoned with a sense of security and safety.

Thus closed the ever-memorable "Stoneman's Raid," leaving as a result the thorough and successful accomplishment of all anticipated, though of no special benefit to our cause, because of the failures of Chancellorsville.

CHAPTER TWELFTH.

Encampments near Bealton—Morrisville and Hartwood Church—March to " Brooks's Station"—Dumfries—After Guerrillas—Encamped at " Catlett's Station"—Great Cavalry Engagement at " Beverly Ford"—Exciting Charge of the Sixth Pennsylvania Cavalry.

ON the 9th of May we marched to Bealton, on the Orange and Alexandria Railroad, and during the day our indefatigable Quartermaster, Lieutenant Theodore Sage, came up from Falmouth with our regimental wagons, and we enjoyed the luxuries of tents, blankets, a change of clothing, and an abundance to eat.

1863.
May 9th.

During the afternoon of the 10th, we marched about five miles towards Falmouth, and bivouacked for the night. A detail was made from our regiment for picket duty. On the day following we marched to near Hartwood Church, where we went regularly into camp. For several days we enjoyed needed rest, the only interruption thereto being our regular tour of picket duty, and an occasional scout for guerrillas.

Morrisville and vicinity was the worst region for the operations of murderous guerrilla bands we ever found. Lieutenant A. P. Morrow, of our brigade, was here captured on the 13th, while engaged in visiting his picket

May 13th.

1863. line. Several other officers of the brigade were captured while within fight of their camps. It was at Elk Run, near here, that Lieutenant Sage was murdered in November of this year.

May 16th. About 4 o'clock on the afternoon of the 16th we broke camp, and after marching three miles, bivouacked for the night. Early the next morning we were again on the road, and marched flowly all day. About 2 o'clock we paffed infide our infantry picket line, and at night went into camp near Brooks's Station, on the Acquia Creek Railroad. Our tents were here pitched on very high ground, with good fhade and water; our camp was well arranged, and prefented a very fine appearance. We remained here in quietnefs, performing no duty but fuch as referred to our own immediate improvement, until the 24th.

Lieutenant William Sproule, Company "F," died in Cavalry Corps Hofpital, at Acquia Creek Landing, on May 19th. the 19th of May. He had accompanied us on the raid, and was taken very fick on the third or fourth day; he however continued with the regiment until its return to Kelley's Ford, when he was taken to the hofpital. He was greatly beloved by his comrades, and poffeffed many admirable qualities. His remains were conveyed to Philadelphia by Captain Davis, of the fame company, where he was buried with military honors.

May 24th. On Sunday, the 24th, the regiment marched to Dumfries, where we remained for five days engaged in picket duty and refitting. While here, and at our previous camp, we parted with the lance, and the whole command was armed with carbines. The lance had been

CATLETT'S STATION.

found to be illy adapted to cavalry fervice, as performed in the wooded country through which we were called to operate. At this date the regiment had ten companies ferving together, with Captain Starr's fquadron only detached, which was ftill with the headquarters of the Army of the Potomac.

1863.

On the 29th we moved towards Warrenton, making a march of twelve miles. On the following day, by a very circuitous route, marched to Bealton, where we arrived about noon. On our arrival there, we learned of depredations committed by a portion of Mofeby's command on the Orange and Alexandria Railroad, near Catlett's Station, during the morning, and we were hurried off in that direction. The rebels had thrown from the track and deftroyed a train of cars loaded with commiffary ftores. After completing their work of deftruction, they fled to the mountains; we purfued, and near evening overtook and captured quite a number of their noted guerrilla band, and with them a fmall mountain howitzer. Late in the evening we returned to Catlett's Station, and bivouacked for the night. The next morning we were ordered to prepare permanent camps. A fine ground was felected on the edge of a wood, near Cedar Run, an excellent ftream of water. We here remained encamped until the 8th of June, engaged in picket and fcout duty to the mountains and the Rappahannock, extending towards Warrenton.

May 29th.

On the 30th, Companies "A" and "D" marched to White Ridge, pofting relays on the road, to carry difpatches between the headquarters of Generals Stoneman and Buford, and remained on this duty until June 3d.

May 30th.

1863. While lying at Catlett's Station, we drew from the Quartermaster wagons sufficient to make up our former allowance. The pack-mule system, introduced by General Hooker, though proving a source of great amusement to the troops, and aggravation to the drivers, was not at all practicable for the active campaign.

June 8th. Early in the morning ammunition, forage, and rations are distributed, and orders issued to be ready to move at a minute's notice. At 2 P.M. the "general" sounds from brigade headquarters, and is re-echoed from every regiment in the command. Saddles are hastily packed, horses mounted, and many speculations indulged as to destination. All indications point to a severe fight, as we know the enemy's cavalry have been concentrating for several days on the south bank of the Rappahannock. We ride down along the line of the Orange and Alexandria Railroad, making rapidly but quietly toward Beverly Ford. Late in the night we arrive behind the wood nearest the river, and bivouac for the night. No fires are allowed, and we make our supper on cold ham and hard tack, spread our saddle-blankets on the ground, and with saddles for pillows, prepare for a night's rest. Our minds are full of the coming battle on the morrow, and various speculations are indulged in regard to our prospects of success. We understand that the cavalry forces of the two armies are to meet at early dawn in what will doubtless prove the greatest cavalry engagement of the war. Our men are confident of success, and eager for the fray. A group of officers together are eating their cold supper, perhaps the last they shall all take together. The morrow will soon break upon us, full of danger and death. Messages are committed to friends to be transmitted to distant loved ones, "in case anything should occur." And after solemn and earnest prayer we are all sleeping soundly.

1863.

At 2 o'clock in the morning the command "to horse" is whispered around, instead of being sounded from a dozen bugles, which would reveal our position to the enemy. Quietly we saddle up, mount, and move stealthily down to the ford. Just as the gray dawn of approaching day begins to brighten up the deep darkness of the hour, we arrive at the river bank. By 4 o'clock our advance guard is across, and surprise the picket of the enemy; and before they have time to fall back upon their reserve, or rub the sleep from their eyes, we are upon and capture them. Now our men dash upon the reserve, and away they run without exchanging a shot. Look there to the right! See that squad flying along the edge of the woods! See how our boys make them run! Hurrah for the advance! A perfect surprise! Now they are lost to sight, and our firing has alarmed the main force of the enemy. Do you hear that sharp bing! bing! bing! of the carbines? Let us on to their support! They have cleared the hill, gained the woods, and roused the whole force of Stuart's rebel cavalry, and now there is earnest work before us. General Gregg, with his division, is crossing, we suppose, at Kelley's Ford, and will march upon our left by 8 o'clock. In the mean time Buford and Kilpatrick must carry on the reconnoissance, feel the enemy, ascertain where the rebel army is, and in what force, &c.; and in doing this, we must meet and master the cavalry force of the Army of

June 9th.

1863. Northern Virginia. On the way up from the river
June 9th. bank we pass General Pleasanton and staff, of the Cavalry Corps, with Generals Buford and Kilpatrick, in consultation. Buford's division has the advance. It is Colonel Davis's brigade that has so nobly opened the day. As we ride on up the hill, heavy artillery firing is heard in the wood immediately in our front. At the command, "Trot, march!" we push rapidly forward. Soon meet anxious and excited messengers, who report having found the enemy in great force. They are fully ready for us. On reaching the edge of the wood, find a rendezvous for wounded. Surgeons are attending to the suffering. Here comes a rough litter bearing an officer. "Who is that, boys?" "Colonel Davis, sir!" "Is it possible!" Noble fellow! "Is he wounded badly?" "A Minie ball through his head, sir!" He is insensible, his hair matted and clotted with blood. God have mercy on the brave, noble, patriot-soldier, the hero of Harper's Ferry! This is our hastily breathed prayer, as we linger for a moment, and then hurry on to join our command. The wounded, dying, and dead, lie on either hand along our way ; but as our own regiment will in a few minutes be in the advance, and relieve those in front, we must hasten on. Our skirmishers are deployed over a rough clearing; every bush, pile of stones, or log of wood, is alive. Here we sit calmly on our horses waiting orders, while over each bush and stone pile lingers a cloud of smoke; and just there, within a few yards of us, are men hidden from our view, who are taking deliberate aim at us, and doing great mischief. We halt, while our skirmishers are sent

forward to clear the field. In a few minutes an orderly dashes up, touches his hat to the commanding officer, and says, "General Buford sends his compliments to Major Morris, and directs him to clear the woods in his front." The proper command is given, and with drawn sabres we promptly press forward into a dense wood. The enemy's skirmishers fly as we advance. On, on we move, expecting each moment to hear the thunder of artillery, and the scream of shell in our very midst; but all is quiet, save the steady tramp of our horses, and the cracking of the fallen branches and undergrowth beneath their feet.

This silence is dreadful: we may expect something desperate soon. They would never allow us to pass through this wood undisturbed by shot and shell, but that they are ready to meet us on the other side. A few minutes bring us to an opening in the wood, some two hundred yards in extent. Under the edge of the wood, immediately in front of us, is a large force of cavalry drawn up to receive us. And now a shower of balls whistle our welcome. Above the rattle of the carbines, the voice of our Major rings forth, in quick succession, the commands "Trot, march!" "Gallop, march!" "Charge!" And with a shout that makes the woods ring, our brave boys of the Sixth Pennsylvania (Lancers) dash across the plain on to the foe. The wildest enthusiasm has seized our men, and at the full speed of their horses they dash forward. We are almost in reach of the enemy: two minutes more, and we will crush that solid column of rebels. A few yards only separate us, when a concealed battery opens on our left, and pours a most destructive

1863. June 9th.

1863.
June 9th. enfilading fire acrofs our path. God of mercy fave us! What an awful fire! fo clofe that we are almoft in the fmoke of the battery. Many of our faddles are emptied, and the horfes, freed from the reftraint of their riders, dafh wildly away; and at the fame moment, hundreds of carbines fend their charges of death into our never-wavering ranks. Our color fergeant reels, and falls from his horfe; another fergeant catches the colors before they reach the ground; and on through the ftorm of death our weakened lines advance until they meet the enemy, and hand to hand the conflict rages. Though we are outnumbered two to one, we break their ranks, and purfue them into the wood. Now the enemy on our right begin to clofe in upon us: our commander has fallen. Major Whelan affuming command, attempts to withdraw us from our terrible pofition. But how are we to retreat? The enemy have completely furrounded us—all is loft! Not yet, thank Heaven! The 6th United States Cavalry has been ordered forward to our fupport, and juft at this moment their yell, as they charge upon the enemy, is heard. They turn to receive them: this is our time. The rebels give way on our right, and a way of efcape opens. All is now in confufion. We are fo few that we cannot hold the pofition, and we are withdrawn again acrofs the field, and through the wood, towards our reinforcements, expofed to a frightful fire from a battery within fifty yards of us. The noife is like deafening thunder; whiftling fhot and fcreaming fhell fall all around us, or go crafhing through the trees, or bury themfelves in the ground, fending a fhower of limbs, twigs, bark, leaves, and earth, all over us, while

the air seems filled with the wickedly-whistling Minie balls. It seems impossible that any of us shall ever get out of this alive. Earnest prayers ascend for Divine protection. We lie close to our horses' necks, and hug still closer as the crashing shot or shell passes within a few feet or inches of us. Our horses are alarmed and excited, and hurry us through the woods, jamming against trees, tearing through brush, and at other times impenetrable thickets, tearing our clothes, and sometimes our skin; but we heed not these little impediments, give the horse the spurs, and in a few minutes are out on the open plain again. Here we meet General Pleasanton, who commands his bugler to sound the "rally." Companies and regiments are all mingled in perfect confusion, all flying for life. But the well-known sound recalls them to thoughtfulness; and in a few minutes the men left of the two Sixes crowd again into column, and await orders. We look around us, and congratulate each other that we, at least, are safe. We miss several valuable officers, and about one half the number of men that filled our ranks a short half hour since. How many, or who of this number may be killed or seriously wounded, is the great anxiety. No one can tell. Such and such ones were seen to fall from their horses, many are known to be wounded, many are doubtless dead on the field. God have mercy on the wounded! We have rescued some few of them that were able to ride.

1863.
June 9th.

But here come the rebels again! They have come around the woods on our right flank. We have reinforcements at hand. "Forward; trot, march!" rings

1863.
June 9th.
forth the command, and away our boys dash again to meet the enemy, while Dr. Coover and I gather up our wounded, and start back with them to a field rendezvous. Our number being large, the enemy doubtless takes us for a demoralized and flying troop; and when we are about half a mile from our forces, a squadron comes charging down upon us. What is to be done? In three minutes they will be upon us, and we will all be prisoners. Our wounded cannot ride rapidly, and we can neither make the ford below us, nor our own forces in the rear. At that moment the thunder of one of our own batteries, concealed within a few feet of us, makes our hearts leap for joy. Never did the roar of artillery and the scream of shell sound so musical in our ears. We halt, and give cheers for Captain Tidball and his splendid battery. The pursuing squadron is thrown into confusion, and wisely conclude to leave that part of the field faster than they came on to it, and we are saved again. From our field hospital we can see the enemy taking their position over an open field some three miles in extent. The ground lies most beautifully for a cavalry and artillery engagement. The country is gently rolling, and divided by an occasional stone wall or hedge. There are no abrupt or high hills. A dozen batteries have taken their position, and by 9 o'clock, when we expected our whole force on the field, we find our two divisions opposing the whole rebel cavalry. Anxious inquiry is made for General Gregg and his division. From 9 A.M. until 3 P.M., the roll of artillery and the clash of arms is unceasing. One of the grandest scenes to be witnessed in one's lifetime lies open before

us; while an occafional fhot or fhell falling or burfting near us, renders the fcene more exciting. But forrow fills our hearts as we fee the terrible refults of the engagement in the maimed, wounded, and dying, that are carried from the field. Oh, horrible, horrible war! A fcore of hills are briftling with the guns of the enemy, while a dozen of our own batteries ftand as a wall of fire between us and the foe. Here and there over the field a cloud of fmoke afcends as the guns are difcharged; the fcream of fhot or fhell is heard at almoft the fame moment, and foon after the deep roar of the piece. Inceffantly the thunder peals, while every few minutes a troop dafh out from the cover of their protecting guns, charging upon the batteries, and ftorming ftone walls, behind which fharpfhooters are firing at the gunners. The fhout of the charge is followed by the clafh and ring of arms; one or the other party foon give way, and fly to the fhelter of their guns. Manfully our troops conteft every foot of ground, but are gradually forced back toward the river until 3 P.M., when rapid firing is heard on our left, and through the fmoke and duft we defcry the gallant Gregg and his divifion. They form a junction with our line, our troops receive frefh infpiration, and a general advance is ordered. Now the rebel line yields; batteries haftily change their pofition and cover each other in their retreat. Charge after charge is made by our brave boys; haftily the enemy flies over the hills, down through the valleys, back through the woods, mile after mile, until we are five miles from the river, where we come upon a ftrong line of infantry, and difcover the Army of Northern

1863.
June 9th.
Virginia, under the command of General Lee, on their march to the invasion of Pennsylvania. Not being exactly prepared to meet the whole rebel army, and as night was almost upon us, and the object of our expedition being fully accomplished, we slowly retired from the field, and again crossed to the north bank of the Rappahannock. Our return was in perfect order in four columns. We had a large number of prisoners, and a number of battle-flags, while above all proudly floated our own triumphant "stars and stripes."

Never did anything appear to our eyes half so beautiful as our returning victorious cavalry force, as they marched quietly and unmolested back again to the ground of their bivouac the night previous. Six of the officers of our regiment who, the evening before, assembled in our friendly group at retiring, were now absent.

The cold form of Captain Davis, one of the noblest of our band, lay in a car—with Colonel Davis—on the road to Washington, there to be embalmed, and sent to a loving and anxious wife. Major Morris, as fine a soldier as ever led a troop, has since died in Libby Prison. Captain Leiper, and Lieutenant Rudolph Ellis, wounded severely; while Lieutenants Lennig and Colladay were captured with Major Morris.

Our loss in non-commissioned officers and privates, during the day, amounted to one hundred and forty.

CHAPTER THIRTEENTH.

The Ninth of June—Brandy Station—Beverly Ford—Full Reports of the Engagement—New York Herald—Philadelphia Evening Bulletin—New York Times—Putnam's Rebellion Record.

NEW YORK HERALD, June 10th: "Yesterday 1863. our cavalry force crossed the Rappahannock,— June 9th. General John Buford at 4 A.M., at Beverly Ford, General Gregg at 7 A.M., and General Duffie at 8 A.M., at Kelley's Ford. One brigade of infantry (Russell's) accompanied the cavalry. As soon as General Buford crossed he encountered the enemy, and sharp hand to hand fighting occurred. It soon became evident that the forces of the enemy, in cavalry, artillery, and infantry, outnumbered our own nearly two to one, with the advantage of position. General Duffie was directed, if possible, to get in the rear of the enemy, and advanced for that purpose, but was recalled when the true state of the enemy's position and force became known, and our whole force attacked the enemy in front. Colonel Percy Wyndham commanded the second brigade of General Gregg's division, and made three successful charges on Brandy Station, and the heights adjacent, where the headquarters of General J. E. B. Stuart were

1863.   situated.   On account of the heavy infantry force there
June 9th. found, he was compelled soon to retire. He captured, however, a large number of papers belonging to the rebel General Stuart, containing valuable information as to the intentions of the rebels. Several prisoners were brought in. Colonel Wyndham's brigade suffered severely.

"The forces under General Buford consisted of the 1st, 2d, 5th and 6th Regulars, and 6th Pennsylvania Cavalry; that under General Gregg, of the 8th and 9th New York, 8th Illinois, and 3d Indiana Cavalry. General Buford's forces being on the right, and crossing very early, first met the enemy's pickets half a mile from Beverly Ford, when a severe engagement immediately commenced, the rebels being in heavy force, and resisting the advance of our troops with continuous hand to hand fighting. When General Gregg brought up his force and became engaged, the enemy gradually gave way, disputing every inch of ground desperately, however. Our men made more than a dozen charges into the rebel ranks, relying almost entirely upon the sabre, which they used with terrible effect. The enemy also repeatedly charged, relying always upon their pistols. Both sides were repeatedly driven back in the course of the battle, though we succeeded in driving the rebels at last (Fitzhugh Lee's and Wade Hampton's division of cavalry, with artillery, all commanded by Major-General Stuart), back to a point about six miles southwest of where their pickets were first encountered, where the enemy were found so strongly reinforced with infantry and artillery, that it was thought prudent to return.

We brought off about two hundred prifoners, our own wounded, and the bodies of our officers killed in the engagement. The Sixth Pennfylvania Cavalry loft heavily, being in the advance all day. Captain Davis was killed, Major Morris wounded and a prifoner, Lieutenant Lennig miffing, Captain Leiper cut with fabre, and Lieutenant R. Ellis wounded. The fields and woods through which we paffed were ftrewn with dead and wounded rebels. The fight clofed at 6 P.M."

1863. June 9th.

PHILADELPHIA EVENING BULLETIN, June 13th: "We have communications from witneffes of the great cavalry fight on the Rappahannock, which fpeak in terms of the higheft commendation of the gallant conduct of the Sixth Pennfylvania Cavalry, formerly known as 'Rufh's Lancers.' This fine regiment, which, by the way, abandoned the lance as unfuited to the fervice, on their return from the late raid, and is now armed with carbines and fabres, was in the extreme advance of General Buford's Divifion, and was on three diftinct occafions during the day engaged in the moft defperate hand to hand conflicts, in all of which it greatly diftinguifhed itfelf by the moft brilliant charges and the moft determined fighting.

"Lieutenant-Colonel C. Rofs Smith was doing duty on General Pleafanton's ftaff during the engagement, and the regiment was commanded by Major Robert Morris, whofe horfe was fhot under him in the midft of one of the fevereft charges when right on the enemy, rolled over on him, and he was captured.

"Captain Charles L. Leiper is fpoken of as fighting

1863.
June 9th.

with defperate bravery. He received feveral wounds, and only left the field at the command of Major Whelan, upon whom the command devolved. Majors Whelan and Hazeltine, Captain Frazier, Adjutant Ellis, Lieutenant White, and other officers, had their horfes fhot under them. Adjutant Ellis was badly wounded.

"It gives us great fatisfaction to award to this fplendid regiment the laurels it has fo proudly won. Circumftances of various forts have hitherto prevented the Sixth Pennfylvania from proving in the field of what manner of metal they were made; but none who knew anything of the quality of officers and men comprifing the regiment, are furprifed at the record it has now made for itfelf. The loffes fuftained by the 'Sixth' are heavy, but principally in prifoners. Captain Davis, a great favorite in the regiment, was killed, and Lieutenants Lennig and Colladay wounded and taken prifoners."

NEW YORK TIMES, June 11th: .... "The right column under General Buford had proceeded about half a mile from the river, when it fell upon General Jones's whole rebel brigade, who had juft fhaken themfelves out of a fleep in time to receive us. A fight thus commenced, which lafted from 4 A.M. to 3 P.M., by which time the entire force of General Stuart, confifting of twelve thoufand cavalry, fixteen pieces of artillery and infantry fupports, had been driven back three miles on the left, and five miles on the right, with heavy lofs. Our forces formed a junction near Brandy Station about 2 o'clock.

"The grandeft charge was made by the 6th Pennfylvania Cavalry, fupported by the 6th United States, when 1863. they dafhed upon a whole brigade of the enemy, and June 9th were taken in flank by another brigade; then, though furrounded, they fought their way out. Two of General Gregg's brigades, under Colonel Wyndham and Colonel Kilpatrick, had hot work all the morning, but drove the enemy from the river to Brandy Station. The enemy had five brigades of cavalry, under Generals Fitzhugh Lee, W. F. H. Lee, Jones, Field, and Robinfon, with artillery under Major Beckham. They had been reviewed the previous day, and were under orders to leave on a grand raid into Maryland and Pennfylvania the next morning. Our forces returned almoft unmolefted."

PUTNAM'S REBELLION RECORD, volume 7th, page 18: "On Saturday evening the compofition of our force was decided upon, and all the cavalry that could be made available immediately, was detailed for the work, under command of General Pleafanton, affifted by Generals Buford, Gregg, and Colonel Duffie, as fubordinate commanders. In addition, two fmall brigades of infantry, under General Ames, of the Eleventh Corps, and General Ruffell, of the Sixth Corps, were detailed to accompany the expedition. A detail of artillery was made of one battery to each brigade, the horfe batteries with the cavalry being in charge of Captain Robertfon, chief of artillery on General Pleafanton's ftaff.

"The infantry force felected challenged particular admiration. The regiments were fmall but reliable. The 2d, 3d, and 7th Wifconfin, 2d and 33d Maffachu-

1863.
June 9th.

setts, 6th Maine, 86th and 124th New York, were amongst the number. General Pleafanton's cavalry rendezvoufed during Saturday and Sunday near Catlett's Station and Warrenton Junction, getting fupplies of forage and food from both places. General Ames's infantry moved on Saturday evening to Spotted Tavern, and on Sunday to near Bealton Station. General Ruffell's brigade moved on Sunday to Hartwood Church, and on Monday to Kelley's Ford. The plan was to rendezvous the command at the two points on the Rappahannock, Beverly Ford on the right, and Kelley's Ford on the left, the two being fix miles apart, and then move the column forward towards Culpepper, on roads converging at Brandy Station, where a junction of the forces was to be formed, or fooner if neceffary. On Monday evening, therefore, General Buford's column left Warrenton Junction, and followed by General Ames's, from Bealton, bivouacked for the night near the Bowen Manfion, about one mile from the ford. General Gregg, taking his own and Colonel Duffie's command, moved to the left from the Junction, and encamped for the night in clofe proximity to Kelley's Ford, where General Ruffell had already arrived. No fires were allowed, and a vigilant watch was kept to prevent difturbances, or anything which might give any indication of our prefence. The orders were to aroufe the command at 3 A.M., and to make the paffage of the river. As foon as it was daylight, General Buford's command was in motion. Colonel Davis's brigade, led by two fquadrons of the 8th New York, and fupported by the 8th Illinois and 3d Indiana, had the advance.

BEVERLY FORD.

The morning was cool and pleasant, a thick mist hung over the river, and objects on the other side were rather indistinct. Our cavalry soon reached the river, dashed in, and dashed up the bank, and were well on the opposite side before the rebels, in their fortifications, were aware of their presence. The suddenness of the movement completely surprised them, and they at once broke for the first friendly timber. General Buford, having driven the enemy's pickets and skirmishers on the right of the road, sent in the Sixth Pennsylvania Cavalry to charge this line on the flank. The Pennsylvanians came up to their work in splendid style. *This is the regiment known as the* '*Lancers*,' and they had a matter of pride to settle in this charge. Steadily and gallantly they advanced out of the woods in excellent order, and then dashed across the field in an oblique direction towards the enemy's guns. They went up almost to their very muzzles through a storm of canister and shell, and would have taken them, when suddenly there dashed out of the woods, on their right flank, in almost the very spot from which they themselves had issued, two whole regiments of the enemy in full charge. The Sixth United States now came to the rescue, but the fire was so severe that even these veterans could not stand it. Retreat was almost cut off, but the regiments, now subjected to a fire in front and on both flanks, fell back with heavy loss. Major Morris, of the Sixth Pennsylvania, was seen to fall from his horse, and is a prisoner. Captain Davis, of the same regiment, was killed. Major Hazeltine had a horse shot under him. Captain Leiper received a severe sabre cut on the head. Captain Dahl-

1863.
June 9th.

1863.
June 9th.
gren, of Major-General Hooker's staff, a model of cool and dauntless bravery, charged with the regiment, and his horse was shot in two places. He describes the charge as one of the finest of the war.

"The enemy was now being reinforced very rapidly, and in a short time General Pleasanton found that Buford's small division was opposed by three strong brigades of cavalry with artillery to match. After the repulse of the Sixth Pennsylvania, the enemy made two attempts to gain our rear, and the approaches to the ford, both on our right and on our left, but particularly on the right; but they were handsomely foiled by Buford, and for two hours there was very sharp fighting, rapid shelling, and admirable manœuvring on both sides, in the open and undulating fields on our extreme right. A brigade of the enemy came down the road which branches off to the right from Beverly, and made a dash for the ford, but they were too late. A regiment and a section of artillery interposed. They never got nearer than a mile to that point, and during these two hours suffered severely from our shell and skirmishers. At this stage of the engagement, General Pleasanton plainly saw that the division under General Buford was far outnumbered, and much anxiety was expressed to hear from Gregg, whose column was considerably stronger than Buford's. Word had been received from him at 8 o'clock, saying that he had crossed with scarcely any opposition, and that he was driving the enemy before him, but his guns had not yet been heard. Matters thus remained until 2 o'clock, nothing being done save some artillery practice, which was pretty accurate on both fides. We difmounted one gun of a fection that the enemy had on the extreme right, and compelled the enemy to move the other. General Ames formed his fkirmifh line, and they picked off the rebel officers without mercy. The enemy were very profufe of their fhell and canifter, and opened upon our troops whenever they approached within range. Many of the men were wounded by canifter fhot, a thing heretofore almoft unknown in the cavalry fighting. At one time, on the left of General Ames's brigade, the rebel cavalry fkirmifhers had advanced and concealed themfelves in fome bufhes, where they were annoying a body of the 9th New York. Major Martin, of that regiment, was finally ordered to take a fquadron and drive them out. This he moft gallantly did, though it was right in the teeth of the enemy's artillery, and he was met by a perfect ftorm of canifter. He captured fifty prifoners. The gallant Major was wounded in the fhoulder. About 1 o'clock Buford again began to prefs the enemy, and this time he fhowed evident figns of uneafinefs, and foon withdrew his force from our right flank, as though he was attacked in rear. About the fame time we heard Gregg's guns; and fome prifoners, taken from Robinfon's North Carolina brigade juft then, reported General Ruffell's infantry advancing through the woods on their right and rear. General Gregg, from the found of the firing, was evidently in the vicinity of Brandy Station. Pleafanton now pufhed forward, and the rebels foon gave way, and fell back rapidly. They were, indeed, in a bad predicament, for Gregg was almoft directly in their rear, Ruffell on the right, and Buford preffing them in front; they

1863.
June 9th.

1863.
June 9th.
therefore made a hasty retreat, abandoning their old camp entirely, part of which we had already occupied. Two of their regiments were very near being cut off as Kilpatrick moved off towards the right to make connection with Buford; they had but a narrow strip not covered by our force through which to escape. General Pleasanton's headquarters were moved forward to where the rebel commander's had been, and the lines of the two columns were soon joined.

"General Gregg reported that his two brigades, under Kilpatrick and Wyndham, had been hotly engaged all the morning, but had driven the enemy uniformly from the river back to Brandy Station. Our troops under Gregg, especially the 1st New York, 1st Maine, and 10th New York, fought most gallantly, and repulsed the enemy in repeated charges, though losing heavily themselves. The 6th New York battery was almost totally disabled; it did excellent service. In the charges by General Gregg's command, a stand of colors and over two hundred and fifty prisoners were taken. Colonel Wyndham captured the heights commanding Brandy Station, and there discovered rebel infantry being brought up by the cars. A spirited engagement here took place for some hours, in which the 1st Pennsylvania Cavalry, Colonel Taylor commanding, did gallant service. Colonel Wyndham was wounded in the leg, and soon after the command devolved upon Colonel Taylor, of the 1st Pennsylvania Reserve Cavalry. Lieutenant-Colonel Broderick and Major Shelmire, of the 1st New York Cavalry, were wounded and captured; Major W. T. McEwen, 1st Pennsylvania, wounded;

Captain Sawyer, 1st New York, captured; Captain Creager, 1st Maryland, killed.

1863.
June 9th.

"While a junction was being effected with Gregg's column on the left, Generals Buford and Ames were pushing out on their right, and with Vincent's battery, Buford had, by 2 o'clock, carried all the crests occupied by the enemy during the forenoon, and had forced him back over three miles from the river. In these exploits the Regulars, especially the 2d and 5th, distinguished themselves by their intrepidity. The 3d Wisconsin and 8th Illinois also won high praise.

"The fact that the enemy were now falling back upon strong infantry supports, and we being already numerically inferior to them, induced the commanders to decide upon a return, and by 4 o'clock our forces began to fall back. On the return we were not molested. General John Buford's division fell back to Beverly Ford, and General Gregg's to Rappahannock Ford, where they crossed. We brought off all our dead and wounded, and also many of the wounded of the enemy. By dark our forces were all on the north side of the river, and the wounded, loaded in box cars, on their way to Washington."

CHAPTER FOURTEENTH.

Thoroughfare Gap—Aldie—Upperville—March into Maryland—Battle of Gettyſburg—Forced March to the Potomac—Rebel Spy—Engagement at Williamſport—Boonſboro.

1863.

June 10th.
June 13th.

THE brigade returned to its previous camping ground, near Warrenton Junction and Catlett's Station, on the 10th. We remained here until the 13th, when we broke camp in haſte, and moved off toward the Bull Run mountains. The night was very dark, and the roads in wretched condition; and the march being a forced one to gain the paſſes in the mountains, was urged with unuſual rapidity. Several men of the command were ſeriouſly injured by falling with their horſes, or being jammed againſt poſts, fences, &c. It was a frightfully wild ride, indeed.

Three regiments, including the 6th Pennſylvania, led by Major Starr, of the 6th United States Cavalry, were delayed by the overturning of a piece of artillery in a narrow road, and when the gun was righted, we puſhed on rapidly to overtake the column. We did not halt during the entire night, and the dawning day found us on the Bull Run battle-field, near Centreville. We here diſcovered that we had marched ſeveral miles out of our way. We retraced our ſteps to the proper turn-

ALDIE.

ing point on our road, and marched to Thoroughfare Gap, where we arrived about 10 o'clock on the morning of the 14th. Having gained poſſeſſion of the Gap, and being thoroughly exhauſted, the moſt of our command were ſoon at reſt, while Captain Treichel, with his ſquadron, was ſent on a reconnoiſſance to Aſhby's Gap. They marched ſteadily all day, returning near evening, and throwing themſelves upon the ground perfectly exhauſted, ſettled themſelves for the night, but in a few minutes orders were received to prepare to move, and we ſtarted on an all night's wearisome march.

1863. June 14th.

At daylight on the 15th, we forded Bull Run at Railroad Bridge, marched to the eaſt, then to the ſouth, then back again to the northweſt, halting at intervals during the day, and near night going into bivouac near Blackburn's Ford, at an abandoned rebel camp of nicely made huts.

The movements this day were perfectly inexplicable, and at night we were utterly exhauſted. We remained here until the 17th, when we marched to Aldie, and after a ſharp engagement, gained the paſs in the mountains, driving the enemy back into Loudon Valley.

On the 20th, the regiment was ſent as a guard to our ſupply train to Fairfax Station, returning on the following day. Our brigade was heavily engaged on the 21ſt, at Middleburg, and on the 22d, at Upperville. The Sixth was held in reſerve near Aldie, uniting with the diviſion on the afternoon of the 23d. We remained in this vicinity, patrolling and reconnoitring the country, and carefully watching the movements of the enemy beyond the Blue Ridge, until the evening of the 26th,

June 20th.

1863. when we started to rejoin the army, already across the Potomac.

While at Aldie, Captain Wesley Merritt, of the Regulars, was commissioned Brigadier-General of Volunteers, and placed in command of the "Reserve Brigade," consisting of the 1st, 2d, 5th and 6th United States, and 6th Pennsylvania Cavalry regiments.

June 26th. At 10 o'clock P.M. of the 26th, we arrived at Leesburg, where we bivouacked for the night, and on the following morning marched by way of Ball's Bluff battle-field to the Potomac, which we crossed at Edward's Ferry. We continued our march all night, halting near morning at Jefferson, Maryland.

June 28th. On the 28th, marched to Middletown, Maryland,
June 29th. and on the 29th, to Frederick City. Our passage through the latter place was a perfect ovation, the officers being welcomed by many friends made during our encampment near the city in the fall of 1862. We halted but for two hours near the city, when we resumed the march, halting near morning at Mechanicstown, after a long and wearisome march.

June 30th. We remained encamped here, guarding trains, and patrolling to Harman's Gap, in the Catoctin range, and on the direct road through the mountains from Hagerstown to Baltimore. On the 2d of July we moved to
July 2d. Emmettsburg, and patrolled and picketed through the mountains. The whole brigade was on duty here, protecting the left flank of our advancing army. On the
July 3d. morning of the 3d the brigade was consolidated, and marched to the left of the Army of the Potomac, and took position in line of battle on the Emmettsburg Road,

near the Round Top Mountain, connecting with the Second Corps (General Hancock's) on our right, we holding the extreme left of our line. The Sixth Pennsylvania, having the advance of our brigade, was the first of the cavalry to become engaged. The men were dismounted, led horses taken to the rear, when we were pushed forward to meet the infantry line of the enemy. The men deployed as skirmishers, and went up boldly over ground interfected by stone walls and fences, but on rising the crest of a hill, they were saluted by a storm of balls that checked their advance. A stone house within range of our men was filled with the sharpshooters of the enemy, doing great mischief to our advancing lines. A section of artillery was immediately brought into position, and opened on the building, causing hasty evacuation of the premises by the enemy. A brisk skirmish was kept up until about 1 o'clock in the afternoon, when the enemy suddenly opened with heavy fire of artillery, and pressed forward upon the left of our line. First, one great gun spoke; and then, as though it had been the signal for the commencement of an artillery conversation, the whole hundred and twenty or more opened their mouths at once, and poured out their thunder. A perfect storm of shot, shell, and ball, rained upon and about us. Every possible shelter was gained behind barricade and stone wall, while the movements of the enemy were carefully watched, and every ordinary advance promptly checked. Our own batteries were splendidly served in reply to the enemy, while the earth trembled beneath the unearthly roar and tumult. The air seemed full of fragments of bursting shell and

1863.
July 3d.

1863.
July 3d.
ball, while the sounds peculiar to the several projectiles told of the determination of the attack. There was the heavy whoo! whoo!—who-oo! of the round shot. The "which-one? which-one?" of the fiendish Whitworth gun, the demoniac shriek of "what-you-doing-here?" of the shells, and the buzzing Minie, all combined to give it the character of a high carnival of powers infernal.

About 3 o'clock the artillery fire slackened, and the smoke lifted to disclose a corps of the rebel army advancing across the long level plain in front of the Second Corps, and extending to our centre, in three magnificent lines of battle, with the troops massed in close column by division on both flanks. Our skirmishers gave them volley after volley as they came on, until they were drawn in to their supports. On came the rebels, with colors flying, and bayonets gleaming in the sunlight, keeping their line as straight as if on parade. Our fire is reserved until they are within a hundred yards of our line. Now our army springs to its feet, and while our artillery pours its storm of death upon the advancing lines, our brave men fire and charge, hurling the first back upon the second line; here they are again rallied, and again press upon our position with determined bravery. Line after line of rebels come up, deliver their fire, and are mown down like the grass before the scythe. They fall back, rally, form, and come up again and again, and are as often met and driven back. By and by the rebel lines come up smaller and thinner, break sooner, and are longer in reforming. Our advantage is pressed, and hundreds of prisoners are captured. At one time in the afternoon, great effort was made on the part of the enemy to turn our extreme left. Our force, which was at firſt to the weſt of the Emmettſburg Road, was forced back a conſiderable diſtance, but our thin line was extended, and every foot of ground fought for deſperately.

1863.

The 5th United States Cavalry made a mounted charge, driving the enemy from an advanced poſition, and giving us great advantage. Gradually the firing ceaſed near night; our forces were conſolidated; held their advanced poſition, but made no attack on the enemy. They were not routed, and can ſcarcely be ſaid to have been driven; they had made attack after attack and been repulſed, and finding that it was uſeleſs to continue the aſſault, they retreated to a ſtrong poſition on the mountain ſlope. The night was ſpent in unceaſing attendance upon the wounded; the dead in the ſtreets of Gettyſburg were removed and buried.

On Saturday morning, July 4th, congratulatory orders were iſſued to the victorious Union Army, and the day was one of unprecedented rejoicings. Never before was the anniverſary of the Nation's Independence celebrated amidſt ſuch ſcenes of blood; and no men felt they had half the right to rejoice on this National anniverſary, as did the faithful ſurviving ſoldiers of the Army of the Potomac, after hurling back the ſolid ranks of the invading rebel army, and accompliſhing the deliverance of the country at Gettyſburg.

July 4th.

Through the night of the 3d we ſtood to horſe, and although we were worn out, by long marches and hard fighting on leſs than half rations, we were ſtarted by 5

1863. o'clock on the morning of the 4th, on a forced march of over seventy miles.

We passed through Emmettsburg early in the afternoon, our march being necessarily very slow. Both men and horses were tired and jaded. For five days we had been without forage for our horses, and in almost constant motion. Hundreds of horses dropped down on this march, and were left on the road with their saddles, blankets, and bridles upon them. Men, whose horses "played out," trudged along on foot through muddy roads and swollen streams without food; the night coming on rapidly, and no shelter from the merciless storm that beat upon us the entire day and night.

During the evening we arrived at Mechanicstown, seven miles south of Emmettsburg, where a halt was ordered for four hours. As soon as the column halted, the men dismounted, and lay down in the muddy roads or fields, with bridle tied to wrist, and utterly exhausted, were soon asleep, and were aroused with great difficulty to pursue the march twelve miles further in dense darkness and heavy rain, halting at 3 o'clock, A.M., after being eighteen hours in the saddle. The ground, though thoroughly saturated, was not more so than the troops, and without tents, fire, or food, we threw ourselves upon the ground to rest.

July 5th. At 7 o'clock the following morning we were again on the road, and about noon arrived at Frederick City. Passing through the town, we bivouacked about a mile to the west, on the Hagerstown Road. Here we were supplied with rations and forage, and took a new lease of life.

BATTLE AT WILLIAMSPORT.

The fun fhone out clear and warm during the afternoon, the night was a fine one, and our fleep found and refrefhing in a ten acre bed.

1863.

During the night a rebel fpy was arrefted by the outer pickets of General Buford. Many papers were found upon his perfon conveying much valuable information for the enemy. He was recognized as being often feen in our camps peddling ftationery. After an examination before General Buford, he was handed over to Company "G," of the Sixth Pennfylvania, then acting as Provoft Guard, with inftructions to hang him before morning. The order was executed fo quietly, that very few of the troops knew of the occurrence until the day dawned, when his lifelefs body was feen hanging from a limb of a large tree within a few yards of our bivouac.

At 5 o'clock on the morning of the 6th, we were again in the faddle. Croffing the mountain, and paffing through Middletown and Boonfboro, we arrived about 4 o'clock on the creft of the hill overlooking Williamsport, on the Potomac. A part of our force, confifting of Colonel Gamble's brigade, was thrown off to the left, ftriking the river at Falling Waters. The 3d Indiana Cavalry charged into the town, and captured feventeen wagons and about a hundred rebel infantry. A confiderable force of the enemy appearing, the 8th Illinois Cavalry was deployed as fkirmifhers to meet them. Three regiments of infantry advanced in line of battle upon our troops. Colonel Gamble's brigade was joined by Colonel Devins's, and every advance of the enemy was met by determined refiftance. Captain Tidball's battery was fplendidly ferved during the fight. Major

July 6th.

1863.
July 6th.
Medill, of the 8th Illinois, fell mortally wounded. Colonel Devins's brigade captured twenty wagons, with full teams, between Williamsport and Falling Waters, and destroyed one of the bridges used by the enemy at the latter place.

Looking down upon Williamsport from our position, thousands of wagons and ambulances, some parked and others moving in long lines, could be discerned; while at the same time we discovered that Lee had not left his line of retreat unprotected. A large force of infantry and artillery attacked us promptly on our appearance, serving their guns with remarkable rapidity and accuracy. A few minutes sufficed to assure us that our cavalry force was largely outnumbered by the infantry of the enemy. They moved upon our thin skirmish line in solid line of battle; and it was only by the determined bravery of our troops, the excellent handling of our batteries, and our advantage in position, that we were able to resist their attacks.

General Kilpatrick passed through Hagerstown, and soon after came upon the enemy. He was forced back upon our right, and came in upon us somewhat demoralized. About 6 o'clock our lines were shortened, our whole force dismounted, and all engaged. We were greatly outnumbered, and that by infantry. We had no support, no reserve, no reinforcements; every man was under fire, and to us it became a desperate fight for existence, and we looked anxiously for night to close upon the scene. Had the daylight lasted another hour, we would have suffered the most disastrous defeat.

About 8 o'clock all firing ceased. Our wounded

were placed in ambulances, and, with our prisoners, captured wagons, and animals, we moved back to the Sharpſburg and Hagerſtown road, where, after throwing out ſtrong picket lines, we bivouacked for the night. 1863. July 6th.

During the fight on the centre of our line, the Sixth Pennſylvania had the advance of the brigade, and was the firſt regiment engaged on the heights of Williamſ-port.

We were under a heavy artillery and muſketry fire, having Captain Graham's battery committed to our defence. We deployed the entire regiment in advance of the battery, and for four hours returned the ſteady fire of the enemy. More than one determined charge of the rebels would have broken our line but for the timely uſe of "caniſter" by Graham's guns.

The regiment and battery ſuffered ſeverely in killed and wounded.

On Tueſday morning we moved back to Boonſboro, the enemy following and attacking our rear-guard. As we were now far away from the ſupport of our army it became neceſſary that we ſhould gain and hold the paſſes of the mountain. A ſtrong force was ſtationed on every road, while the main portion of the cavalry was drawn up in line of battle about a mile in front of Boonſboro, acroſs the Hagerſtown road. At 4 o'clock P. M., the 1ſt United States Cavalry was ordered on a reconnoiſſance toward Hagerſtown. After proceeding about two miles they came upon a regiment of cavalry, which they immediately charged and routed, killing and wounding ſeveral of the enemy and taking ten priſoners. Lieutenant Burns was wounded, while three enliſted men were July 7th.

1863. killed in the charge, and buried by the roadside near
July 7th. Boonsboro.

The 6th United States made a reconnoissance in the evening, met the enemy and had a brisk fight, in which they lost nine men wounded. The night was spent dismounted in a ploughed field in line of battle, in a heavy storm of rain, without fires and with clothes thoroughly saturated; without either noonday or evening meal; standing in mud to our knees, every horse remaining saddled and in position, and every man at his horse's head, the prospect of rest for our exhausted cavalry force was very unpromising.

This was one of the most wretched nights of all our experience in the cavalry service. It seems inexplicable how human nature could endure such continued hardship and exposure; but we were yet far from the end.

CHAPTER FIFTEENTH.

Engagements at Boonſboro—Funkſtown, near Hagerſtown—Our Cavalry Batteries—Operations of our Noble 100—Falling Waters—Again in " Dixie"—Wapping Heights—Brandy Station and Culpepper—Camp Buford.

AT 10 o'clock on the morning of the 8th of July the enemy again advanced in force in an effort to gain poſſeſſion of Turner's Gap in the mountain back of Boonſboro. They opened with artillery and muſketry, and at one time during the afternoon forced us back to within one mile of the town. Shells from the enemy's guns fell in the ſtreets of Boonſboro, creating great conſternation among the citizens. The fight laſted until dark, and the enemy withdrew during the night.

_{1863.}
_{July 8th.}

We lay in line of battle all the night and following morning. During the afternoon of the 9th, our diviſion was reinforced by General Kilpatrick's, and near ſundown our whole line was advanced. We came upon the enemy ſome two miles out, and forced him back over Beaver Creek and beyond it ſome two miles, the fight continuing for an hour after dark.

_{July 9th.}

1863.
July 10th.
We rested on our arms, and early on the morning of the 10th renewed the attack, driving the enemy through Funkstown, acrofs the Antietam Creek, to within fight of Hagerstown.

We had a very fevere fight all day, the enemy making stubborn refistance near Funkstown, and having great advantage in pofition.

In thefe engagements we loft heavily; our wounded being fent back to Boonsboro.

During the afternoon, and juft as we had about exhaufted our ammunition, we were cheered by the appearance upon the field of the Eleventh Corps of the Army of the Potomac. Great was the rejoicing of our exhaufted cavalry force when they faw the infantry lines moving up to take their places in line of battle. In the laft fixteen days we had engaged the enemy in ten battles, had marched over two hundred miles, with but little fleep and on half rations, and in every engagement fighting againft fuperior numbers of infantry.

We had deftroyed nearly 800 wagons, captured 3000 horfes and mules, and over 4000 prifoners of war.

We had met, defeated, and deftroyed, as a fighting organization, General Stuart's boafted rebel cavalry, fending what remained of his once proud riders acrofs the Potomac utterly demoralized.

In all thefe actions, Pennington's, Graham's, Elder's, and Tidball's batteries ferved with the cavalry moft efficiently; they fhare equally in the honor of the achievements of the cavalry fince the engagement at Beverly Ford.

Towards evening on the 10th we were withdrawn

from the front, paffed through Boonfboro, over the mountain, and went into camp on the Catoctin Creek near Middletown. We here had accefs to our wagons; put up our tents, and luxuriated in clean linen, and an abundance of commiffary fupplies, enjoying pofitive reft for two days.

1863. July.

While the regiment had been thus engaged, 100 men of the command had been detached, under Captain W. P. C. Treichel, for fpecial duty.

On the 2d of July, while the Referve brigade was lying at Emmettfburg, 100 picked men were felected from the Sixth Pennfylvania Cavalry, under command of Captain Treichel, with Lieutenants Morrow, White, Whiteford, and Herknefs, and were ordered to report to Captain Ulric Dahlgren, then on General Meade's ftaff, for fpecial duty.

The fmall force moved that night to Ridgeville, and on the morning of the 3d along the roads in the rear of Lee's army over which his trains muft pafs. They were joined by a large number of citizens mounted and armed with fhot-guns, while others carried axes to be ufed in the deftruction of wagons. On arriving near Greencaftle they were informed that the enemy's cavalry held poffeffion of the town. Our little band, led by Captain Treichel, charged through the ftreets, furprifing the enemy and taking 84 prifoners. Lieutenant Morrow received a flight wound while leading a portion of the force in this charge, while his horfe was killed under him.

On the 5th, one of their fcouts reported the movement of General Earley's trains, ftrongly guarded, on

1863.
July.

the Williamſport and Chamberſburg road, about three miles diſtant from their bivouac of the night previous. The command was moved near to the road and lay concealed until about 300 wagons had paſſed, when, the force being divided between Lieutenants Morrow and Herkneſs, they charged to the front and rear of the train at the ſame time. With the aſſiſtance of citizens they deſtroyed 130 wagons and run the horſes off to the woods, captured two iron guns, and 200 priſoners. The ſtrong infantry guard of the train ſoon appeared in overwhelming numbers, and a ſevere fight enſued, in which we loſt nearly all the priſoners we had previouſly taken, and a number of our own men captured. Lieutenant Herkneſs received a ſevere ſabre cut and was taken priſoner.

Our men fled to the woods and were ſcattered in ſmall ſquads during the night. They rendezvouſed at Wayneſboro, Pa. On the following morning they ſucceeded in bringing to Wayneſboro about thirty priſoners.

They were at this time reduced to about eighty men; but, learning that a force of rebel cavalry under Jenkins had demanded a tribute of the authorities of the town that it might be ſaved from deſtruction, aſſiſted by citizens, they attacked the enemy, ſurpriſed them in the ſtreets, and drove them from the town, purſuing them about ſix miles. After the purſuit was diſcontinued, another train of wagons was attacked, a large number deſtroyed, and ſome priſoners taken; our party retreating before heavily attacked.

At times during the expedition the command was

greatly scattered, being secreted by loyal citizens. Lieutenant Whiteford, with a squad of ten men, were thus sheltered in Hagerstown while Longstreet's Corps passed through the town.

1863. July.

With the same party he afterwards captured a rebel messenger and paymaster with a guard of fifteen men, with dispatches from Richmond and eight thousand dollars in Confederate currency and Southern State bank notes.

On the 7th of July, about sixty men of the party rejoined the regiment at Boonsboro and were sent to Frederick City to refit; they returned to the regiment on the 12th.

On this expedition they had destroyed over two hundred wagons, loaded with valuable supplies, that had been stolen from the farmers and merchants of Pennsylvania. At one time they held more than double their number of prisoners, many of whom escaped during their several engagements, although they succeeded in bringing in to General Buford's headquarters between seventy and eighty of them.

It was this party of 100 men under Captain Treichel (to whom was chiefly due the success of the undertaking), that won for Captain Dahlgren his colonelcy, as he was nominally in charge of the force and reported directly to General Meade, who recommended him for promotion.

We would not dim by the slightest breath the gilded fame of one so fondly cherished as the noble, brave, and worthy Colonel Ulric Dahlgren, but would join in

1863. ascribing to him all deserving praise, and would write his name in imperishable characters amongst the bravest of the defenders of our country's honor; and yet we claim only justice for one of "*Ours*" when we ascribe the success of this expedition in an equal degree, at least, to Captain W. P. C. Treichel, of the Sixth Pennsylvania Cavalry.

We remained in camp near Middletown until the
July 12th. afternoon of the 12th, when we recrossed the mountains in a heavy storm of rain, and bivouacked in front of Boonsboro, where we remained until the morning of
July 14th. the 14th, when we made a rapid march to Falling Waters, joining General Kilpatrick in an attack upon the rearguard of the rebel army. We endured a pretty severe shelling from guns stationed on the heights on the south side of the Potomac.

We marched back from the river about two miles,
July 15th. and bivouacked for the night. On the 15th, we marched to Harper's Ferry, over Maryland Heights; thence down the Potomac to Berlin; thence in the evening to Petersville, where we remained in camp several days, refitting and preparing for an advance into Virginia.

The army crossed the Potomac into Virginia on the
July 16th. 16th and 17th. The Reserve Cavalry Brigade followed
July 18th. on the 18th, marching until near midnight, when we halted at the foot of the Blue Ridge Mountains near Hillsborough.

General Lee, having passed into the Shenandoah Valley, no sooner found that we were close upon his heels than he made a feint, as if he would return and recross the Potomac. General Meade paid no attention to his movements in that direction, but pushed his advance rapidly southward until he held all the passes in the mountains down to Manassas Gap. The occupation of this important pass was given to the old First Cavalry Division of General Buford. On the 19th, his scouts reported the approach of two corps of the enemy from Port Royal. He engaged the advance of the rebel army, and a heavy skirmish ensued.

1863.

July 19th.

Reinforcements were called for, and in the emergency, the 3d Corps, then guarding Ashby's Gap, was ordered down to our support. They moved in the afternoon, and during the night found Buford ten miles in advance up the Gap, in the vicinity of Linden. On the following morning our line of battle was formed, looking down upon the beautiful valley through which was rapidly pressing the "Army of Northern Virginia."

July 20th.

Generals French and Buford attacked the enemy early in the morning, and a severe engagement ensued lasting all day, with wavering fortunes and heavy losses on both sides. The ground over which the battle raged was a succession of hills, known as Wapping Heights, and was favorable to defensive warfare. The enemy attacked with overwhelming numbers, and General French withdrew to a strong position on the mountain side for the night.

General Meade came up during the evening and received information of the return of the rebel force that during the day had moved down the valley, and every indication pointed to a renewal of the attack, and a severe engagement on the following day. Acting upon the in-

1863.
July 20th.

formation gained, General Meade ordered up the bulk of his army in anticipation of a decisive battle at that point.

A reconnoissance made early in the morning revealed the total disappearance of the rebels from our front. By the movement of the army into Manassas Gap we lost nearly two days in our southerly march, thus enabling Lee to reach the Rappahannock and effect a crossing unmolested.

Aug. 1st.

The 1st Cavalry Division started at 3 o'clock on the morning of the 1st of August, and forded the Rappahannock at the ford below the railroad crossing, while a pontoon bridge was being constructed above; by 9 o'clock they came upon the pickets of the enemy and discovered cavalry camps about two miles out. The object of the expedition was to ascertain the exact position and force of the enemy.

About noon we became heavily engaged near Brandy Station, and by hard fighting forced the enemy back to within a mile of Culpepper, where they came upon their infantry supports. Our men stood up bravely against the overwhelming fire of the enemy notwithstanding the disparity of numbers. The Reserve Brigade under General Merritt had the advance on the extreme right and made several charges upon the enemy; the Sixth Pennsylvania, commanded by Captain Lockwood, being heavily engaged all day.

Terrific charges were made upon the enemy's line when near Culpepper, in which we drove the cavalry in dismay back upon their supports of infantry, who, coming up in regular and solid line of battle with their long

Enfield rifles, were too strong for our cavalry division, and we were withdrawn in perfect order to Brandy Station, our rear-guard resisting the advance of the enemy. During our engagement General Meade had advanced his infantry across the river and established his lines out nearly to Brandy Station, and extending from Waterloo to Falmouth.

1863.

Another cavalry skirmish occurred on the 5th of August, when we were attacked about 2 o'clock in the afternoon. Our line of battle was soon formed, with the Sixth Pennsylvania in the advance and on the right of the brigade, under Captain Lockwood. The rebels had only a brigade, which they pushed forward to reconnoitre our front, doubtless supposing that our main force had recrossed the river. Our men did not wait for an attack from the enemy, but promptly advanced to meet them, fighting dismounted and with artillery admirably served. We succeeded in driving the enemy back some three miles, capturing several prisoners and leaving many rebel dead upon the field. The Sixth Pennsylvania lost one killed and three wounded.

Aug. 5th.

We remained encamped in the vicinity of Brandy Station, until the 15th of August, when the Reserve Brigade under General Merritt was withdrawn from the front under orders to proceed to Washington. Their horses, arms, and all public property were turned over to the quartermaster of the division, and the brigade sent by rail to Alexandria. On the 16th we crossed the Potomac, and went into camp on the heights overlooking the river near Giesboro Point, between Forts Greble and Carroll.

Aug. 15th.

Aug. 16th.

1863.   Captain Lockwood commanded the regiment, which was now reduced to about two hundred men prefent for duty. We were ordered to this point to recruit, refit, and reorganize, and after our long campaign, of unprecedented marching and fighting, greatly needed the reft thus fecured to us.

CHAPTER SIXTEENTH.

Major Robert Morris, Jr.—Rejoin the Army in Virginia—A Night Advance—A Fight at Briſtow—Deſtruction of Railroad—Captain Lockwood Inſide the Enemy's Lines—Guerillas at Morriſville—Murder of Lieutenant Sage—Acroſs the Rappahannock—Engaged near Culpepper.

EARLY in September, while at Camp Buford, we received intelligence of the death of Major Robert Morris, Jr., while a priſoner of war at Richmond, Virginia.

1863. September.

He was the ſon of Dr. Morris, of Philadelphia, and a great-grandſon of Robert Morris, the Revolutionary financier, and was at the time of his death in the 27th year of his age. At the outbreak of the war he entered the military ſervice in the " City Troop," and, on their return from the three months' ſervice, he aſſiſted in recruiting the Sixth Pennſylvania Cavalry.

He diſtinguiſhed himſelf in the early campaigns of the regiment on the Peninſula and in Maryland in 1862. Commanded the regiment during Stoneman's raid in May, 1863, and in the great cavalry engagement at Beverly Ford on the 9th of June. On the latter occaſion he was captured while leading a daring charge upon the enemy. He was conveyed to Richmond and con-

1863. fined in Libby prison, where the dreadful treatment given to our prisoners soon broke his constitution and rendered him peculiarly susceptible to the disease of which he died on the 12th of August, after a short illness. His remains were interred at the Oakwood Cemetery, being followed to the grave by Chaplain McCabe, U. S. A., and Lieutenants Lennig, Colladay, and Herkness, of the Sixth Pennsylvania Cavalry, his fellow prisoners. Major Morris was a brave and able commander; a thorough disciplinarian; of purest principles and noblest impulses; reliable as a friend, and a model soldier. He was loved by many, honored and respected by all.

Oct. 10th. On the 10th of October the quiet of our camp life was suddenly broken by orders for immediate movement of the brigade to the front. The rebels were attempting a great flank movement in Virginia, and the Army of the Potomac was falling rapidly back upon Centreville. Every indication pointed to a third engagement on or near the old Bull Run battle-field. We were hurriedly armed and mounted, the most of the brigade being ready to move by 5 o'clock P. M.

The "general," sounded from brigade headquarters; tents were struck, wagons loaded, horses saddled and packed, while the men lounged about waiting for further orders, which did not come until 7 o'clock the following morning. We left Camp Buford on the morning Oct. 11th. of the 11th, passed through Washington, over Long Bridge, and out as far as Bailey's Cross-roads. On the 13th we moved to Fairfax Court-house, and on the Oct. 16th. 14th joined the army near Centreville. On the 16th were fent on reconnoiffance, returning towards midnight. On the 17th, Captains Starr and Carpenter, who, with Companies "I" and "E," had been on duty at headquarters of the army, rejoined the command, and from this date our regimental organization was kept intact. At 3 P. M. we ftarted on a reconnoiffance with the Referve Brigade, Captain W. P. C. Treichel, commanding the Sixth Pennfylvania. We croffed Bull Run at Blackburn's Ford, and paffing beyond our lines about dufk, pufhed out towards the Orange and Alexandria Railroad, under inftruction to gain and hold Manaffas Junction, if poffible.

1863.
Oct. 17th.

The night was clear and ftarlight; we marched with great caution, and about 9 o'clock in the evening came upon the enemy's pickets, and foon after a heavy force oppofed our march, and a brifk fkirmifh enfued, with but little injury to either fide until we had forced them back to the railroad, where a more determined ftand was made, and where by the light of burning railway ties we could more clearly difcern their line. Five rebels, who were killed during the advance, were buried by our troops on the following morning.

Our lofs confifted of three flightly wounded. On Sunday, the 18th, General Merritt came up, and affuming command of the brigade, ordered the Sixth Pennfylvania to make a reconnoiffance toward Briftow, and "draw the fire of the enemy."

Oct. 18th.

We advanced a ftrong fkirmifh line, and foon came upon and drove in the pickets of the enemy; they were ftrongly reinforced, but were flowly forced back for about one mile, when they opened upon us a battery of

1863. seven guns from a very favorable position, throwing solid shot and shell into our line, but with little effect. The 5th United States was ordered up to our support; but being satisfied that we were largely outnumbered, and under orders simply to learn the position and force of the enemy and not precipitate an engagement, we withdrew to Manassas Junction. In this skirmish the Sixth lost two men wounded; one but slightly in the hand, from the effects of which he afterwards died in hospital in Washington.

Oct. 19th. A reconnoissance on Monday morning developed the withdrawal of the rebels from our immediate front, and the brigade was sent forward in three columns to Catlett's Station, where we halted, and sending a party forward some two miles, found their picket line again established.

Oct. 20th. On the 20th we were ordered back to Bristow Station, and on the return met General Warren with his corps marching to the front; that evening he established our advance picket line near Catlett's Station. The railroad was most effectually destroyed; every cross-tie being burned and every rail bent by fire; culverts and bridges were burned or torn up, and every deep cut filled in with earth.

A large construction force was immediately put upon the road, and in a few days cars were running out as far as Warrenton Junction, which was made the depôt of supplies.

Oct. 23d. On the 23d the brigade was ordered to Gainesville. We moved up in the morning in a heavy storm of rain, and returned in the evening wet, cold, and hungry, and not fully persuaded that the long march thus taken was of the leaſt importance, as we were within fight of our infantry camps all day.

1863.

We again eſtabliſhed camp at Manaſſas Junction about 9 o'clock in the evening, where we remained in quiet until the 27th.

During the evening of that day, while the officers were nearly all gathered around our large headquarters fire, orders were received to make preparation for immediate movement.

Oct. 27th.

By 9 o'clock tents were ſtruck, wagons packed, troops mounted and in line of march, moving in two columns along the railroad.

About midnight we halted at the recently abandoned fires of the 2d Corps near Catlett's Station for about one hour, when we again moved on, halting at half-paſt four A.M., near Germantown. The night was ſtormy, and we ſuffered greatly from cold.

Erected temporary ſhelter at daylight, and remained in our uncomfortable camp all day. Captain Lockwood with his ſquadron being ſent on picket duty.

Oct. 29th.

On the 30th, Captain Lockwood having returned from a hard tour of picket, was ſent with two engineer officers from General Meade's headquarters on a reconnoiſſance four and a half miles beyond our lines. Paſſing inſide the enemy's pickets, they moved down to, and along the Rappahannock, diſcovering the poſition of the enemy, and gaining much other valuable information. They returned ſafely to camp about 10 o'clock the following morning.

Oct. 30th.

During the afternoon of Saturday, the 31ſt, we moved forward to Elk Run, and on Tueſday, the 3d of Novem-

Oct. 31ſt.

Nov. 3d.

1863. ber, to Morrisville, where the brigade encamped in a denfe pine wood, our regiment being fent on picket to Kelley's Ford, Hartwood Church, and towards Bealton. The regiment was relieved from picket and returned to camp the next morning.

Nov. 4th. While lying at Morrisville on the 4th of November, Lieutenant Sage, acting brigade quartermafter, was killed by guerillas. The following obituary gives a juft mention of this brave young officer:

"The officers of the Sixth Pennfylvania Cavalry are called upon to mourn the lofs of another valued and gallant comrade in the death of Lieutenant Theodore M. Sage, Regimental and Acting Brigade Quartermafter, who, on the 4th of November, was killed in cold blood by guerillas in the vicinity of the camp of the regiment, near Morrifville, Va. As he was riding through a wooded road, in the difcharge of the duties of his office, and in company with Lieutenant Walker, of the 1ft United States Cavalry, and two orderlies, the party were fired upon by cowardly murderers concealed in a thicket by the roadfide, one of the fhots ftriking Lieutenant Sage in the lower part of the back and proving almoft immediately fatal. Lieutenant Walker, with the orderlies, efcaped.

"Lieutenant Sage had won the confidence and hearty friendfhip of all his comrades in arms by untiring attention to his duties, by his generous and manly fpirit, by his gallantry in the field, and by all the traits characteriftic of one who would never fail his companions in any of the viciffitudes of the life in which he was engaged."

In April, 1861, he enlifted in the "Philadelphia

Grays," forming a part of the 17th Pennsylvania Infantry. He returned home in July, and in the month following entered the Sixth Pennsylvania Cavalry as corporal in Company " B." On the 3d of January, 1863, he was commiffioned Quartermaster with the rank of 1st Lieutenant. On the day that he was murdered his body was sent to Washington in charge of the Chaplain of the regiment. It was there embalmed and encafed in a richly ornamented coffin and delivered over to members of the family, the expense being borne by the officers of the Sixth Pennsylvania Cavalry.

1863.

Nov. 4th.

The following Order was published from brigade headquarters in reference to the occurrence:

"HEADQUARTERS CAVALRY RESERVE BRIGADE,
November 5th, 1863.

"GENERAL ORDERS, No. 32.

"It is with sincere regret that the Brigadier-General Commanding announces officially to the Reserve Brigade an occurrence which all have heard informally with unfeigned sorrow and indignation, the death of First Lieutenant Theodore M. Sage, Regimental Quartermaster of the Sixth Pennsylvania Cavalry, and Acting Brigade Quartermaster.

"He was murdered on the highroad, near Elk Run, while in the discharge of his duty, by a band of armed men in the rebel service.

"Lieutenant Sage entered the service of the Government over two years since as an enlisted man, and soon, by his unceasing attention to every duty and pre-eminent capacities as a soldier, gained the unanimous indorsement of his superior officers for a commission in the regiment; since that time, he has steadily made his way to a high position among the best of officers and soldiers. His quiet, unobtrusive, and amiable manners made him beloved and sought for as an associate; his high sense of honor, and zeal in the performance of his duty gained him the most implicit confidence of his superior officers, and the unquestioning obedience and trust of his inferiors in rank; his qualities of mind and heart won for him respect from all who knew him.

"His untimely death will be mourned by the entire brigade, and every

1863. soldier will remember his cowardly murder by the dastard cut-throats who waylaid him, as one of the unsettled accounts with the rebels.
"By command of
"Brigadier-General WESLEY MERRITT.
"JAMES F. McQUESTION,
"First Lieutenant 2d U. S. Cavalry, A. A. A. G."

On the same day on which Lieutenant Sage was killed, General Merritt was fired upon by guerillas, while visiting our picket line.

The day previous, five men belonging to our division, while guarding cattle near Warrenton Junction, were captured and the cattle driven off. It was near this same point that Lieutenant Morrow was captured in the month of May.

Nov. 6th. On the 6th, our division moved to near Warrenton Sulphur Springs, and occupied an advanced position, having a slight skirmish during the day.

Nov. 7th. On the 7th, we were relieved by infantry, who, pushing forward their lines, had a spirited engagement during the afternoon.

Nov. 8th. On the morning of the 8th, the 1st Cavalry Division crossed the river at Sulphur Springs, and moved down towards Culpepper, passing through Jefferson to Rixey's Ford on Hazel River. They drove before them from the Springs a few squadrons of the enemy's cavalry, who had been picketing in that vicinity; and, at the ford above mentioned, they found the 10th Virginia Cavalry, which also retired before them. They pushed forward to within four miles of Culpepper, when they came upon Wilcox's rebel division of Hill's corps.

Colonel Chapman's brigade, with Lieutenant Wil-

lifton's battery, was formed on the left, while General 1863.
Merritt's brigade, with Lieutenant Butler's battery was Nov. 8th.
on the right, and farther advanced. The enemy moved
forward their infantry in heavy line of battle, supported
by artillery, against our single division of dismounted
cavalry. The 3d Indiana, 8th Illinois, and 6th Pennsylvania received the greatest attention from the enemy;
we were forced back a short distance, but after a sharp
fight, lasting about one hour and a half and terminating
at dark, the enemy retired from their advanced position;
the Sixth Pennsylvania being left to picket the ground.
Our division went into camp about three-quarters of a
mile to the rear.

Our entire loss was something over fifty, including
Lieutenant Butler of the battery, and Lieutenant Stevens of the 8th Illinois Cavalry.

The former was wounded in the ankle quite severely,
and during the night it was found necessary to amputate
his foot.

Lieutenant Butler had won golden opinions throughout the brigade, and it was with deep sorrow that we
learned of his injury and removal from the field.

During the night the enemy withdrew, and on the
morning of the 10th, General Merritt moved forward Nov. 10th.
and occupied Culpepper, establishing his picket line two
miles out.

CHAPTER SEVENTEENTH.

Engagement at Rappahannock Station—Mine Run Expedition—In Camp near Culpepper—Death of Major-General John Buford—Changes in Field, Staff, and Line.

1863.
Nov. 8th.

WHILE our cavalry were moving in the vicinity of the Sulphur Springs on the 7th, General Sedgwick with the 5th and 6th Corps advanced upon the enemy, ſtrongly intrenched at Rappahannock Station. They had thrown up fortifications on both the north and ſouth bank of the river. The enemy's ſkirmiſhers were driven in by the rapid advance of our troops, until our guns occupied the creſt of a hill leſs than one mile from their works. An artillery duel commenced as ſoon as our guns reached this favorable poſition, and during its progreſs a ſtorming party, confiſting of four regiments of Ruſſell's brigade, and two of Colonel Upton's, was organized, who, with loud cheering and fixed bayonets, made a deſperate aſſault upon the forts and rifle pits. To reach the works, half a mile of open plain had to be traverſed; but, regardleſs of the heavy fire that was opened upon them, they moved ſteadily forward at double quick, without firing a ſingle ſhot, until they reached the works; here a deſperate hand to hand ſtruggle commenced and continued for about twenty minutes, 1863. resulting in a complete victory for our troops, and the surrender of the entire force of the enemy; four guns and two thousand stand of arms were captured, and about eighteen hundred officers and men taken prisoners.

On the 10th, our cavalry established their camps about one mile in front of Culpepper, doing advanced picket duty. Nov. 10th.

On the 18th, the regiment was sent on a scout out the James City Road some three miles beyond our lines; we returned near night with several prisoners and some information in reference to the position of the enemy. Nov. 18th.

Our picket line was now established from James City to Cedar Run. We took our regular tour of picket on this line, until the afternoon of the 25th, when we changed our picket line and the whole division moved to the east of Culpepper, preparatory to an early movement the succeeding morning. Nov. 25th.

This was a night of frequent alarms in consequence of repeated attacks upon our pickets.

On the 26th, we left camp at 8 A. M., and moved with the brigade to Stevensburg, where we bivouacked for the night. On the march, received telegrams from the War Department announcing the great victories of General Grant at Lookout Mountain and Missionary Ridge. The reports created great enthusiasm amongst our troops. Long and loud cheers were given for Grant and the Army of the Cumberland. Nov. 26th.

General Buford being sick in Washington, the 1st division was commanded by Brigadier-General Merritt,

1863. and the Reserve Brigade by Colonel Alfred Gibbs, of the 19th New York Cavalry, a regiment recently added to the Reserve Brigade.

Nov. 25th. The Army of the Potomac had crossed the Rapidan in three columns on the 25th, and severe skirmishing had been going on at different points. On the 27th, General Kilpatrick attempted to cross the river at Raccoon Ford under fire of rebel batteries, but was driven back from the river.

Nov. 27th. At 8 A. M. on the 27th, we left Stevensburg and marched about five miles, when we overtook the 1st and 6th Corps wagon trains, which this division of cavalry was to guard, and also act as rear-guard for the army towards Fredericksburg. The wagons of the Cavalry Corps were soon after added, and an immense park was established near Ely's Ford on the Rapidan. During this day was fought the battle of Locust Grove, which resulted in the success of our arms and the retreat of the enemy with heavy loss.

Nov. 28th. On the 28th, a portion of the regiment was sent on picket down the Rapidan and back towards Fredericksburg; heavy artillery and musketry firing could be heard across the river in the direction of Chancellorsville much of the time on the 28th and 29th. The corps of Generals French, Warren, and Prince had pretty heavy skirmishing with the enemy. General French, commanding the 3d Corps, lost heavily, but succeeded in driving the enemy and capturing 900 prisoners; during the advance and fight, the 6th Corps was thrown forward to his support. The 5th Corps train was attacked in flank on the plank road and fifteen wagons were deſtroyed. General Gregg's cavalry was attacked, and 1863. though taken by ſurpriſe, ſoon rallied, had a ſevere fight with rebel cavalry, and drove them back upon their infantry, and were then driven back upon the 5th Corps, who in turn drove the rebels from the field. On Monday evening the two armies were ſeparated by Mine Run Valley, which croſſes the Frederickſburg and Orange Plank-road twelve miles from Orange Courthouſe. General Lee was ſtrongly intrenched in this poſition ; earthwork roſe above earthwork, and all of a very ſtrong character.

General Warren was ordered to attack at daylight on the 30th, but during the night the enemy's works were greatly ſtrengthened, and it was deemed impracticable to carry them without too great a ſacrifice of life. General Meade viſited the left and countermanded the order for an advance, and although conſiderable artillery and ſome muſketry firing continued throughout the day, yet no attack was made in force. During the night of the 1ſt of December our troops were quietly withdrawn to the Rapidan, and on the following day the army moved back to its former camps in the vicinity of Stevenſburg, Culpepper, Brandy Station, and Warrenton, while a large portion were ſtretched along the Orange and Alexandria Railroad for its protection. Nov. 30th. Dec. 1ſt.

The humane ſpirit actuating the truly great Commander of this army is ſhown in the following extract from a letter from General Meade to a friend in Newark, about the time of the Mine Run movement :

"I am fully aware of the great anxiety in the public mind that ſomething ſhould be done ; I am in receipt of

1863. many letters, some from persons in high position, telling me I had better have my army destroyed and the country filled up with the bodies of the soldiers than remain inactive. Whilst I do not suffer myself to be influenced by such communications, I am, and have been most anxious to effect something, but am determined at every hazard not to attempt anything unless my judgment indicates a probability of accomplishing some object commensurate with the destruction of life necessarily involved. I would rather a thousand times be relieved, charged with tardiness or incompetency, than to have my conscience burdened with a wanton slaughter, uselessly, of brave men, or with having jeopardized the great cause by doing what I thought wrong."

It was this regard for the lives of his soldiers, and the great odds against him at Mine Run, with the fact that winter was upon him with all its uncertainties of weather, and danger of breaking up of communication and interference with supplies, that led General Meade to decide upon a return without giving the enemy battle.

Dec. 2d. Reveille sounded in our camp at 4 o'clock on the morning of the 2d of December, the regiment leaving camp at daylight and marching to Stevensburg, when, after resting for two hours, we again mounted and proceeded to Culpepper.

Scouts were sent out in all directions, and near night our picket line was again established far in advance of our old line, the Sixth Pennsylvania being sent out on this duty, and relieved the following morning by the 19th New York Cavalry.

Dec. 4th. On the 4th, an alarm was created in camp at 3 o'clock in the morning in confequence of a reported attack upon 1863. our picket line. The regiment was quickly in line, and after an hour or two of ftanding to horfe, the men were allowed to tie their horfes to their picket ropes, where they remained ready faddled until near noon, when the regiment was fent on fcout to Cedar Mountain. We remained in this camp preparing permanent winter quarters until the 25th of December, when we celebrated Dec. 25th. our Chriftmas by a removal of camp to near Mitchell's Station.

We left comfortable quarters, built with great care, in which we had expected to winter, and moving out fome four miles, fpent the afternoon in vain efforts to arrange fome comfortable bivouac with fhelter tents. In confequence of recent heavy rains the ground was very wet and fpongy. The night was cold and ftormy, and in the greateft difcomfort its hours wore through. Thoughts of home and the feftivities of the Chriftmas feafon added nothing to our enjoyment of that difmal Chriftmas night in the extreme front of the Army of the Potomac.

On the 18th, our divifion was made forrowful by the announcement of the death of General John Buford, which occurred at the refidence of General Stoneman, Wafhington, D. C., from difeafe contracted in the fervice. General Buford was born in Kentucky, but removed to Illinois at an early age; was appointed from that State to the Military Academy at Weft Point. Graduating in 1848 he entered the 2d U. S. Dragoons as fecond lieutenant.

He ferved with his regiment until the outbreak of the

1863.
December.

war, when he was transferred to the Infpector-General's department. In 1862, he was appointed to the command of the regular brigade of cavalry.

In the fpring of 1863, he was affigned to the command of the 1ft Cavalry Divifion, which pofition he held with the rank of major-general at the time of his death. A feries of refolutions, expreffive of the feelings of the divifion in his lofs, were prepared at a meeting of his ftaff officers and prefented to the officers of the divifion for their approval, as follows:

"*Firft*. That we, the divifion officers of the late Major-General John Buford, fully appreciating his merits as a gentleman, foldier, commander, and patriot, conceive his death to be an irreparable lofs to the cavalry arm of the fervice. That we have been deprived of a friend and leader whofe fole ambition was our fuccefs, and whofe chief pleafure was in adminiftering to the welfare, fafety, and happinefs of the officers and men of his command.

"*Second*. That we deeply fympathize with his bereaved family, and tender them our heartfelt appreciation of his merits in this their hour of affliction. That we look upon his character as a model of high integrity and modefty united with the fympathies of a heart alive to every tender emotion as well as indifference to perfonal inconvenience and danger. That to his unwearied exertion in the many refponfible pofitions which he has occupied, the fervice at large is indebted for much of its efficiency, and in his death the cavalry has loft a firm friend and a moft ardent advocate. That we are called to mourn the lofs of one who was ever to us as the kindeſt and tendereſt father, and that our fondeſt deſire 1863. and wiſh will ever be to perpetuate his memory, and emulate his greatneſs."

December.

The funeral ſervices were held at Rev. Dr. Gurley's Church, Waſhington, D. C., December 20th, and were largely attended by officers of the army and navy, members of Congreſs, and a large concourſe of citizens, crowding the church to overflowing. The ſermon was an able one and worthy the occaſion, from which we can only make this brief extract, which preſents ſomething of the characteriſtics of our honored chief:

"He was modeſt, yet brave; retiring, yet efficient; quiet, but vigilant; unoſtentatious, but prompt and perſevering; careful of the lives of his men with an almoſt parental ſolicitude, yet never ſhrinking from action, however fraught with peril, when the time and place for ſuch action had come. His ſkill and courage were put to ſtern and deciſive teſts on many hardfought fields, and they were always equal to every emergency."

Major-General Stoneman commanded the military eſcort on the occaſion, conſiſting of a regiment of infantry; Battery "L," of the 5th Regulars; one ſquadron of cavalry, and prominent officers and citizens. The remains were taken to Weſt Point and there interred with military honors. A ſufficient ſum was contributed by the officers of the diviſion to erect a ſuitable monument over his grave.

The following changes in the ſtaff and line, hitherto unnoticed, occurred during the year, or previouſly.

Firſt Lieutenant William Odenheimer reſigned in February, 1863, in conſequence of diſeaſe contracted in

1863.
December.
field-fervice. He entered the regiment at its organization as a private in Company "A," Auguſt, 1861, and, before the regiment left Philadelphia, was appointed 2d Lieutenant of Company "H." In November, 1862, was promoted as 1ſt Lieutenant of Company "M."

William White, of Philadelphia, was appointed 2d Lieutenant of Company "D," November 1ſt, 1862, and promoted to 1ſt Lieutenant in ſame Company, February 11th, 1863; had previouſly ſerved for "ninety days" as private in Company "F" ("Waſhington Grays"), 17th Pennſylvania Infantry.

Rev. S. Levis Gracey, Paſtor of the Methodiſt Epiſcopal Church at Media, Delaware County, was invited to the regiment, and by the unanimous voice of the officers choſen its Chaplain, and was commiſſioned and muſtered accordingly, November 20th, 1862.

Surgeon John B. Coover was commiſſioned as ſuch, and aſſigned to the Sixth Pennſylvania Cavalry, in December, 1862, ſerved faithfully with the regiment during all its campaigns in 1863.

George Meade, of Philadelphia, ſon of Major-General George G. Meade, entered the regiment as 2d Lieutenant of Company "C," November 20th, 1862, having ſpent the two previous years at the Military Academy at Weſt Point. He ſerved faithfully with the regiment in all its campaigns until May 22d, 1863, when he was appointed a Captain and Aide-de-camp on the ſtaff of his father, then commanding the 5th Corps. Went with General Meade when he was aſſigned to the command of the Army of the Potomac, and ſerved on the ſtaff to the cloſe of the war, being greatly expoſed in every engagement of the army in its advances upon Richmond. At this writing (Auguſt, 1866), he is ſtill borne on the ſtaff of Major-General Meade, with the brevet rank of Lieutenant-Colonel, a rank and poſition fairly earned by long and faithful ſervice.

1863.
December.

Major George E. Clymer reſigned February 5th, 1863. He had been faithful in every poſition in the regiment during its arduous campaigns, and was greatly beloved by the entire command.

On the 24th of February, 1863, Captain F. C. Newhall, Company "K," was appointed Acting Aſſiſtant Inſpector-General on the ſtaff of Major-General Stoneman, who had been recently aſſigned to command the Cavalry Corps.

At the above date, his ſervice with the regiment virtually ceaſed. Captain Newhall entered the regiment as 2d Lieutenant in Company "A," but only remained on duty with the company for a few days, when he was muſtered as Adjutant of the regiment, with the rank of 1ſt Lieutenant, on the 31ſt of October, 1861.

On the 27th of March, 1862, he was muſtered as Captain of Company "K," vice Ellis reſigned. He ſerved with his company until the battle of Frederickſburg, when he was appointed Provoſt-Marſhal of the 6th Corps, which poſition he occupied until his appointment as above, on the ſtaff of General Stoneman. When Major-General Pleaſonton aſſumed command of the Cavalry Corps, Captain Newhall remained in the ſame poſition, and continued to fulfil the duties of his office faithfully, and when General Sheridan was ordered to the command of the Cavalry he was retained upon

1863.
Dec. 31ft.
his ftaff, ferving in all the campaigns of this brilliant Cavalry leader.

On the 6th of February, 1865, at the requeft of Major-General Sheridan, Captain Newhall was appointed by the Prefident Affiftant Adjutant-General of the Middle Military Divifion with the rank of Lieutenant-Colonel. He retained this pofition on the ftaff of General Sheridan until after the clofe of the war, and won the higheft praife for faithfulnefs of fervice.

Sergeant Bernard H. Herknefs, Company "C," promoted 2d Lieutenant in Company "G," April 1ft, 1863.

Captain Robert Milligan, Company "F," refigned in January, 1863. He ferved with the three months' troops as Captain in the 1ft Delaware Infantry, and at the expiration of their term of fervice entered the Sixth Pennfylvania Cavalry with the fame rank. He was with the regiment when it ftarted from Philadelphia, and through the Peninfula and Maryland campaigns, and at the battle of Frederickfburg. In the latter engagement he ferved with his company as Provoft-Guard for General Franklin's Grand Divifion.

Sergeant Archer Maris was appointed 2d Lieutenant Company "I," April 1ft, 1862, having ferved faithfully with the regiment fince its organization. He was placed on detached duty on the 4th of November, 1863, being appointed Provoft-Marfhal of the Referve Cavalry Brigade.

Lieutenant E. P. Bertrand was detached from the regiment June 26th, as Aide-de-camp to Major Starr, 6th United States Cavalry, then commanding the brigade; his fervice with the regiment ceafed on that date, for on the 29th, General Merritt assumed command of the brigade and retained him as personal Aide-de-camp on his staff, which position he retained until the expiration of his term of original enlistment, November, 1864, when he left the service. 1863. Dec. 31st.

The health of Captain H. P. Muirheid being completely broken, he was compelled to resign on surgeon's certificate of disability, April 2d, 1863.

He entered the regiment with the rank of 2d Lieutenant, September 10th, 1861; promoted to 1st Lieutenant, October 1st, 1861, at Camp Meigs, Philadelphia, and to a captaincy, March 28th, 1862. During a part of the Peninsula campaign was detached from the regiment as Provost-Marshal of the 6th Corps, Major-General Franklin commanding, and also served with him during the first Maryland campaign. He served with the regiment at the battles of Hanover Courthouse, Gaines's Mill, White Oak Swamp, and Charles City Cross-roads. At the battle of South Mountain he acted as Aid on General Franklin's staff. He left us while encamped at White Oak Church, Virginia.

Major John H. Gardiner resigned February 5th, 1863, on surgeon's certificate of disability.

At the breaking out of the war he commanded a company in the 17th Pennsylvania Regiment, Colonel Frank Patterson, and, at the expiration of their three months of service, he engaged in recruiting for the Sixth Pennsylvania Cavalry, and entered the regiment as Captain of Company "B." Promoted Major, November 1st, 1862. Suffered greatly from sickness during the

1863.
Dec. 31ſt.

winter of 1862, and was compelled to leave the field-ſervice in the ſpring of 1863.

Major J. Henry Hazeltine was promoted from Captain of Company "E," February 5th, 1863. Commanded the regiment after the Beverly Ford engagement through the ſummer campaign in Pennſylvania, at Gettyſburg, and the battles at Williamſport, Boonſboro, Funkſtown, Falling Waters, &c. Reſigned, November 12th, 1863.

Thomas O. Mailey entered the United States Army as Quartermaſter-Sergeant in the famous 2d United States Cavalry (now 5th), in the early part of 1855; his term of ſervice having expired in 1860 he returned to civil life.

On the 5th of Auguſt, 1861, joined the Sixth Pennſylvania Cavalry with the rank of 1ſt Lieutenant and Regimental Quartermaſter and Commiſſary, and ſerved in that capacity until April 14th, 1862, when he was commiſſioned in and transferred to the 5th United States Cavalry, of which regiment he is ſtill a member. The experience he brought to the Quartermaſter's and Commiſſary's Departments was of vaſt benefit to the regiment in its organization, when nearly every officer was inexperienced in military matters.

Firſt Lieutenant T. W. Neill, reſigned in Auguſt, 1863, in conſequence of failing health; he firſt entered the ſervice as Orderly-Sergeant of the Commonwealth Artillery, ſtationed at Fort Delaware. Entered the Sixth Pennſylvania as 2d Lieutenant of Company "K," at formation of regiment. Served faithfully through all the operations of the regiment while on the Peninſula and in Maryland.

Affiftant-Surgeon Thomas L. Morrifon was commif- 1863. fioned as fuch and affigned to our regiment January 31ft, Dec. 31ft. 1863. Refigned, June 30th, 1863.

Second Lieutenant J. Hinckley Clark promoted 1ft Lieutenant Company "K," April 6th, 1862; Captain Company "M," March 16th, 1863.

Charles M. Ellis, M.D., of Elkton, Maryland, entered the regiment at its formation with the rank of Affiftant-Surgeon, and ferved with the regiment during the Peninfula, Firft Maryland, and Fredericksburg campaigns. When our army fell back from near Cold Harbor, leaving our hofpital with its inmates to the mercy of the enemy, Dr. Ellis voluntarily remained in charge of the fick and wounded; was taken with them to Richmond and confined in Libby prifon until the latter part of July, when he was exchanged, and rejoined the regiment. He was the only furgeon with the regiment during the Antietam and Fredericksburg campaigns. Refigned January 18th, 1863, while we were encamped near White Oak Church, Virginia.

Edward Whiteford was appointed 2d Lieutenant in the regiment in May, 1863. He is the fon of a Britifh officer belonging to the 13th Light Infantry ("Queen's Own"), and was born in County Dublin, Ireland. After a liberal education in early life he went to Dublin and entered as a ftudent in a military inftitution, expecting a commiffion in a cavalry regiment. Whilft waiting for pofition in the Britifh Army the civil war broke out in the United States, and he refolved to enter the Union Army, and thus fee active field-fervice. Notwithftanding the proteftation of friends, and efpecially

1863.
Dec. 31st.
that of an uncle, Sir George Whiteford, with whom he had made his home for feveral years, he failed for America in the fpring of 1861.

Soon after landing in the States he entered the fervice in the Firft Lincoln Cavalry of New York. This organization failed, and he entered the 5th New York Cavalry in the fpring of 1862. He ferved with this regiment in the campaigns of the Shenandoah under General Banks, after the fecond battle of Bull Run, in which he rendered diftinguifhed fervice. Lieutenant Whiteford was fent to Wafhington fick; while there he refigned. In November, 1862, he again defired to enter the fervice, and was invited by a general officer of the 2d Corps to a pofition on his ftaff with the rank of 1ft Lieutenant, which he accepted; but, defiring to return to the cavalry fervice, entered the Sixth Pennfylvania as above mentioned. He rendered very efficient fervice with the regiment, proving a fearlefs, dafhing cavalry officer. He remained in fervice with the regiment, commanding different companies, until Auguft, 1864, when he was ordered to the ftaff of General Merritt, 1ft Cavalry Divifion, as Aide-de-camp.

Later in the year he returned to the regiment as Captain of Company "G," and remained in active fervice until the clofe of the war.

CHAPTER EIGHTEENTH.

Winter Quarters near Mitchell's Station—Reconnoiffance to Robertfon's River—General Cufter's Raid to Charlottefville—Stormy Night Rides in Midwinter—Flight of the Contrabands.

DURING the early part of January we eftablifhed permanent winter quarters near Mitchell's Station on the Orange and Alexandria Railroad, five miles beyond Culpepper; our camp being three miles in front of the moft advanced infantry lines, and our picket lines five miles to the front; extending from Robertfon's River on the right, by Cedar Mountain to Somerville Ford, thence along the Rapidan to Raccoon, Morton's, and Mitchell's Fords. Very excellent log huts were erected, in regular ftreets and of uniform dimenfions. The regimental headquarters were taftefully arranged. A large chapel was built of logs, covered with heavy canvas furnifhed by the Chriftian Commiffion, in which religious fervices were held each Sabbath, and three evenings of each week. A Sibley tent, mounted on a ftockade, and fupported from the exterior, furnifhed a very beautiful and attractive club tent for the ufe of the officers. It was the fcene of much good cheer and amufement.

1864.
January.

1864. A ſtring band was organized by the enliſted men, which furniſhed entertainment during many of the long winter evenings; as there were alſo three good braſs bands in the brigade, and as the regiments were encamped within a ſhort diſtance of each other, we had the advantage of the entire army in this reſpect.

While here the offer was made to pay a bounty and give a furlough of at leaſt thirty days to thoſe who would re-enliſt for three years; about one hundred and forty men re-enliſted and were ſent home on furlough.

Captain W. P. C. Treichel was muſtered as Major; Lieutenant Frank Furneſs as Captain, and 2d Lieutenant William White as 1ſt Lieutenant, on the 11th of January. A few evenings afterward a ſerenade was tendered them by the band of the 1ſt United States Cavalry, and ſeveral officers of the regular regiments called to congratulate the Major.

Jan. 11th.

Feb. 6th. The Reſerve Brigade, Colonel Gibbs commanding, left camp at daylight; marched to, and croſſed Robertſon's River, and proceeded to within a mile of Barnett's Ford on the Rapidan, when we turned into a fine grove of pines and ſtood to horſe all night. The deſign of the reconnoiſſance was to aſcertain the poſition of the enemy towards Orange Court-houſe, and create a diverſion in favor of the advance of a portion of the 1ſt and 2d Corps towards Raccoon and Morton's Fords. General Sedgwick commanded the infantry force on this occaſion.

The 2d and 3d diviſions of the 2d Corps under General Warren croſſed the river at Morton's Ford; they ſoon encountered a pretty ſtrong line of the enemy, when a confiderable fkirmifh followed, in which we loft between two and three hundred killed and wounded. General Kilpatrick croffed with his divifion at Culpepper Ford and fcoured the country to the left as far as Frederickfburg, but found no traces of the enemy in that direction.

1864.

On the morning of the 7th, our brigade advanced a fhort diftance, the Sixth Pennfylvania being thrown out to the left to eftablifh videttes. We had feveral fkirmifhes during the day, our artillery being ufed effectively. Near night, having accomplifhed all that was defigned by the expedition, we ftarted on our return to camp, and by 9 o'clock that evening we were again in our comfortable quarters. The infantry returned to their former camps on the 7th and 8th.

Feb. 7th.

On the 15th, a complimentary dinner was given by the officers of the regiment to General Merritt; a large number of the officers of the brigade being prefent.

Feb. 15th.

On the 27th, a detail of one hundred men from each regiment of the brigade, under Major Treichel, were ordered to prepare for a raid on the Virginia Central Railroad at Charlottefville, to be conducted by General Cufter. On the fame day General Kilpatrick ftarted on his raid towards Richmond.

Feb. 27th.

The detail from our regiment was commanded by Captain B. Lockwood. We moved at 7 o'clock in the evening to Pony Mountain, where we went into bivouac about 9 o'clock, the night being very bluftery and cold. As we had no tents and but little fire, we fuffered much from the keen northeaft winds. Near noon on the 28th we marched to Robertfon's River near Madifon Court-houfe,

Feb. 28th.

1864. and found the 6th Corps there in bivouac under shelter tents, having come out thus far from their winter quarters to cover our expedition. Reveille sounded at midnight, and after breakfast on "hard tack" and good hot coffee, we started on the march beyond our lines·at 2 o'clock in the morning of the 29th.

Feb. 29th. We left the 6th Corps quietly sleeping, and passing through Madison Court-house, and beyond our infantry picket lines, were once more loose in "Dixie."

Our regiment had the advance of the brigade, being led by an advance guard under Captain Clark. We pushed rapidly forward in the still night through a country alternately open and wooded, toward the Rapidan. All went quietly until we reached Wolftown, where a picket fire was observed, and Captain Clark immediately charged upon the startled enemy. A few shots were exchanged, but in the darkness of the night all escaped, and we pushed on rapidly towards Charlottesville.

Near Stannardsville, Captain Clark captured a small party of rebels with wagons loaded with flour, hams, and potatoes. As we proceeded we found a tolerably well-cultivated and high-rail-fenced country, the farmers ploughing in the fields; when the horses were worth it they were taken from plough, cart, or stable, in the name of the United States. Frequently, some of the men would make a descent upon the poultry yards along our line of march. A fine horse was found tied in front of a house on the roadside, and as some of our men were about claiming him by authority in them vested, they discovered a lady's saddle upon him, and the fair owner came from the house to remonstrate against the capture,

saying she was there from a neighboring farm on a short 1864.
visit, and she "hoped her horse would not be taken;" Feb. 29th.
of course, there was no soldier of the command proof
against her eloquent pleadings, and she was allowed to
return unmolested to her own home. Nearly all the
male citizens along our route were taken along as prisoners, as a precaution against bushwhacking and to prevent information being conveyed to the enemy.

In the town of Stannardsville the people came out to
see the troops, looking on with great curiosity, as we
were the first representatives of the Union Army that
had ever been in their vicinity. The post-office was
ransacked, and all public buildings in the town searched,
though nothing was disturbed but public property. The
men were exceedingly disgusted when they found they
had to accompany the column as temporary prisoners.
We picked up several rebel soldiers who were enjoying
furloughs from military service. The female relatives
of one Confederate thus captured clung to him, and,
with distressing outcries and shrieks, protested against
his being regarded as a spy, assuring us that he had only
been home from the army for a few days, and begging
that he should not be hung; he was captured as we
went out, and on our return was allowed to stop and
see his family again, to assure them that no harm should
come to him.

In the afternoon we crossed the Rivanna River and
found the enemy in force near Charlottesville. On approaching the town we were opposed by a strong infantry force in line of battle, and a brisk shelling immediately began. After skirmishing for an hour, we were

1864.
Feb. 29th.
satisfied that an overwhelming force of the enemy opposed our advance, and that our safety demanded a rapid retreat. A squadron of the 5th United States, under Captain Ash, scouting on our left, came so suddenly upon an artillery camp that the gunners had barely time to run off their guns by hand, and before they had recovered from their surprise, the camp was fired in several places, a number of caissons were blown up; harness, forges, and battery-wagons destroyed. Captain Ash, with his handful of men, being attacked by a heavy force, retreated in great haste, losing some prisoners. Train after train of cars, in the mean time, had arrived from Gordonsville, all loaded with troops, and, forming in line, advanced upon our weak force; we were then withdrawn across the Rivanna, our pioneers soon had the bridge in flames, and our two pieces of artillery brought to bear upon the only ford of the stream.

A large mill, near the bridge, filled with corn-meal and flour for the rebel army, was destroyed by fire.

We marched five miles towards Stannardsville, the Sixth Pennsylvania forming the rear-guard, and were followed and fired upon all the way back. We then halted for four hours, fed our horses, and had rather a poor meal for ourselves, having eaten nothing since leaving Madison Court-house on the night previous.

About 10 o'clock we again took up the line of march through a very heavy rain that began to fall about dark. After spending two hours in marching one mile, General Custer determined to halt until daylight; rain mingled with snow fell during the entire night; we all had to lie upon the wet ground and were unprotected from the pelting storm. The only wood accessible was green and wet, and it was impossible to have even a good fire; the rain froze upon our clothes and the limbs of the trees, so that by morning everything appeared to be cased in crystal, and when, during the succeeding morning, the forces of the enemy got in our way to contest our return, the cannon-shot made a wonderful crashing among the frost-bound limbs of the forest.

1864

We started out at daylight on the morning of the 1st of March, through very muddy roads, and a heavy storm of rain and sleet. Captains Starr and Clark, with the rear-guard, skirmished with the enemy all day. Sergeant Wright, of Company "I," was badly wounded. After passing Stannardsville we were opposed by a large force of the enemy when attempting to cross one of the branches of the Rapidan. The 5th United States, and a section of artillery, the latter commanded by Lieutenant Essex Porter, engaged them; some excellent shots were made by the battery, and a portion of the rebel force driven by the 5th Cavalry.

March 1st.

We then made a detour to the right toward Orange Court-house, where General Lee's headquarters were established; when within five miles of that place we turned, and riding rapidly back to the road on which we were previously marching, crossed the stream without opposition and hastened on, as rapidly as the wretched condition of the roads would admit, to Madison Courthouse, the 6th Corps having sent out a force to meet us near Wolftown. Like lost children, the command was welcomed back into the lines by General Sedgwick and the officers of his corps. After a halt of three

1864. hours, during which time our prisoners were turned over
March 1st. to the Provost-Marshal of the 6th Corps, and men and horses fed and warmed, the night being wet and cold, Major Treichel determined to march the command to their comfortable quarters near Mitchell's Station. A heavy storm of snow continued all night, and we suffered greatly with cold, our clothing being thoroughly soaked since the night previous.

We arrived at our winter home about 1 o'clock in the night, having marched over fifty miles through wretched roads and heavy wintry weather.

In the rear of our column, and only protected by the rear-guard, there followed hundreds of contrabands, of all shades, sexes, ages, &c. Who that has not seen a flight of the contrabands can have any conception of such a scene? It was impossible to keep them from joining the column, and our appearance in their neighborhood was the signal for their hasty preparation for flight from homes of bondage, and perhaps oppression, to liberty. Old and young, male and female, in wagons and carts, on mules, horses, or oxen, trudging along on foot, any way and every way, hurrying on after the column, encouraging each other and enduring unimaginable hardships. As the advance of the enemy would press our rear-guard, the officers would urge them on, and their frantic efforts to keep up with the column were both pitiful and ludicrous in the extreme. Here are men yelling and swearing; women screaming and weeping; children crying; horses, mules, and oxen running, kicking, and jumping, while some obstinately stand still, and others lie down in the mud in exhaustion and despair.

Juſt imagine a man, frightened half out of his wits, riding a refractory mule ſtubbornly refuſing to move forward one ſtep, while the ſhots of the enemy came nearer and nearer, then again ſtarting forward as though an incarnation of all modern ideas of progreſſion, running, kicking, and braying hideouſly, to the diſcomfort of all the maſs of fugitives and amuſement of the troops.

1864. March.

Men were riding that day from the tail to the ears of their animals, and ſome holding on to both ends. On others, there were man and wife riding together, the latter clinging to the former, and their rapid bouncing on rough horſes, the flogging of mules, and amuſing expreſſions, awoke irrepreſſible laughter.

One ſcreams out, "Git up here!" another, "De Lord have mercy on dis nigger!" "Stop dat mule!" "Git out de way dar!" "De rebels will git dis nigger, ſure." "I'ſe bound for de happy land of Canaan!" A mule lies down in the mud with man and wife; after vain efforts to get him up, the diſguſted contraband ſays: "Go, you ſtubborn mule, I'ſe gwan on foot; de rebels don't cotch dis child." Then, men in wagons waling away at their horſes or mules, with their wives and all her relations of the "female perſuaſion," jumping and clapping their hands, and ſhouting to frighten the jaded animals into running away. The pedeſtrians trudge on, through mud, rain, and cold, towards the great Union Army, the repreſentative to them of the great idea of freedom. One large and very dilapidated family carriage was particularly noticeable: it was crowded to burſting with women and little pickaninnies; the animals drawing it were one lean, lank horſe and a dwarf-

1864.
March.

ifh mule; the harnefs, old and fubjected to conftant ftrain, broke frequently, when the male members of the families being benefited would fall to work to mend it up, or putting their fhoulders to the wheel would lift it out of mud-holes and pufh up the hills; thus, they managed to keep up with the command until near noon on the fecond day, when it became immovably fixed in deep clay foil; the enemy were clofe upon us; there was a fudden abandoning of carriage and everything but its living freight; three women were mounted on each animal, and each with a little child in her arms, while a child was alfo borne by each of the men. We fkirmifhed with the enemy a confiderable time to give them a chance to gain the main column, and their gratitude fully repaid for the rifk and trouble. Nearly all arrived at Madifon Court-houfe in fafety, and there reported to the Provoft-Marfhal, and were fent to Wafhington.

CHAPTER NINETEENTH.

Reorganization — Spring Campaign — In the Wilderneſs — Great Flank Movement of the Army of the Potomac — Todd's Tavern — Firſt and Second Day — The Wounded — Sheridan's Raid.

THE 1ſt and 3d Corps of Infantry, and the 1ſt Diviſion of the Cavalry Corps, Army of the Potomac, were reviewed to-day near Culpepper by Lieutenant-General Grant, accompanied by Generals Meade, Warren, and Merritt.   1864. Mar. 29th.

Nothing of ſpecial intereſt tranſpired in our army during the month of April, and it was not until the early part of May that the army was called upon to reſume the offenſive. In the meantime it had been reorganized, recruited, and otherwiſe increaſed in efficiency, and now numbered, in all, about one hundred and fifty thouſand men. The five corps had been reduced to three; the 1ſt and 3d having been diſtributed between the 5th and 6th. The 9th Corps, General Burnſide commanding, had alſo been aſſociated with the Army of the Potomac, and a new power added to it by the immediate preſence of the ranking officer of the armies of the United States, — Lieutenant-General U. S. Grant.

1864.
May 4th.
On the 4th of May, we moved from our camp near Culpepper to Stevenſburg, where we halted for two hours, and then continued our march to Stevens' Mills by night, and encamped until ſunriſe on the 5th, when the regiment croſſed the Rapidan at Ely's Ford, and marched by way of the old Chancellorſville battle-ground to Aldrick's houſe, where we ſtood to horſe until night ſet in.

General Gregg's and Merritt's diviſions advanced to Ely's Ford on the 4th, and General Wilſon moved to Germania Ford, each being provided with pontoons.

At midnight, the 2d Corps, under General Hancock, which had been encamped near Culpepper, marched out towards Germania Ford, and at daylight on the morning of the 4th, the 5th Corps under Warren, the 6th under Sedgwick, and the reſerve artillery, began a forward movement on the ſame road. The ſupply train, ſixty miles long, compoſed of 8000 wagons, followed the 2d Corps.

The enemy was encamped near Orange Court-houſe, watching from his elevated lookout at Clark's Mountain for the firſt ſign of change. On obſerving our movements, General Lee put his army in inſtant motion to ſtrike the advancing column as they croſſed the Rapidan.

Burnſide was ſtill lying on the north bank of the Rappahannock. It was underſtood that the 9th Corps was to be a reſerve to protect the Capital, but at nightfall on the 4th, the ſhelter-tents were folded, and the men of the 9th were on the march along the foreſt road, lighted only by the ſtars, to join the main army at Germania Ford, where they arrived on the morning of the 5th.

1864.
May 5th.

Early on Thurſday morning the Union forces had taken up the march, their location being as follows: Sedgwick's Corps extended from Germania Ford foutheaſt to the Wildernefs Tavern; Warren's Corps was at Belmont Farm; Hancock's Corps at the old Chancellorfville battle-ground. Hancock began his march toward Spottfylvania, but was ſhortly recalled and ordered to advance his line to the ſouthweſt from Chancellorfville toward Shady Grove Church.

The Union Army was formed on a line running northweſt and ſoutheaſt, with Hancock on the left, Sedgwick on the right, and Warren in the centre. This difpofition was not perfected before the enemy approached in ſtrong force. The country was very unfavorable as a battle-field. Its ſurface covered with denfe forefts of low pines and ſcrub oaks, with impenetrable growth of hazel; the roads were narrow and eafily choked up with troops, and there was no opportunity for uſing artillery; a few guns were interfperfed here and there in any open ſpace by the roadfide, but the great artillery trains of both armies were filent in the rear. The engagements that enfued were ſtrictly infantry battles. About noon, General Griffin, commanding the 1ſt Divifion of Warren's Corps, advanced his lines and became engaged with Ewell's Corps. A ſharp fight of one hour's continuance followed, when our troops were drawn back to the main column; the enemy continued their attack and heavy fighting enfued. Thus were opened the great battles of the Wildernefs, and for

1864. eight confecutive days the armies fought face to face; fome portions of the ground between the lines were fought over four or five times.

May 6th. The battle of the 6th was a feries of fierce attacks by both combatants, and almoſt entirely by muſketry; this terrific infantry conteſt cloſed on a diſputed field, neither army having gained great advantage.

General Meade had about the fame poſition as on Thurſday. During Friday night the right was ſtrengthened by earthworks, and the armies reſted behind their rifle-pits and breaſtworks, while the broad ſpace between them was occupied by the dead and wounded of both.

May 7th. The battle was renewed at daybreak by the Union Army, and a feries of ſharp conflicts enſued, in which our troops were generally victorious; but it became evident by noon that General Lee was retreating with his main army towards Spottfylvania Court-houſe. Our army was immediately put in motion, marching ſouthward by a road nearly parallel with the enemy's.

At the opening of the ſpring campaign, our diviſion, the firſt, was commanded by General Torbett, the Reſerve Brigade by General Merritt, and the Sixth Pennſylvania by Major James Starr.

On the 6th we marched to the Furnace, in the Wilderneſs, to fupport General Cuſter. That General had been ſkirmiſhing during the morning with the enemy's cavalry, and in the afternoon had a fevere fight, in which he was ſuccefsful without our active affiſtance.

So far we had only heard the diſtant thunders of the infantry battle in the Wilderneſs, and the rapid ſharp firing of the other brigades of the diviſion in our imme-

TODD'S TAVERN.   235

diate front; but, about 4 P.M. on the 7th, our turn came. The 1st and 2d Cavalry Divifion had concentrated at Todd's Tavern, from whence, now taking the lead, the Sixth Pennfylvania ftarted on the road to Spottfylvania Court-houfe. We foon came upon the enemy, found afterwards to be Hampton's and Lee's cavalry. They had a heavy line of fkirmifhers, well covered by the character of the ground. Captain C. L. Leiper with his fquadron was deployed mounted on the left of the road; Captain Clark with his was deployed difmounted on the right, where the woods were impaffable for horfes, and Captain Carpenter with the third and remaining fquadron was held in referve in the road. We advanced promptly, driving the enemy fome diftance, when they made a ftand. The remainder of the brigade now came up; Captain Carpenter was fent in with his men on the left, while Colonel Gibbs and the 19th New York Cavalry went in on the right with Captain Clark, and the line was preffed forward. We were now at clofe quarters; the enemy fought ftubbornly, and taking advantage of a weak place in our line made a dafh through it. It was here that moft of the cafualties of the day occurred. Lieutenant William Kirk, acting adjutant, received a ball in his thigh, which broke the bone and difmounted him, and from which he died in hofpital at Alexandria, June 24th, 1864. Major James Starr, whofe horfe had already been hit, was wounded in the face by a piftol-ball, making him fpeechlefs, and forcing him to go to the rear, and Captain E. M. Carpenter and Lieutenant E. Hazel, while gallantly attempting to fave Lieutenant Kirk from falling into

1864.
May 7th.

1864.
May 7th.

the hands of the enemy, were themselves captured, and remained prisoners until Sherman "opened wide their iron doors." The wounded man was left on the field, minus boots and what could be quickly stripped from him, according to rebel custom. But this damage to our advance was more quickly repaired than it takes time to narrate it. The command of the regiment was at once turned over to Captain Charles L. Leiper, fresh troops thrown into the break, and another attack made, before which the enemy gave way, and retired fighting for about a mile and a half, when night came on and ended the battle, leaving the dead and wounded of both sides in our hands, besides a number of prisoners.

Our losses were, in addition to those mentioned, First Lieutenant Charles B. Coxe, wounded in the arm; Sergeants Golden, Kirk, Scott, and Booz, wounded; Corporals Keyfer and McCord, killed; Corporal Gilbert, wounded; and Privates Lyndford Bowers, Preston A. Saxton, E. B. Strong, Hackett, Miller, Scypes, Henderson, Harden, Cassiday, Finney, Boon, Heckler, Martin, Richardson, and Burk, wounded.

May 8th

On the 8th, we were again engaged at daylight, and after severe fighting for about two hours, we drove the enemy from their breastworks, and they retired to their intrenchments some distance to the rear. We were then relieved by the 5th Corps, and marched back to Todd's Tavern, where we halted for about two hours, groomed and fed our horses, and after eating our own spare meal we were again mounted, and marched to Aldrich's house, where the Cavalry Corps was concentrating.

On this day, the brigade lost one of its most brave

and dafhing officers, Captain Afh, of the 5th Cavalry, who was killed while gallantly leading into the fight fome of the infantry who had relieved us. 1864. May 8th.

A portion of our army occupied Frederickfburg on the morning of the 6th, and made arrangements for the reception of the wounded from the fields of battle.

(Correfpondence of the "Inquirer.")

"TODD'S TAVERN, May 8th, 1864.

"By noon yefterday it was whifpered around that the enemy were falling back. Soon there was great buftle and moving about of wagon-trains, and thefe, with ambulances containing wounded, followed by droves of cattle, with artillery wagons, and everything not available for fervice at the front, were, before dark, in motion, down the Frederickfburg Pike. Many of the uninitiated fuppofed they were on another fkedaddle, as one could perceive by the remarks heard in paffing along the crowded road; but on arriving a few miles beyond Chancellorfville, and finding themfelves turned to the right up the Catharpan Road, they were fuddenly undeceived. It was no retreat, but an advance ftill deeper into the heart of Seceffia. The troops were withdrawn from their pofition during the night and early morning, and were now within a few miles of Spottfylvania Courthoufe. Arriving in this vicinity about 10 o'clock this morning, we found a portion of our cavalry engaged in fkirmifhing with the enemy between Piney Branch Church and Spottfylvania Court-houfe, and alfo in front of Todd's Tavern.

1864.
May 8th.

"At the latter point the enemy had a battery, the shells from which reached near to the road along which the infantry of the 2d Corps was marching in close column; but our cavalry held their ground firmly, keeping the enemy far enough back to secure the troops on the road from molestation. This afternoon they were relieved by infantry, and retired towards the rear to renew their supply of subsistence and forage.

"The possession of Todd's Tavern has been the subject of frequent skirmishing for two or three days, and yesterday that point was the scene of a pretty severe contest. The enemy, with Fitzhugh Lee's division, held possession of it on Saturday morning up to nearly noon, our cavalry having retired on Friday along the Catharpan Road to the neighborhood of Piney Branch Church, and as that position commanded the road along which our infantry, coming down from the left of our lines at the Wilderness, would have to pass, it was necessary to regain possession of it, and of the Spottsylvania Road as far as possible. Our line was formed with Custer's brigade of Torbett's division on the right; Colonel Gregg's brigade of General Gregg's division next; then General Merritt's brigade of the 1st division, and, on the extreme left, Davies' brigade of Gregg's division, and extended across the Catharpan Road between Todd's Tavern and Piney Branch Church, nearly parallel with the Brock and Spottsylvania Court-house Roads. We advanced shortly before noon, and after considerable hard fighting, drove the enemy back upon the Catharpan Road about four miles to Corbin's Bridge. At that point Stuart had massed his entire force, and while his centre was retiring, it was obferved that he was 1864. throwing his troops forward on our flanks, with the evident intention of entrapping us. We, therefore, retired again to a good pofition, a little in front of Todd's Tavern, fo as to keep control of the road, which was our only object.

"A fection of Martin's battery was pofted on a hill near the Tavern, and a fection of King's battery further to the left, when we awaited further demonftrations on the part of the enemy.

"General Merritt had the right, where the fire was the hotteft. The Referve Brigade fuffered the moft, as it was moft hardly preffed, and moft nobly did they meet the defperate onflaught. Our cavalry were all difmounted, for the conteft occurred moftly in thick woods, where horfes could not be ufed to advantage."

On the 9th, Sheridan ftarted on his raid to the rear May 9th. of the rebel army, to cut off their fupplies and communications, and otherwife cripple him to as great an extent as poffible. Three days' rations were iffued to the men, as all the wagons were to be left behind, except the ammunition wagons and two ambulances to each brigade. Thus unincumbered, the command moved at daylight on the 9th, taking the Telegraph Road between Richmond and Frederickfburg, marching fteadily all day. We croffed the North Anna at Reed's Mills, paffing the enemy's right flank, to the fouth of Spottfylvania Court-houfe towards Childfburg. General Cufter, who had the advance during the day, preffed forward rapidly to Beaver Dam Station on the Virginia

1864.
May 9th.

Central Railroad, where he captured and deftroyed two trains of cars and a large ftorehoufe filled with government ftores. Here, our force alfo furprifed a rebel provoft-guard with three hundred and feventy-eight Union prifoners, who had been captured the day previous at Spottfylvania Court-houfe. Our own foldiers were releafed, and the captors were themfelves led captive. A detachment was alfo fent to Afhland, on the Frederickfburg Railroad, where they deftroyed the ftation, a large warehoufe filled with ftores, and eight miles of railroad; after a fharp fkirmifh with the enemy they rejoined the main column. The divifion went into camp at night, half a mile fouth of the river. The Sixth Pennfylvania was fent during the evening to Beaver Dam Station to deftroy the railroad; we moved out rapidly and without oppofition, worked on the road until 2 o'clock, tearing up and deftroying the track, culverts, &c., and returned to the divifion near morning.

CHAPTER TWENTIETH.

Sheridan's Raid—Captain Miller—Engagement at Yellow Tavern—Meadow Bridge—New Market—White Houſe—Mechanicſville—White Chimneys—Aylette—Hawes's Shop—Battle at Betheſda Church.

AT dawn on the 10th, while we were preparing or eating our breakfaſt, we were ſtartled by the familiar "whir-r-r-bomb," of ſhell, and there came ſcreaming through the air the compliments of the enraged enemy in the ſhape of 12-pound ſhot and ſpherical caſe. Our breakfaſt was left unfiniſhed, and the echo of the guns had ſcarcely died away ere we were mounted and in line ready for action. The attack was from the rear, and General Gregg, not having croſſed the river the night previous, led the 2d diviſion upon the enemy, our regiment being ſent to co-operate with him. After a ſhort engagement the enemy were driven off, and our march was reſumed. 1864. May 10th.

General Gregg, with the 2d diviſion, had the advance of the column; the 3d diviſion, General Wilſon, being in the centre, and the 1ſt diviſion, temporarily commanded by General Merritt, in the rear. During the day we had occaſional ſkirmiſhing with the enemy.

Captain Arnold, of the 5th Cavalry, was ſent off to

1864. deftroy Davenport's Bridge, and, meeting a large force, came near being captured with all his men. Lieutenant Emmons, A. A. G. of Colonel Gibbs' ftaff, went out to his affiftance with Sergeant Miller, of Company "L," Sixth Pennfylvania Cavalry, and a fquad of five men. Captain Arnold fucceeded in deftroying the bridge, although he loft heavily; he alfo captured an officer of the engineer corps, with his implements of fervice. Lieutenant Wilfon, of the 5th United States, and Sergeant Miller, with part of his men, were captured.

On the banks of the South Anna we felled trees in our rear, thoroughly blocking up the road, and had a flight fkirmifh near night. Went into camp after dark near Ground Squirrel Bridge, the foe continuing their moleftation all through the night.

May 11th. At 3 o'clock A.M., on the 11th, General Davies' brigade was difpatched to Afhland Station, feven miles to the eaft, on the Richmond and Frederickfburg Railroad; they fired the warehoufe and deftroyed large quantities of ftores; tore up fix miles of railroad, three culverts, two treftle bridges, and deftroyed a locomotive and three trains of cars. On their return to the main column they were attacked, and loft about thirty men.

At 5 A.M., the 1ft divifion moved down the turnpike towards Richmond, the Sixth Pennfylvania Cavalry having the advance. One-half of the regiment was deployed in front as fkirmifhers on both fides of the road, whilft Captain Leiper marched with the other half on the turnpike. A long line of flankers on each flank connected with the advance, the whole of the Referve Brigade thus acting as the advance-guard of the cavalry corps. It was well so careful a formation was observed, for after having pushed on some ten miles, and having crossed the Richmond and Fredericksburg Railroad at Allen's Station, the advance skirmishers flushed the rebels, and after reconnoitring them for half an hour, about noon developed nearly the whole of the rebel cavalry corps under General J. E. B. Stuart. We learned of their presence in an odd way. The skirmishers were spread across the country, and moved straight ahead, despite of fences, barn-yards, woods, or anything else. It proved that one of Stuart's captains took advantage of his being in the neighborhood of his home to ride over and see his family, and whilst enjoying his visit the cry was suddenly raised that the Yankee cavalry were coming. To avoid capture he rushed into the thick pine woods near the house and climbed a tree, feeling sure that we would ride by and never see him. A bright-eyed youth of the Sixth happening to direct his glances that way, he was ordered to withdraw from his undignified and unwarlike position. A more sullen, uncommunicative rebel was never gobbled. We were approaching Yellow Tavern, the intersection of the plank road from Hanover and the turnpike.

1864.
May 11th.

When, on the evening of May 9th, General Lee discovered that Sheridan was off for a raid in his rear with a powerful force, he at once dispatched General Stuart in pursuit, to take care of us as best he might. By dint of forced marches he overtook us here; but no sooner was Sheridan well assured of the position of affairs than he ordered up Custer's and Davies' brigades to support the advance, and then at the word of command the divi-

1864.
May 11th.
sion charged, capturing two guns, numerous prisoners, and killing General Stuart, Colonel Piatt, and others of less note,—thus opening the road to Richmond, and warning the rebels to be careful how they placed themselves across the path of the Cavalry Corps of the Army of the Potomac.

The command remained near Yellow Tavern until midnight, and then moved on towards Richmond. A regiment of Davies' brigade pushed down to the very gates of the city, but, finding them well guarded, waited for daylight. The night was very wet and dark, the road choked with the column, and the march flow and painful. Suddenly we heard three explosions in front, and supposed that the artillery of the Richmond fortifications had opened upon the advance; but it turned out that the rebels had planted torpedoes in the road, with wires ingeniously attached, for the horses to trip over. Three had been thus exploded, killing several horses of Sheridan's escort, the General himself, and some of his staff, narrowly escaping. The rebel prisoners in our hands were forthwith set to work to dig them up, and these particular representatives of the chivalry agreed with us that it was an ignoble system of warfare.

Daylight came at last, and an examination proved that though we were within the outer line of fortifications, Richmond was too strong for us, so the column was turned off to the left towards Mechanicsville. General Wilson with the 3d division had the advance, and pushed boldly on towards the Chickahominy, having been assured by the guide he had picked up that the road led outside the rebel line of works.

He found to his coſt that it did not, for his advance came ſuddenly upon the fortifications of Richmond, and the enemy opened upon them with artillery, throwing his command into confuſion. Gregg, with the 2d diviſion, was ordered to ſupport Wilſon, whilſt the 1ſt was maſſed to await developments. The rebels ſeemed to think they had us where they wanted us, for about 10 o'clock there ſallied out a diviſion of infantry, with the amiable intention of bagging us all. With them came a newſ-boy from Richmond, who ſneaked into our lines and ſold us the morning papers, in which we read that Preſident Davis in perſon, and General Bragg, then General-in-chief of the Confederacy, had taken the field againſt us; that we were ſurrounded, cornered; that not a man of us ſhould eſcape. The occaſion was certainly full of intereſt; and there may have been, that wet, muddy, cheerleſs morning of the 12th of May, ſome of Sheridan's bold riders who did not ſee their way very clearly out of the ſcrape. The General did not ſeem to be of the number, however, for finding, after a ſpirited, ſtubborn fight, that Gregg and Wilſon could hold their lines againſt the attack of the rebel infantry, the 1ſt diviſion was ordered to open the road acroſs Meadow Bridge, a little more to our left. This was an exceedingly awkward thing to do, for the enemy had deſtroyed the bridge, and were in ſtrong force acroſs the road on the other ſide. General Merritt promptly diſmounted all of the diviſion but three regiments, and the men toiled painfully acroſs the broken bridge, forming in line of battle in the ſwamp beyond, whilſt the pioneers repaired the bridge as well as they could with fence-rails and ſuch means as were at hand.

1864.   All being prepared, the charge was founded, and the difmounted regiments rufhed on the rebels, whilft a mounted column, led by Colonel Gibbs, confifting of the 1ft New York Dragoons, 5th United States Cavalry, and 6th Pennfylvania Cavalry, croffed the bridge and charged along the caufeway beyond. This was a fearful moment, for the road was but twelve feet wide, bordered on both fides by deep fwamps, and nearly a mile long, and could have been fwept by the enemy's artillery. Had they fought with any fpirit our lofs muft have been frightful. But we found we were fighting our opponents of the 11th, and they had not forgotten Yellow Tavern. After a moderate refiftance, which inflicted confiderable lofs upon us, however, for the ground was greatly againft us, they took to their horfes and difappeared.

The Referve Brigade was now ordered ahead to Mechanicfville, which they held until the reft of the command came up, when they pufhed out again and ftruck the rebel cavalry. The enemy was at once driven half a mile or more, when the column turned to the right, and made for Cold Harbor. All three divifions of the cavalry corps had thus been engaged at once, but after beating off the enemy in rear, and brufhing away the obftacles in front, we moved fteadily along, and went into camp near Cold Harbor at 9 o'clock P.M., in a drenching rain, as wet, tired, and uncomfortable as it is permitted man to be.

May 13th.   Friday, 13th, we moved without moleftation to Bottom's Bridge, where, finding the bridge deftroyed, we went into camp until it could be repaired. We had now quite exhaufted our rations and forage, and fent off foraging parties into the adjoining country. They returned empty-handed, for the moſt part, for it is a wretched country, and had not been improved by the campaign in 1862. Neither his excellency the Preſident of the Confederacy, nor his General-in-chief, diſturbed us, and the command was quite as much at home within twelve miles of Richmond as we ever found ourſelves on the "ſacred ſoil."

1864.

The following morning, May 14th, we croſſed the Chickahominy and moved down through White Oak Swamp to Malvern Hill and Hackſall's. Never were tired men and horſes more delighted to leave the doubtful regions of the hated Chickahominy and reach terra firma. As the head of the column approached the James River the gunboats ſent a few ſhells after them, but our ſignal officers ſoon made it apparent who we were, to our mutual ſatisfaction. How the hungry jaded horſes did ſnort as we went into camp in a clover field on Malvern Hill, and ſhake themſelves when their ſaddles were removed for the firſt time in ſeveral days.

May 14th.

That night, the Sixth Pennſylvania Cavalry was ſent on picket, to keep their hands in. The regiment ſtarted at 9 o'clock that black ſummer night (black as tar, as Sergeant Wagner very properly ſaid), to find a road that no one in the command knew anything of. This road led to Carter's Mill, where we arrived about midnight. From here the commanding officer was ordered to run a line of videttes acroſs the country to a houſe three miles off, where ſomebody elſe's pickets were to be found. To march acroſs a well-wooded, well-watered, well-ditched rolling new country, as the crow flies, on a night when the men could not ſee their file-leaders, was ſlow

1864. work, and it was long after daylight when the line was established.

May 15th. We returned to camp at Malvern Hill on the evening of May 15th, and were awakened from our sleep at
May 16th. daylight of the 16th by the sound of distant artillery. This was Beauregard pitching into Butler, on the south side of the James, which ended in the thrashing of the latter, and his being bottled up in Bermuda Hundred.

That afternoon our brigade went out with an enterprising staff-officer of Butler's on a reconnoissance towards Richmond, to look up some imaginary works of the enemy near Newmarket, but finding none we returned to camp.

May 17th. At 10 o'clock P.M. of the 17th, we broke camp and marched all night. At daylight a halt was ordered at Pleasant Hill for two hours, when we again moved forward to within three miles of the White House, where we halted for several hours, to feed and rest both men and horses. In the afternoon we marched to Baltimore Store, and at 5 o'clock P.M. went into camp.

May 19th. On the 19th, Captain Leiper was sent out with the regiment on a reconnoissance. He proceeded to within four miles of Cold Harbor, where he encountered the pickets of the enemy. After a sharp skirmish with a rebel brigade, and developing a superior force of the enemy, he returned to the main command and reported the presence and force of the enemy.

May 20th. On the 20th, General Custer was sent on a reconnoissance towards Ashland Station; General Gregg being sent at the same time towards Hanover Station.

May 21st. On the 21st, we marched to the White House and

encamped on the Pamunkey. We were engaged in repairing the bridge over the river at this point until near night on the 22d, when we croſſed and went into camp. 1864.
May 22d.

We left camp at daybreak on the ſucceeding morning and marched ſteadily all day, paſſing through King William's Court-houſe, halting at 5 o'clock P.M. at Aylette's, on the Mattapony, oppoſite Dunkirk.

We reſumed the march early the next morning, moving ſlowly all day; halted at night near White Chimneys. Our regiment picketed that night between our column and the army under General Meade, the latter being within a few miles of us without our knowledge. May 24th.

We moved early on the 25th, and near Cheſterfield Station paſſed within the lines of the army, and were rejoiced to receive our mails and full rations, having been abſent from army headquarters and our mail communications for three weeks. May 25th.

On Friday, May 20th, began another grand flank movement by the Army of the Potomac. About noon, a portion of our cavalry force advanced to Downer's Bridge, about a mile ſouthweſt of Guinea Station, where their further progreſs was oppoſed by rebel cavalry. The 5th New York Cavalry charged the enemy, who fled before them. They puſhed on ſouth to Bowling Green. At Milford Station they ſcattered a force of the enemy, capturing ſeventy cavalrymen.

At midnight on the ſame day the 2d Corps followed on the road opened by the cavalry, and arrived at Milford Station at 3 P.M. on Saturday.

On the 21ſt, General Hancock croſſed the Mattapony at Milford Bridge, and, forming in line of battle, ad-

1864. vanced a short distance, when a terrific fire was opened upon him from some twenty pieces of artillery. The troops were drawn under shelter, and after a harmless shelling of about two hours, the enemy withdrew.

On the 23d, they crossed the North Anna at Jericho Ford about 5 o'clock in the evening; soon after crossing they were attacked, and a severe battle raged until dark, when the enemy withdrew.

Our entire army was now between the North and South Anna Rivers, and within twenty-five miles of Richmond.

May 26th. Our division left camp at noon on the 26th, and marched rapidly until dark, making a march of twenty-five miles. We then halted for two hours, prepared our supper, fed our horses, and then moved on to the Pamunkey, going into bivouac at Edwards' Ferry, throwing out our pickets along the river and to the rear.

May 27th. As soon as it was light, we discovered the pickets of the enemy on the opposite shore. General Custer was soon ordered to cross the river, which he did, under a heavy fire. He drove the enemy back from the river about three miles, where they made a stand, and a severe fight ensued, resulting in their being driven from their position and again forced to retreat. Custer captured about sixty prisoners. We bivouacked for the night on the field of the morning's engagement, the killed and wounded of the enemy falling into our hands; the dead were properly buried and the wounded cared for.

May 28th. On the 28th, we were relieved at Hanovertown Ford on the Pamunkey, by the 2d and 5th Corps, when we moved to the left toward Hanover Court-house. Near

Hawes's Shop we ſtruck the rebel lines, and immediately 1864. an engagement opened with great vigor.

Generals Gregg and Cuſter, on the right and centre, fought deſperately, and ſuffered more heavily than did our diviſion on the left. General Gregg found the enemy ſtrongly entrenched in a thick woods, and having heavy guns mounted in poſition, and with every advantage on their ſide. The fight raged with great fury, General Gregg continuing the unequal conteſt bravely from noon until near 2 o'clock, when General Cuſter came up to his aſſiſtance; he formed his ſquadrons in line, and a general charge was ordered upon the enemy's works. Moſt nobly did they ruſh upon the enemy's guns through a ſtorm of grape and caniſter and muſket-balls, and many a brave fellow fell in this daring aſſault; but the enemy yielded, and were forced to abandon the field, and fled in great confuſion, leaving their dead and wounded in our hands, beſides over one hundred priſoners.

Our regiment was ſent to operate upon the left flank of the enemy; as we advanced and preſſed cloſe upon their lines, they opened upon us with caniſter from two guns, which checked us. About 5 o'clock we were joined by the 19th New York Cavalry, when we again charged diſmounted, and drove the enemy back about a mile and a half.

Late that night we returned to Hanovertown Ferry, paſſing through our own infantry camps.

We left camp at noon on the 29th, marching until 6 May 29th. P.M., when we halted on Colonel Ruffin's farm and went into bivouac in a magnificent clover-field, the headquarters of the regiment being eſtabliſhed under a

1864. very large and beautiful oak tree in the centre of the field.

At this time, the entire army was succesfully acrofs the Pamunkey, and formed in a line fronting to the fouthweft and extending about three miles from the river. The lines were moved cautioufly forward, as an attack was momentarily expected from General Lee; but in this they were miftaken, for no enemy appeared, and the only firing during the day was by a reconnoitring party towards Hawes's Shop.

May 30th. On Monday, the 30th, Lee's army was afcertained to be on the Mechanicfville Road fouth of the Tolopatomy Creek Road, between that ftream and Hawes's Shop, their right refting on Shady Grove Church.

General Warren's Corps was the firft to meet the enemy; he reached Shady Grove Church about 2 o'clock P.M., and began fkirmifhing, but was foon after withdrawn to the Mechanicfville Road, where the men threw up long earthworks. Near fundown the whole of Ewell's rebel corps emerged from the woods, formed in three lines, and advanced to the charge. Scarcely had they ftarted before a fevere crofs-fire was opened upon them, which changed their courfe fomewhat; but ftill they preffed on towards a fence and fome bufhes that concealed our rifle-pits and men from their view. They came up to that line in excellent order, when our whole line opened upon them a crufhing fire of mufketry, while the artillery poured in canifter and one-fecond fufe fhells. Their repulfe was inftantaneous and complete; thofe who were not killed or wounded of the firft line threw themselves upon the ground and surrendered, the other lines precipitately fled.

1864.
May 30th.

General Hancock made an attack just before dark, in which he was succesful in capturing the rifle-pits of the enemy, which he held all night, notwithstanding the many efforts made to dislodge him.

CHAPTER TWENTY-FIRST.

*Battles at Old Church and Cold Harbor—Bottom Bridge—
Raid on the Virginia Central Railroad—Battles at Trevillian Station—Return March to the White Houſe.*

1864.
May 30th.

GENERAL TORBETT, commanding the 1ſt Diviſion of Cavalry, met the enemy near Old Church on the 30th, about noon. Colonel Devin's pickets were attacked and driven in by a heavy force. General Merritt was ſent forward with the Reſerve Brigade, and a battery of Napoleon guns, when the advance of the enemy was checked. A ſevere battle enſued, continuing until after dark. The Sixth Pennſylvania was ſent in on the left of the line, and charged the rebel flank; a hand to hand encounter followed, in which our brave boys fought with deſperation, though loſing heavily. Captain Charles L. Leiper, commanding the regiment, was ſeverely wounded, and Lieutenant Martin inſtantly killed. Captain Clark aſſumed command, and being joined by General Cuſter on the right, a general charge was ordered, when the rebels were ſwept before our reſiſtleſs ſquadrons. They fled precipitately on all parts of the field, leaving a large number of dead and wounded and priſoners in our hands. Charles W. Horner and Thomas Whalley of the Sixth Pennſylvania, were killed. We pushed rapidly forward, driving the enemy to Cold Harbor, where we went into camp at 10 o'clock at night.

1864.

Our regiment bivouacked on the same ground occupied by us two years before, and fastened our horses to picket-posts put up by the regiment under Colonel Rush during the Peninsular campaign.

We saddled up at 3 o'clock next morning, and stood to horse until 5 P.M., when we advanced our cavalry mounted, and soon came upon the enemy strongly entrenched, when we were suddenly transformed into infantry, under the order "prepare to fight on foot." We pushed forward, and were soon joined by Devin's and Custer's brigades on the right. We drove the enemy from his works by a determined charge, and pursued him three miles beyond Cold Harbor, when he received heavy reinforcements, consisting of three regiments of North Carolina infantry.

May 31st.

As we were ordered to hold this position, our fight was even more desperate than on the previous day. We held our own until darkness closed upon a disputed field. Lieutenant Murphy was killed this day while bravely encouraging his men on the skirmish line.

The 6th Corps came up in the evening and formed near us. Our line now being established from Tolopatomy Creek across the Cold Harbor Road to the Chickahominy, with cavalry on both flanks, advanced beyond the infantry line.

During the night we had constructed a barricade in front of our bivouac, and early in the morning had an opportunity to prove its usefulness, as we were attacked

June 1st.

1864. by rebel infantry and artillery in heavy force; several unsuccessful attempts were made during the morning to dislodge us, but with our carbines alone we repulsed Hoke's division of infantry, who charged upon us with fixed bayonets.

About 12 o'clock we were relieved by the 6th Corps, and soon after the 18th Corps came upon the field.

Our brigade was moved back to near Old Church, and bivouacked for the night at Paysley's Mills.

Our infantry attacked about 3 o'clock. A ploughed field stretched before them, and beyond that was a strip of pine forest, in which the enemy lay entrenched. A charge of two divisions was ordered in the centre; they dashed across the field and into the woods, while a deadly storm of musketry and artillery raked the line. The charge was made upon the run, and both divisions rushed upon and over the rebel earthworks with great spirit, taking and holding their first line of rifle-pits, and about six hundred prisoners. The battle continued with great desperation until late in the night, the Union loss being very heavy.

During the day severe fighting also occurred near Bethesda Church. Taking the day through it resulted favorably for the Union army, as we secured on the left the possession of Cold Harbor, a point of much importance, not only in reference to the subsequent crossing of the Chickahominy, but also as commanding the road to our base of supplies at White House.

June 2d. At 8 o'clock A. M. on the 2d, we marched about three miles towards Cold Harbor, when we halted until 3 o'clock in the afternoon, and then moved to Bottom

Bridge, on the Chickahominy. We arrived there in time to fee a column of rebel cavalry moving on the other fide of the river. They halted, and occupied a ftrongly fortified pofition in earthworks thrown up during the campaign of 1862. We had a flight fkirmifh with them, when both parties brought ftrong batteries in pofition, and a very loud but not very damaging artillery converfation took place, continuing until night. After dark we fell back a fhort diftance and went into bivouac, leaving our pickets along the bank of the Chickahominy. 1864.

On the fucceeding morning our infantry attempted to crofs the river, but every effort was fuccefsfully refifted. At 7 o'clock P.M. the rebels attacked Smyth's brigade, of the 2d Corps, and a battle raged with great fury for half an hour, the enemy being everywhere repulfed. June 3d.

The lines of the hoftile armies were now eftablifhed only a few rods apart, intrenchments being thrown up by both parties, behind which they lay for the next ten days.

During all this time there was not a day of quiet, and fcarcely an hour, day or night, that did not refound with the fharp crack of the mufket, or the heavier report of artillery. Early on the morning of the 3d, our regimental train came up, and as it was the firft time we had had accefs to our wagons fince May 25th, we were enjoying the luxuries furnifhed by them, when our camp was alarmed by an active demonftration of the enemy upon General Gregg's command. Our wagons were hurriedly packed, and in a few minutes our horfes were faddled and regiments in line awaiting orders to move.

1864.　We stood to horse until 4 P.M., when we again unsaddled and bivouacked for two hours, when the Sixth was sent on picket. We were relieved by infantry the
June 4th. next morning; rejoined the cavalry corps, and early in the day started with Sheridan on a raid upon the communications of the rebel army towards Gordonsville. The corps was kept well together, and after a steady march of ten hours, encamped at night at Old Church, where the promotion of Sergeants Lanigan and Wint to Second Lieutenancies, was published.

Several new recruits reported to the regiment to-day from rendezvous in Philadelphia.

June 5th.　At 10 o'clock A.M. on the 5th, we moved to near Hawes's Shop, where we found General Wilson, with his command. We stood to horse until 2 o'clock, when we went into bivouac on Norman's farm, near the Hanover and Richmond Cross-roads. On the following day we marched to the Pamunkey River near New Castle, where we crossed on a pontoon bridge in the night.
June 7th. The march was continued on the 7th, and the column halted at night near Aylette, on the Fredericksburg Railroad. After a good night's rest, we started at 5 o'clock
June 8th. on the morning of the 8th, marched rapidly all day, and halted near night at a mile beyond Polecat Station.

At this point, and also at Chesterfield and Aylette Stations, the railroad was destroyed for a considerable distance. This uneventful marching continued the next day when we passed through Childsburg, New Market, and Mount Pleasant, not halting in our march until 9 o'clock at night, when we went into bivouac at Young's Bridge.

BATTLE AT TREVILLIAN STATION.

The intention of the General commanding, now, was 1864. to strike the Virginia Central Railroad at Trevillian Station, march thence to Mechanicsville, where he should cut the Gordonsville Road, and press rapidly on to Charlottesville.

On the 10th, we crossed the South Anna at Becker's June 10th. Store, and when near Buck Childs', which is within three miles of Trevillian Station, came suddenly upon a force of rebel cavalry. As our men seemed to take special delight in worrying rebel cavalry, the prospect of an increase of interest to our further march was very promising.

As the enemy retreated and darkness was deepening about us, we drew off from the road and established our bivouac for the night. Our scouts reported the enemy in force near Trevillian Station.

The 11th dawned clear and delightful, and if previous June 11th. days had been monotonous, this contained enough of incident to at least relieve the tedium of travel. Early in the morning we moved forward cautiously. General Torbett, with Merritt's and Devin's brigades, moved up towards the station.

Merritt, being in the advance, soon came upon the outposts of the enemy, when Lieutenant Horrigan of the 2d United States, was ordered by Captain Rodenbough, commanding the regiment, to charge them, and press forward as far as possible. He dashed at them promptly and with such determination that the enemy fled before him and were closely pressed for nearly two miles, when his supports were reached and a line of battle was formed across the road, and extending into a heavy woods.

1864.
June 11th.
The 2d United States was now difmounted and fent forward to charge the enemy; this they did in fplendid ftyle, though encountering a moft determined foe. From carbines they came to piftols; from piftols to fabres, and a defperate hand to hand fight enfued. Lieutenant Horrigan croffed fabres in a fight with a rebel officer, and after wounding him, compelled his furrender.

General Merritt led in the 1ft United States, commanded by Captain Sweitzer, and the Sixth Pennfylvania, Captain J. Hinckley Clark, to drive the rebels from the railway cut and a brick kiln, behind which they had entrenched themfelves. The enemy being found in large numbers and ftrongly pofted, General Torbett ordered Devin's brigade to attack on our right. All our troops were difmounted and fought defperately, gradually forcing the enemy back towards Trevillian.

General Sheridan, with his ftaff, was alfo up in the centre of thefe operations, where fhot and fhell flew uncomfortably clofe, but where he could perfonally fuperintend all movements.

During the night of the 10th, General Cufter had been directed to move by a wood road to the left and rear of the enemy, beyond Louifa Court-houfe. When near Trevillian he encountered a ftrong force, which he attacked vigoroufly, and after a fharp fight completely routed; the dead, and many of the wounded of the enemy, fell into his hands, and his captures at one time numbered twenty officers, five hundred enlifted men, and three hundred horfes.

When the 1ft and 2d divifions advanced on the right, the enemy were between two fires, and were forced back by Sheridan upon Cuſter's ſmall brigade. By flanking Cuſter's force they got to his rear, when all his priſoners were ſet at liberty, and many of our own men captured; the enemy decamping with General Cuſter's headquarters wagon, his pack mule train, and five caiſſons of Pennington's battery.

1864.
June 11th.

Several ineffectual attempts were made by General Sheridan to communicate with Cuſter, and, at length, Captain Dana, A. A. G. of the 1ſt Cavalry Diviſion, ſucceeded in running the gauntlet of the enemy's lines, and gained Cuſter in time to communicate movements, which, with his co-operation, would enable them to form a junction of the forces. The directions were promptly acted upon, and the corps, once more united, made a vigorous charge upon the enemy near the ſtation, and drove them from their haſtily conſtructed works.

By determined charges they were forced back, until night cloſed the operations, leaving us in poſſeſſion of the field.

Colonel Sackett, of the 9th New York Cavalry, and Lieutenant Ogden, of the 1ſt United States, were killed; Captain Rodenbough and Lieutenant Horrigan, of the 2d United States, were wounded, in the early part of the day.

The Sixth Pennſylvania was ſeverely engaged the entire day, and loſt heavily in wounded. Among the number were Lieutenant P. H. Ellis, Sergeants Pennington, mortally, William Denney, John Algie, W. A. Gurance, and P. Burns; Corporals George Wattis and John Moyer; Privates Theodore McNamee, Oliver A. Hoffman, William Jones, J. Johnſon, John Hopkins, George Stout, George W. Harper, John Smith, Company "G."

1864. Alexander Smith, John H. Leipſen, James Hoap, Kirby
June 11th. Smith, John A. Carr, Daniel Dougherty, James Bennett, Anthony Shriver, Charles Shields, John F. Baynes, William Gringee, Samuel Weaver, William Irvin, Samuel F. Aſh, M. Farrell, James Dobſon, James Stokes, C. Shearer, J. C. Maleſberger, Thomas McNee, James Coffee, D. Smith, Oliver Thomas, John C. Simpſon, and N. J. Adams.

The enemy fell back towards Gordonſville, and Gen-
June 12th. eral Torbett was ſent in purſuit this morning. When within five miles of Gordonſville, he found them ſtrongly intrenched and heavily reinforced with infantry. As their poſition was too ſtrong for him to carry alone, he waited the arrival of other troops. Our whole cavalry force fought all day diſmounted, being oppoſed by infantry behind earthworks and barricades. The Reſerve Brigade made a determined charge upon their rifle-pits, but were refiſted by ſuperior numbers, and every future effort confirmed the impoſſibility of their capture. While our battle was raging, another force was buſily engaged deſtroying the railroad for ſeveral miles. Our loſs was ſix killed, twenty-ſix wounded, and four priſoners. The brigade loſt, in total, one hundred and fifty.

The heavieſt loſs of the enemy was in the killing of General Roſſer.

The fighting on the 12th, was, if poſſible, more deſperate than that of the day previous, and having demonſtrated to our ſatisfaction,—and to General Sheridan's, which was a little more difficult,—that further advance in that direction was impracticable, in conſequence of the heavy reinforcements received by the enemy, and their strongly intrenched position; and as our store of ammunition was running quite low, our horses suffering for forage, and our men exhausted by hard marches and fighting, General Sheridan decided upon a withdrawal, and shortly after dark we commenced our retreat. The command marched all night, crossed the South Anna on the morning of the 13th, and pushed on as rapidly as possible until 4 o'clock in the afternoon, when we halted at Prospect Hill. The march was resumed at daylight on the 14th, without food for either men or horses; the day was quite warm, and the roads dusty, making our ride very unpleasant. We halted at 3 P.M. at Shady Grove Church, fully appreciating its shade and rest. On the succeeding morning we moved at 5 o'clock, and during the morning passed through Spottsylvania Courthouse, and the battle-ground of a month previous.

1864.

June 13th.

June 14th.

The debris of the battle strewed the ground; large trees were seen cut nearly in two, scarred and shattered by solid shot, shell, and musket-balls, while heavy lines of earthworks marked where the severest charges were made and resisted. The graves of those who fell on this terrible field were on every hand. At night, we halted near Guinney's Station.

On the 16th, 17th, and 18th, we made long marches. The weather was warm, and the roads very dusty, and as our regiment marched in the rear of the column, we became unpleasantly familiar with the "sacred soil."

June 16th, 17th, 18th.

On the 19th, we crossed the Mattapony, on a pontoon bridge, at Dunkirk.

June 19th.

CHAPTER TWENTY-SECOND.

Engagement at White House—General Gregg engaged at St. Mary's Church—March to Wilcox's Wharf, on James River—Wilson's Raid—Camp near Windmill Point.

1864.
June 20th.

ON the evening of Monday, June 20th, after one of the hottest and dustiest marches, of even that week of dust and exhaustion, we reached Fiskhall, a station on the Richmond and York River Railroad, on the east side of the Pamunkey, opposite White House, when we learned that General Lee, of the rebel cavalry, had that day attacked the depot at White House, where were parked upwards of six hundred wagons and ambulances belonging to the Cavalry Corps of the Army of the Potomac.

The trains had been left here by General Grant when he moved to Petersburg, and were under the protection of General Getty, who, having recovered from wounds received in the Wilderness, was on his way to rejoin the army. His force consisted of a regiment of colored troops, part of a regiment of the Invalid Corps, and a detachment of dismounted cavalry, and with this provisional brigade, aided by a couple of gunboats, he had kept the rebels off from the much-coveted wagons. The trains had been hurried across the river over the old railroad bridge, which was repaired

ENGAGEMENT AT WHITE HOUSE.

for the occasion, and our arrival was opportune, for these rebels were coming too close.

Accordingly, at daylight of the 21st, our long line of cavalry pushed across the bridge by twos, and Generals Gregg and Custer and Colonel Devins moved against the enemy, whilst, for once, the Reserve Brigade was held in reserve,—that is, massed in an open dusty plain, with the thermometer at ninety in the shade, if there had been any, but there was not. The rebels withdrew without serious opposition, and in the evening we went into camp on the hills overlooking White House, on the very spot where the enemy's battery, that had so terrified the Invalids and dismounted men, had been the day before. Here some of us are said to have bathed and changed our clothes for the first time in two weeks, the latter part of which statement seems more credible than the first, for, ever since June 7th, when we started on the Trevillian raid, we had marched daily at 5 o'clock P.M., not reaching camp often until after dark, after such days of heat and dust as choke one to look back upon. All our wardrobe was on our backs, so that our camp here, where our wagons rejoined us, was an oasis. Here, too, we got the mail, which was wonderfully acceptable, and Major Treichel rejoined the regiment on his return from sick leave, relieving Captain Clark from the command of the regiment, which he had held since May 20th. Lieutenant Coxe came, too, hardly recovered from his wound received at Todd's Tavern, May 7th, both full of stories of friends and home.

June 22d, we saddled up at daylight and prepared for an attack from the rebel cavalry, but as they did not

1864. come, we unfaddled again and remained in camp until 1 o'clock in the afternoon, when we ftarted for Jones's Bridge on the Chickahominy, where we encamped at fundown. For a wonder, we found this wretched ftream quite clear, and we enjoyed a bath in it, fo delicious that it made us forgive the treacherous flood for many previous difappointments and labors.

June 23d. Thurfday, June 23d. We remained quietly in camp at Jones's Bridge, and in the afternoon, our wagon train, which was following us, began to arrive. The operation which General Sheridan was now conducting was a very delicate one, viz., that of marching from White Houfe to Peterfburg, taking with him his immenfe trains, on the flanks of which hung Hampton with his cavalry corps, longing to make a fwoop, to capture or deftroy. We had been fent ahead to open the way, and keep it open, whilft the other brigades marched with the wagons and in rear. Colonel Devins, who guarded the trains on the 23d, was attacked, but quickly beat off the enemy, whilft General Gregg with his divifion croffed the Chickahominy at Long Bridge, feveral miles above us, thus interpofing between the enemy and our long column.

June 24th. June 24th, we marched from Jones's Bridge to Charles City Court-houfe, and encamped in the evening fome two miles beyond, in a fplendid field of clover, on one of the fineft eftates in Virginia. This day, General Gregg ftill marched on our flank, being thus neareft the enemy, but near enough to us, it was thought, for our help, fhould he be attacked. General Hampton, finding that here was one of Sheridan's divifions marching detached from the main body, threw a few squadrons in Gregg's road to intercept his messengers, and then, having severely engaged him at St. Mary's Church, hurled upon him the whole of his corps, which charged, mounted and dismounted, with the intention of capturing or destroying the whole division. Gregg had hard work to hold his own, but, by dint of desperate fighting, assisted nobly by his unsurpassed horse artillery, succeeded in falling back from one position to another until he rejoined the main force near Charles City Court-house. He had sent aids and couriers to General Sheridan begging for reinforcements, but they had all been intercepted by the enemy, and we first knew of Gregg's desperate encounter when his shattered column appeared amongst us. Our camp this evening was but a few miles from Harrison's Landing, where we had spent some wretched weeks in the summer of 1862. General Hampton, not knowing of our whereabouts, put his troops in camp within a short distance of us, and we were equally unaware of his presence until after 9 o'clock in the evening, when Captain McQuesten, of Merritt's staff (a noble fellow, afterwards killed at Winchester), riding around to visit our pickets, stumbled upon a rebel vidette and rode almost into their camp. Boots and saddles was at once sounded, and, rousing ourselves from deep slumber, we saddled our weary horses and stood to horse until morning.

Saturday, June 25th, was an intensely hot day. We moved up to Charles City Court-house and stood to horse for several hours in the blazing sun, when, towards evening, the enemy not attacking, we followed our

1864.

June 25th.

1864. wagons down to Wilson's Wharf on the James River.
June 28th. Here we remained until June 28th, the trains being ferried across the river to Windmill Point. Our brigade was the rear-guard, the last to cross, and our regiment passed a wretched night, picketing towards the rear, and expecting the enemy to repeat his tactics of the 24th, and crush us whilst separated from our supports and unable to get away.
June 29th. But, at daylight on the 29th, we joyfully crossed the James in a dilapidated ferry-boat, that rocked so much as to threaten to spill all the horses into the river, and was not steadied until its side-wheels were put in motion. Arrived at Windmill Point, we went into camp, hoping to enjoy some days of rest, and as the river was full of transports, we had hay to issue to our horses, the first they had tasted for weeks. This was a great feast for them, as the pastures had all been dried up by the drought; but they were not permitted to enjoy it long, for, at sundown, we were again in the saddle, marching to the relief of Wilson, who had got into trouble at Ream's Station. We reached Prince George Court-house at midnight, after a dark, wretched march,
June 30th. and on the 30th pushed on to Ream's Station. Here we waited several hours, and finding that we had come the day after the fair, marched back to Warwick Swamp and encamped there.
July 1st. Friday, July 1st. We marched up and down the Jerusalem Plank Road, and the sun blazed so and the soil was of such nicely powdered sand that it really seemed as if there were some of the horrors of heat and dust that we had not previously fully appreciated. Having duly realized the beauties of the position we went into camp

five miles from Prince George Court-houſe, and a good drink of water for man or beaſt would have commanded a handſome premium that night.

Saturday, July 2d, the very hotteſt of thoſe dreadful days, we marched back through Prince George Court-houſe to Jordan's, or Light-houſe Point, on the James River, where we bivouacked after dark, and made ourſelves as comfortable as we could, without wood or water, or anything to eat.

Sunday, July 3d, we joyfully picked out a camp, where we got our long-promiſed reſt,—delightful word, after the fatigues of the previous ſixty days. Since May 4th we had been conſtantly in the ſaddle, and had not been longer than eighteen hours in camp at any one time, whilſt our poor horſes were ſo uſed up that we had to try and reſtore them by giving them plenty of oats and hay, bathing them in the river, and healing their galled backs. Here we remained encamped for ſeveral weeks, remounting and refitting the command, with an occaſional tour of picket duty, and a ride over to Peterſburg to view the ſtupendous warfare there carried on, liſtening to accounts of Earley raiding it near Baltimore and Waſhington, and of gold ſelling at $2.80 in New York.

July 12th, Major Starr rejoined us, hardly recovered from his ſerious wound received at Todd's Tavern, May 7th, and on the 13th aſſumed command of the regiment, Major Treichel having reſigned on account of ill health.

CHAPTER TWENTY-THIRD.

Feint on the Enemy's Left on the North Side of the James—Fight at Darby's Houſe—Burnſide's Mine—March to Lee's Mills—Return March to City Point and Embarkation for the Shenandoah Valley.

1864.
July 15th.

ABOUT this time, a propoſition was made to Major-General Sheridan, then commanding the Cavalry Corps, to have the regiment ſent to Pennſylvania to recruit its ranks and reorganize. High bounties were being paid at home, and we were aſſured that we could fill up our ranks with firſt-claſs material, beſides retaining in the field many of the old officers of the regiment, whoſe term of ſervice would expire in the coming autumn, but who agreed to continue in ſervice in conſideration of the reſt they would have. General Sheridan heartily approved of the plan, and perſonally exerted himſelf to ſecure, and did ſecure, the neceſſary authority from General Grant. A formal application was made, which received indorſements from Brigade, Diviſion, and Corps Headquarters moſt ſatisfactory to us; but General Meade declined to make an exception in our favor, as many other regiments were applying for the ſame privilege, and the project fell through. The Sixth

Pennsylvania Cavalry was but the skeleton of a regiment for the rest of the war.*

1864.

We enjoyed such repose as the extreme heat would allow in our camp near Light-house Point, until the 26th, when, with the usual three days' rations for man and horse, we started at 3 P. M. with our division toward the James.

July 26th.

Through the newspapers, for it was from them only we heard the rumors from the front of our own army, we read about a mine being made under the enemy's lines, secretly, as to position, to all but the Generals and those immediately engaged in the work. The crisis of this gunpowder plot had been for days eagerly expected by the North, whose listening ear waited impatiently for the noise thereof. As our column headed northwardly we began to have an idea of what we were doing; and when we heard of the Second Corps ahead of us, and already across the James, we recognized a feint on the enemy's left.

That same evening we crossed the Appomattox into General Butler's domain, as yet untrodden by any of

---

* It will be well to note here one of the evils of the volunteer system in our State. New regiments were raised at every call of the President, and officered, in many cases, by men as inexperienced as those in the ranks, while the old regiments in the field, depleted by the casualties of war, were allowed to remain so, and meritorious officers, schooled by active campaigns, often saw themselves ranked by men who had yet to hear the sound of bullets, and brave soldiers saw little hope of promotion. Ambition, a quality to be fostered in a soldier, found a severe check under this system. This evil could have been entirely avoided by having and keeping recruiting parties through the State, and by raising no new organizations until the old were filled.

1864. us. That night we made a toilsome march through a dense, dreary pine forest, the darkness of which was made visible by guide fires, lighted and kept up by the 1st New York Mounted Rifles, to show our road, and without which we should not have got out of the woods.

July 27th. Daybreak found us at Jones's Neck on the James. After an hour or two of rest, we crossed the bridge, well strewn with hay, &c., to muffle our sounds. Our column numbered three hundred and twenty-six enlisted men. We pushed on gradually across Deep Bottom to the Richmond and Charles City Road, where part of the 2d United States Cavalry charged and routed a small body of rebel cavalry awaiting our approach. That night we encamped on the roadside.

July 28th. At daylight of the 28th we saddled up and waited, as Micawber did, and as often we had waited before, for something to turn up, and, as usual, night did not bring us disappointment.

About noon we saw Gregg lead his division by us, going to see what the Confederacy was doing on our right toward Charles City. About an hour after we hear his guns and begin to look for news of him, but soon our attention is called to our own front, and there our picket line, the 2d and 5th United States, had been sharply attacked and pressed back; the 1st United States Dragoons was sent to help them, and then the 1st Cavalry, but still the enemy advanced until their Minie bullets began to come among our horses. "Our turn comes next," said one of our officers, and very soon an aid gallops to us with orders to go in on foot at once. At double quick we marched to a group of farm-houses, owned by one Darby, in front of which the enemy was 1864. advancing over an open field, in folid infantry line, with three flags flying. We halted at the houfes and fired feveral rounds rapidly into their ranks, which ftaggered them with their muzzle-loaders, and cut down one of their color-bearers. The command was then given to charge, and the forward movement was promptly taken up by the other regiments in our line, and by the 2d brigade on our left, and together, we drove this North Carolina brigade off the field. They left their killed and wounded, their three ftands of colors, and many prifoners in our hands, who faid they could not ftand before fuch firing, it was too faft for them. We did not purfue the retreating North Carolinians, but remained on the field we had won until relieved by the infantry. In this fight, Adjutant Lanigan was feverely wounded in the thigh, and fix enlifted men were wounded, one of them mortally. It was here, too, that Lieutenant Thomas E. Maley, of the 5th United States Cavalry, our firft regimental quartermafter, was terribly wounded in the face by a Minie ball. That evening we retired to the flats on the banks of the James and unfaddled, expecting to enjoy a reft, we thought, well earned; but at 1 A. M., orders came to recrofs the river. At the bridge we found the 1ft divifion of the Second Corps croffing, and the compliments, ufual when cavalry and infantry meet in a crowded road, paffed between the two columns.

At 3½ o'clock A. M. we were back at our camp of July 29th. the night of the 26th, but ftaid only to feed ourfelves and horfes.

1864. There is one thing that a cavalryman very naturally protefts againft, and that is, being transformed into an infantry foldier; fighting on foot he objects to,—but he can often fee the neceffity of it, but he cannot be made to underftand that it may perchance be his duty to leave his horfe behind and turn tramper. This is what our divifion was called upon to do this hot July day. The Mine, fo far as we knew, was not exploded yet, but part of the Second Corps had left us, while the neceffity ftill remained of fhowing a force on the north fide of the James.

At 6 o'clock A. M. we croffed the river and deployed in line on the plains beyond. At noon, our regiment was allowed to take fhelter from the fun in the woods on its immediate left, and there we remained until night, when we recroffed and got back to our horfes about 11 o'clock P. M.

July 30th. Here we found a mail, but not reft, for, at 2 o'clock A. M., we were in the faddle, and on the road to rejoin the Army of the Potomac.

At 5 o'clock A. M. we halted for breakfaft, and about 6 o'clock refumed our march. Paffing near General Meade's headquarters, we learned the failure of the affault made that morning in front of General Burnfide's line. The Mine had done its work well; hundreds of unfortunates, within range of its influence, had perifhed miferably in its explofion, " and the colored troops fought nobly," as the fcores of wounded, being conveyed to the hofpitals, fhowed too plainly; but nothing had been gained, the why and wherefore of which will, probably, be ever a difputed queftion. Continuing our march on the Jerusalem Road, by the left of the army, under a terrible sun, that struck many from our ranks, and through dust so thick that a few paces distance showed a rider in front only in vignette, we reached Finn's house at noon, wellnigh exhausted. Here, the only water we could find was in the old clay well-holes of a deserted camp, and the only shade the withered boughs collected by those who had been there before us. At 2 o'clock P. M. we were again on the road, and encamped that night near Lee's Mills. It was a distressing day's ride; the failure of the morning had cast a gloom over the whole army, and the character of the country we were in, its scorching sun, its choking dust and ugly pine swamps, had little tendency to excite a flow of spirits.

1864.

This morning we were told to prepare for a raid, and received our three days' rations. In due time the column moved off, but soon turned to the left, a direction which excited curiosity. Various opinions were advanced as to where the road went to; finally, some one asserted that he knew it went to the James River. Our regiment leading the brigade, and the brigade being first in column of the division, we were not far from the General, so that when we halted, at a place we all recognized as not many miles from City Point, General Merritt asked how we should like a trip on steamers to Washington, and a campaign in the Valley of the Shenandoah. The change which came over all as this passed down the column can only be understood by those who actually felt it. The prospect ahead compensated fully for the sufferings of the past five days; we were going to leave the desert for the region of green fields and pure air and

July 31st.

1864. water, and with Sheridan as General, to try our hands at the hitherto unsolved problem of the Shenandoah Valley.

All night of the 31st we worked with a will at shipping the command on transports at City Point, and about sunrise steamed down the James River.

Aug. 2d. About noon we reached Giesboro' Point, below Washington, and encamped on the flats near the river, to await the arrival of the remainder of our division.

CHAPTER TWENTY-FOURTH.

General Grant viſits Hunter at Monocacy—Grant's Inſtructions—The Middle Military Diviſion—Sheridan Succeeds Hunter—Skirmiſhes at White Poſt and Newtown—Deſtruction of Baggage Train—Skirmiſh at Front Royal—Withdrawal to Halltown—Skirmiſh at Kearneyſville.

AT the opening of the new campaign in the Shenandoah Valley, deſtined to be ſo different from the former difaſtrous ones in that region, and to make famous the name of General Sheridan, it may not be out of place to inſert an extract from General Grant's report, ſhowing how General Hunter was relieved, and embracing the order for the deſtruction of army ſupplies in the Valley, which, together with ſundry ſevere whippings adminiſtered by his cavalry, made Sheridan's name ſo deteſtable to its inhabitants.

1864.

"On the 2d of Auguſt," writes General Grant, "I ordered General Sheridan to report in perſon to Major-General Halleck, Chief of Staff, at Waſhington, with a view to his aſſignment to the command of all the forces in the Department of Weſt Virginia, Waſhington, Suſquehanna, and the Middle Department.

Auguſt 2d.

"At this time, the enemy were concentrated in the neighborhood of Wincheſter, while our forces under

1864. General Hunter were concentrated on the Monocacy, at the croſſing of the Baltimore and Ohio Railroad, leaving open to the enemy Weſtern Maryland and Southern Pennſylvania. From where I was I heſitated to give orders for the movement of our forces at Monocacy, left by ſo doing I ſhould expoſe Waſhington.

Aug. 4th. Therefore, on the 4th, I left City Point to viſit Hunter's command. On arriving there, and after conſultation with General Hunter, I iſſued to him the following inſtructions:

"MONOCACY BRIDGE, Aug. 5, 1864, 8 P.M.

"GENERAL:

"Concentrate all your available force without delay in the vicinity of Harper's Ferry, leaving only ſuch railroad guards and garriſons for public property as may be neceſſary. Uſe, in this concentrating, the railroads, if, by ſo doing, time can be ſaved. . . . . From Harper's Ferry, if it is found that the enemy has moved north of the Potomac in large force, puſh north, following and attacking him wherever found; following him, if driven ſouth of the Potomac, as long as it is ſafe to do ſo. If it is aſcertained the enemy has but a ſmall force north of the Potomac, then puſh ſouth with the main force, detailing, under a competent commander, a ſufficient force to look after the raiders, and drive them to their homes. In detailing ſuch a force the brigade of cavalry, now *en route* from Waſhington, via Rockville, may be taken into account.

"There are now on their way to join you three other brigades of the beſt cavalry, numbering at leaſt five thouſand men and horſes. Theſe will be inſtructed, in the abſence of further orders, to join you by the ſouth ſide of the Potomac. One brigade will, probably, ſtart to-morrow.

"In puſhing up the Shenandoah Valley, where it is expected you will have to go, firſt or laſt, it is deſirable that nothing ſhould be left to invite the enemy to return. Take all proviſions, forage, and ſtock wanted for the uſe of your command; ſuch as cannot be conſumed, deſtroy. It is not deſirable that the buildings ſhould be deſtroyed, they ſhould rather be PROTECTED; but the people ſhould be informed that, ſo long as an army can ſubſiſt among them, recurrences of theſe raids muſt be expected, and we are determined to ſtop them at all hazards.

"Bear in mind, the object is to drive the enemy south; and to do this, 1864. you want to keep him always in fight. Be guided in your course by the course he takes.

"Make your own arrangements for supplies of all kinds, giving regular vouchers for such as may be taken from loyal citizens.

"U. S. GRANT,
"Lieutenant-General."

"The troops were immediately put in motion, and the advance reached Halltown that night.

"General Hunter having, in our conversation, expressed a willingness to be relieved from command, I telegraphed to have General Sheridan, then at Washington, sent to Harper's Ferry by the morning train, with orders to take command of all the troops in the field, and to call on General Hunter at Monocacy, who would turn over to him my letter of instructions. . . . .

"On the 7th of August, the Middle Military Department, and the Departments of West Virginia, Washington, and Susquehanna, were constituted into the Middle Military Division, and Major-General Sheridan was assigned to the command of the same. The divisions of Generals Torbert and Wilson were sent to Sheridan from the Army of the Potomac."

On the afternoon of August 5th, our regiment broke Aug. 5th. camp at Giesboro' Point, and leaving behind us the men of Company "G," whose term of service was to expire on the 8th, started at 7 P. M. on the new campaign. Once more we marched through the streets of Washington, and then on beyond Tenallytown, where we encamped.

On the 6th, we made twenty-three miles, to Hyatts- Aug. 6th.

1864. ville, and on the 7th, twenty-six miles, to Maryland
Aug. 7th. Heights. Here Captain Leiper rejoined the regiment. On his return from leave, on account of wounds, to Washington, at the time of Earley's raid, he had, with others, been put on duty with the troops around the capital, and had subsequently been taken by General Wright on his staff.

Aug. 8th. On the 8th, we again crossed into Dixie, and reached our camp-ground just beyond Halltown that afternoon. General Torbert, who had now joined us with the remainder of our division, was made Chief of Cavalry to General Sheridan's army, and General Merritt was assigned to the command of the old First Division.

The concentration of our army at Halltown caused the enemy to withdraw all his forces to the south side of the Potomac, and to take up his position at Bunker Hill, twelve miles south of Martinsburg.

Aug. 10th. At 6 o'clock A. M. on the 10th, the advance began; we soon passed the infantry, and our regiment, in advance of the army, passed through Charlestown, and took the turnpike road to the left, to Berryville. As we marched we got reports of sundry detachments of the enemy, who for the time had turned their "spears into pruning-hooks," and were engaged in reaping the crops; from one of these parties we received a few harmless bullets, and from another, Lieutenant Price, of Company "I," took one prisoner, and two wagons and a threshing-machine, which he destroyed. About noon, the advance-guard came up with a fortunate contraband, who, well mounted, was carrying lunch to a Major Richardson, rebel, of those parts. The horse was promptly reconstructed, and the lunch, needless to say, never reached Major Richardson. Passing through Berryville we marched on toward White Post, our destination for that day. A few miles from this place we struck the enemy's cavalry in small force, and pushed them about a mile, when they left our front. That night our regiment picketed to the left and rear.

1864.

The enemy had now moved to the west bank of the Opequan, occupying the line between the points where the Winchester and Potomac Railroad and the Berryville Pike cross that stream.

On the 11th, General Sheridan intended to cross the Opequan to the left of the enemy and give him battle; but the discoveries made by our division changed these plans. We were ordered up the Millwood Pike, and found the enemy's cavalry covering that road west of the Opequan. We attacked at once and pushed them toward the Valley Road. Our regiment, which the day before had had the advance, was this day in rear of the brigade, and had been engaged in guarding the ammunition train. It was now afternoon, and fighting having begun, we were brought to the front, and from our position, supporting the brigade battery, could see the struggle going on. The enemy's cavalry had been driven behind his infantry, which, posted in a belt of woods and behind a rail barricade, successfully prevented our further advance. One regiment after another of our division was put in, and tried hard, but without success, to drive the rebels from the woods. Finally, our turn came; Captain Clarke's squadron was detached and sent to the left, while the two remaining squadrons, under Major

Aug. 11th.

1864. Starr, advanced difmounted, and "in fplendid ftyle," as General Merritt faid, who was in the front eagerly watching the fight, over an open field in full view of our protected enemy, who received us with a fevere fire. Not a man flinched, and the line moved forward fteadily, without firing a fhot, to a fence about a hundred yards from the woods. There we found parts of the 1ſt and 2d Cavalry, and halted a moment, but finding it too hot, and feeing a ditch a few yards in front which would protect the men, we leaped the fence and put ourfelves under its cover. From this natural rifle-pit a rapid fire was kept up until our battery opened, making fome fine fhots over our heads, and forcing the enemy to keep clofe. There we remained until relieved foon after dark, when we found we had been fighting Gordon's divifion of infantry, which had been thrown out to cover the flank of the main army of the enemy in its retreat up the Valley.

Aug. 12th. The enemy interfered with our early breakfaſt this morning by feeling our picket line. There were but a few parting fhots. At 5 o'clock A. M. we were on the march; we paffed through the barricades which had obſtructed us the afternoon before, through Newtown, and then to the left up the Valley Pike and through Middleburg to Cedar Creek. Arrived there, we found that our fkirmifh line of infantry had been thrown acrofs and was exchanging fhots at long range with the rebels who occupied the heights north of Straſburg.

Aug. 13th. The next day our divifion made a reconnoiffance to Straſburg, taking the back road, which is about two and a half miles weſt of the main pike. We met no opposition, but lost one or two stragglers from the column, who were picked up by rebel scouts. From Strasburg, with the assistance of field-glasses, we could plainly see the enemy on the hills south of us, and his signal station on Three-top Mountain. Before sunset we got back to camp, and there found our sutler, Jackson Groves. His presence was generally a good sign, for it would tell us that our trains had come up, which were to bring us forage and rations. But now the sign failed, for the sutler's face was long and troubled; he brought rumors of an attack on the trains by the irrepressible Moseby, and their total destruction,—a dismal thought to sleep on that night. Forage and rations could be replaced, but in that train was all our camp equipage, all the few luxuries we could carry along with us, and, still worse, all the records of the old division, of the Reserve Brigade, and of the several regiments, the loss of which could never be replaced, and would involve company commanders in untold difficulties, such as those only can appreciate who have been responsible to the Government for its property, and been bound by its fetters of red tape. This operation of Moseby caused a severe loss to one of his rebel brethren, too; for the men hearing they were to get no rations that night made a vigorous attack on a fine flock of sheep grazing near the camp, which attack furnished food not only for the men, but for very severe comments on the part of General Merritt.

On the 14th, our regiment, under orders from General Merritt, crossed Cedar Creek in front of our lines, on a reconnoissance to ascertain the enemy's line at Stras-

1864.
Aug. 14th.
burg. We expected to find our infantry pickets where we had left them the day before, on the heights directly north of the town. We pushed on, confidently, paſt a picket-poſt we took for a reſerve, until halted by ſhots from the enemy. We found that our picket line had been retired in the night, and that the enemy occupied thoſe hills with infantry and in force much ſuperior to our ſkeleton of a regiment. Retiring behind our pickets, parties were ſent to the right and left to find the extent of the enemy's lines. This being done, Major Starr reported to General Merritt in accordance with the facts, and we waited for orders. About ſunſet, General Wright, with one diviſion of the Sixth Corps, attacked the enemy's line, and after a briſk ſkirmiſh, drove them from the hills and through Straſburg. On our return to camp that evening, the rumor of the loſs of our wagons was confirmed. Moſeby, with his little band of bold riders,—they cannot *rightly* be called ſoldiers,—had attacked the trains near Berryville, had ſcattered General Kenley's gallant brigade of 100 days' men, and had fired and deſtroyed the wagons of our diviſion. The only ſatisfaction we had was that he burnt up our records and baggage, and did not carry them off to furniſh comfort and entertainment to his followers. He was too hurried to realize on his venture, for, on the approach of a body of our cavalry, he diſappeared, and left behind him a paymaſter's ſtrong box, full of greenbacks.

Aug. 15th. The arrival of Major Nichols in camp, with four months' pay, ſomewhat relieved the loſs we had met with on the 13th. The day was ſpent in paying the men. At 9 o'clock P. M. Captain Clarke with his ſquadron

relieved the pickets of the 1st Cavalry, and at 3 A.M. 1864.
Captain Leiper, with the other two squadrons, was sent
to strengthen his line.

For several days past it had been reported that the
enemy was moving a column toward Front Royal through
Chester Gap, by which he could gain the rear of our
army. To watch for such a movement, Devins's brigade of our division had been sent to Front Royal on the
14th. On that day General Sheridan received dispatches
from Washington confirming this report, and causing
him to move back, as will be seen.

On the morning of the 16th our regiment was re- Aug. 16th.
lieved from picket by Colonel Lowell, and marched
through Middleburg and took the road to the east, to
Cedarsville, which we passed, and went into camp about
3 o'clock P.M., on the Winchester and Front Royal
Pike, with the rest of the Reserve Brigade. About sunset a brisk cannonade opened near Front Royal, and we
at once recognized the expected flank attack being now
made, at the crossing of the Shenandoah, on Devins's
brigade and on Custer's, which, on the 15th, had been
sent to his support.

The enemy attacked with infantry and cavalry, forced
a crossing of the bridge and ford, and charged boldly
upon our lines; but our artillery was well served and
checked their further advance, while Colonel Devins
with his brigade charged their left in flank and drove them
routed across the river again, capturing two stands of
colors and many prisoners. On our left, Custer, after
severe fighting, succeeded also in routing the enemy, but
not until after dark. At one time, the battle looked

1864. dubious, and our brigade was ordered to fupport, but it had been handfomely won before we reached the ground.

Aug. 17th. On the 17th, the following order was publifhed to our divifion:

"HEADQUARTERS MIDDLE MILITARY DIVISION,
CEDAR CREEK, VA., Auguft 16, 1864.

" *To Brigadier-General A. T. A. Torbert,*
Chief of Cavalry, Middle Military Divifion.

"GENERAL: In compliance with inftructions of the Lieutenant-General commanding, you will make the neceffary arrangements and give the neceffary orders for the deftruction of the wheat and hay fouth of a line from Millwood to Winchefter and Petticoat Gap. You will feize all mules, horfes, and cattle that may be ufeful to our army. Loyal citizens can bring in their claims againft the Government for this neceffary deftruction. No houfes will be burned; and officers in charge of this delicate but neceffary duty, muft inform the people that the object is to make this Valley untenable for the raiding parties of the rebel army.

"Very refpectfully,

"P. H. SHERIDAN,
"Major-General Commanding."

Our regiment avoided the detail for this unpleafant duty, and marched in rear of the deftroyers, who, ftretched in long line acrofs the Valley, did their work thoroughly. We reached Berryville by 6 o'clock P. M., and went into camp about two miles out of the town, on the Snicker's Gap Pike.

The day had been an unpleafant one; the weather was hot and the roads very dufty, and the grief of the inhabitants, as they faw their harvefts difappearing in flame and fmoke, and their ftock being driven off, was

SAD SCENES IN BERRYVILLE.

a fad fight. It was a phafe of warfare we had not feen 1864. before, and though we admitted its neceffity, we could not but fympathize with the fufferers.

For feveral days, now, we had not feen any of our infantry; but, on the 18th, on our march to Berryville, Aug. 18th. we met the Sixth Corps coming through the town, with a quick fwinging ftep and their ranks clofed, which denoted work in fome quarter. The army was falling back.

We moved through Berryville and took up a pofition on the Winchefter Pike, where we ftood to horfe all day, anxioufly awaiting developments. It was a dull and rainy day, and it feemed almoft endlefs. The ruins of our burnt train were the only objects of intereft near us, and they were not very agreeable ones, as they only reminded us that if they had not been fo burnt, we fhould not have been, as we were, out of rations.

The following day brought little change for us until Aug. 19th. the evening, when we received fupplies for man and horfe, and a mail, which was very acceptable. There were fad fcenes in Berryville this day and the next. Mofeby and his men, in retaliation for our deftruction of the crops, had killed a number of his prifoners, and had given us to underftand he would continue fo to do. To ftop this work, all the males of age in Berryville had been taken as hoftages, to the great diftrefs of their families.

At 3 o'clock P. M. on the 20th, we ftarted to run a Aug. 20th picket line, to join Cufter at Berryville, with the infantry on our left, and remained on picket until noon of the day following, when we fell back toward Charlef- Aug. 21ft

1864. town. The enemy, who had been marching almoſt parallel with us on the weſt ſide of the Opequan, now threw a heavy force acroſs that ſtream at Smithfield, drove in our cavalry pickets, and advanced as far as the picket line of the Sixth Corps near Flowing Springs, which being a heavy one, ſucceſsfully reſiſted the attack after a very ſevere ſkirmiſh. In ſound of this fighting, and anxious as to its reſults, our diviſion retired by brigades in echelon on the Berryville and Charleſtown Pike, and reached Charleſtown about 9 o'clock P. M., going into line of battle on the plain northeaſt of the town, and remaining ſaddled all night. The infantry during the night fell back to Halltown.

Aug. 22d. The morning of the 22d opened with a ſkirmiſh between our cavalry pickets and the enemy, who had puſhed up to our poſition, but they made no attack.

At 5 o'clock A. M. we ſtarted for Shepherdſtown, and arrived at 9 o'clock A. M. without meeting any oppoſition. There we remained ſaddled all day in line, on a limeſtone ridge outſide of the town, waiting the approach of the enemy, who did not make his appearance.

Company "A," of our regiment, which had been on duty at General Torbert's headquarters, was muſtered
Aug. 24th. out on the 24th, and thoſe of its members whoſe term of ſervice had not yet expired, rejoined the regiment.

Aug. 25th. On the morning of the 25th, General Merritt's and General Wilſon's diviſions of cavalry were ordered to attack the enemy's cavalry at Kearneyſville, on the Baltimore and Ohio Railroad. We left camp at 6 A. M., and marched unoppoſed acroſs the railroad weſt of the ſtation. About 11 o'clock A. M., Cuſter's brigade in the advance came, very unexpectedly to both sides, upon the rebel infantry in large force, marching toward Shepherdstown; a severe skirmish followed, and proved the enemy to be too strong for us, and we withdrew slowly toward the Potomac. The enemy followed us step by step with great tenacity as far as Shepherdstown, and there succeeded in isolating Custer's brigade, and forcing him acrofs the ford to the north side of the Potomac. We continued falling back from Shepherdstown towards our infantry lines at Halltown, the enemy marching acrofs the country and harafling our flanks until night ended this hard day's work, and we went into camp a few miles from Harper's Ferry on the river road to Shepherdstown.

1864.

On the night of the 26th, the enemy left our front and removed his infantry back to Bunker Hill, leaving his cavalry at Smithfield and Leetown, so that the two armies were, on the 27th, in almost the same position they were in when this campaign opened on the 10th.

Aug. 26th.

CHAPTER TWENTY-FIFTH.

Engagements at Leetown and Smithfield—Regiment ordered to Pleafant Valley to be muftered out—Death of Surgeon John B. Coover.

1864.
Aug. 28th.
ON the morning of the 28th, a new advance was begun by the whole army. The infantry was moved in front of Charleftown, while our cavalry divifion was ordered to attack the rebel cavalry at Leetown, on the Winchefter and Shepherdftown pike. Before leaving camp the men of "B" company, whofe term of fervice had expired, were fent to Harper's Ferry to be muftered out.

We marched without oppofition paft Duffield Station to within a fhort diftance of Leetown, where the 2d U. S. Cavalry, which had the advance, came upon the enemy. They were too ftrong for the 2d to handle alone, and they fent to General Merritt for affiftance. Major Starr was then ordered with the 6th Pennfylvania to fupport the 2d, and taking command of the advance to pufh on up the pike towards Smithfield. As foon as we had joined the 2d Cavalry, Major Starr fent Captain Morrow, of the 6th Pennfylvania, with his fquadron to the left acrofs the country in hopes of getting in rear of the rebels, and then ordered the 2d and 6th forward. The enemy did not wait for us, but retreated precipitately up the pike, we following for a mile or more. A halt was 1864. then made and word fent to General Merritt, who at once came up to our pofition.

The divifion then advanced fteadily up the turnpike, General Cufter's brigade on the right; Colonel Devins' brigade, temporarily commanded by Colonel De Cefnola, on the left, and the Referve brigade, under Colonel Gibbs, in the centre, on the pike. We puſhed the enemy, who offered no real refiftance, until we came within two miles of Smithfield, when the 5th U. S. Cavalry, now leading the Referve brigade on the road, charged them with the fabre, and drove them in confufion, capturing a number of prifoners of Bradley Johnfon's command. In this charge Lieutenant Hoyer of the 5th was killed.

The character of the country prevented us from reaping the full advantage of this charge. The ftone wall fences delayed our movements through the fields, fo that the troops on the flanks could not keep up with thofe in the road, and thus the enemy got away from us for a while.

This charge fomewhat diforganized our advance, and that no time fhould be loft our regiment again took the lead.

The rebels made their laft ftand on the hills between Smithfield and the Opequan, leaving their fkirmifhers in the town and fweeping the road with their artillery, which was admirably well ferved. But their attention was foon taken from the road by one of our batteries, which was promptly put into pofition, and which was intended to keep them bufy until Cufter, who had gone,

1864. under cover of the woods, to the right, could strike them in flank and cut off their retreat across the Opequan. The first shot from Custer's skirmish line warned them of their danger, and they retreated in haste to the west side of the stream at the very moment we were about to charge them, leaving us in possession of the town and the heights, upon which the division was now formed to await further developments. But the sun was setting, and darkness coming on, we bivouacked for the night without change of position.

Aug. 29th. At dawn we saddled up and soon after opened the day's work by a reconnoissance by Custer's brigade on the west side of the Opequan. His column marched over the bridge and disappeared in the woods beyond.

We had not to wait long before we heard the sounds of a brisk skirmish apparently favorable to us, for a few prisoners came in and the sounds became fainter. An hour or more passed when Custer's column appeared coming back, and before we could learn the results of the reconnoissance, the enemy opened on us with several pieces of artillery, throwing canister in a most reckless manner among our horses and men, who being entirely exposed on the hills furnished a fair target. The momentary confusion was soon brought into order, the horses were led behind the hills, and part of each brigade was deployed on foot to meet the expected attack, which soon came.

Custer, as had been invariably the case for the last year, had driven the rebel cavalry to the cover of his infantry, and now the infantry had come out to offer battle. They advanced steadily to a ford not far below the bridge over the Opequan, and attacked the 19th New York and our regiment holding that part of the line. They were too ſtrong for us, and driving us from the ford, croſſed in large force, endeavouring to turn our left. A ſevere ſkirmiſh now began, which laſted all of that long day. Inch by inch we diſputed the advance, taking advantage of every tree, fence, or elevation to make a ſtand, but we could not hold them in check. Before noon our cartridges were exhauſted, and freſh ammunition was ſent for, which was diſtributed by mounted men with great difficulty and danger. Driven into Smithfield, we held the town for a time, but here De Ceſnola unaccountably withdrew his brigade from our left, leaving a fair opening for the enemy, who at once took advantage of it, and attacking us in flank, forced us to retire. Once out of the town the enemy opened his artillery on us with moſt uncomfortable accuracy. The ammunition was now again exhauſted, and we were retiring over an open field, partly ploughed, eagerly preſſed by the enemy, when General Merritt and ſtaff rode up to Major Starr. "Is this your regiment?" ſaid the General. "Yes, ſir," was the reply; "my men are out of ammunition, and well-nigh exhauſted; our left is entirely expoſed; you can ſee the rebels cloſing on us through that cornfield." "Turn about," ſaid the General, "you muſt make a ſtand; uſe your piſtols, if you have no carbine ammunition." The command was at once faced to the front again, and with a cheer advanced to a ſtone wall and fence between us and the enemy. But we could not ſtay there. Cuſter on our right was falling back, and we had either to do the ſame or be captured.

1864.
Aug. 29th.

1864.
Aug. 29th.

Word was sent to Colonel Gibbs, commanding the brigade, that our men were exhausted and if not relieved would be made prisoners, and the 2d Cavalry was deployed mounted to keep the enemy occupied while we dismounted, passed through their files to the rear, to our horses. This was no easy matter, for the enemy was shelling us vigorously and pressing on their infantry lines. Twice the 2d Cavalry was driven back, but the third time we succeeded in getting inside of their line, and reaching our horses, mounted them, with the feeling of intense relief and comparative security. It was in this last struggle that 1st Sergeant Staley, of " M " company, a most gallant soldier, was mortally wounded ; his comrades tried their best to carry him with them to the rear, but they were forced to leave him, and he fell into the hands of the enemy. The whole division now fell back about half a mile, where we met the head of General Rickett's Division of the 6th Corps of infantry coming to our assistance, and with them General Sheridan and staff, all of whom were welcomed most heartily.

The generals at once met in council, but did not take into account the near presence of the enemy, who fired into the group and killed Dr. Rulison, Medical Director of the Cavalry.

The new dispositions were promptly made. The infantry took the left of the road leading from Charlestown to Smithfield, on which we had been retreating, our brigade the right, skirmishers and supports being in line, and the generals in the centre, on the road, with their staffs and escorts. The 2d U. S. Cavalry formed the skirmish line, the 19th U. S. Dragoons and the 6th Pennsylvania the line of battle of the cavalry. Thus we advanced through the woods, the enemy retiring with little oppofition, which difappointed us, for we felt ready to cope with them now, and confident that we could return with intereft what we had been receiving all day. The men manœuvred admirably in forming column to get through breaches in the ftone walls, and reforming line when the obftructions were paffed. They were in fine fpirits, for they had received unqualified praife from General Merritt for the day's work, and were confcious that it had been well done. Near Smithfield a body of rebel cavalry made a fhow of refiftance, but being charged by the 2d U. S., quickly retired to the weft fide of the Opequan. Thus we recovered all the ground we had loft during the day. The body of Sergeant Staley was found where his comrades had left him; it was lifelefs, and had been ftripped of all but the underclothing. Pickets of our divifion were left at the Smithfield bridge, and we marched feveral miles towards Charleftown, and went into camp. Our lofs in this engagement was two killed and fixteen wounded.

1864. Aug. 29th.

This day is one of the moft memorable in our hiftory, for it was the laft time that the original regiment met and fought the enemy.

As our men and officers had been muftered individually, we had no date of regimental mufter, and claimed to be difcharged at the expiration of individual terms of fervice. This was practically impoffible in the front, while active operations were going on; and as we were lofing, by killed and wounded in every fight, men who had already ferved their terms well and faithfully, we now applied to

1864. be sent to Pleasant Valley, to muster out those entitled to discharge, and reorganize the regiment upon the nucleus composed of those who had re-enlisted, the '62 men, and such few recruits as we had received from time to time.

Aug. 30th. On the 30th, Major Starr was ordered to Washington, to replace, as far as practicable, from copies, the papers destroyed by Moseby's attack on our train, leaving the command of the regiment to Captain C. L. Leiper. In the afternoon of the 30th, the regiment moved with the division to Berryville, and from then to the 8th of September was employed on picket duty or on scout and reconnoissance, first on the left of the army toward White Post, and then on the right toward the Opequan.

Our army was now holding a line from Clifton to Berryville, the enemy being in position on the west bank of the Opequan, about six miles from Clifton. The object of these frequent scouts was to hold all the country between our lines and the creek.

Sept. 6th. On the 6th, Captain C. L. Leiper was mustered as Major.

Sept. 8th. On the 8th, our application to be sent to Pleasant Valley was returned granted, and at 2 P. M. we started in company with the 2d Maryland Cavalry, and arrived Sept. 9th. that night. The following day Major Leiper, by General Sheridan's orders, took command of the Remount Camp, turning over the regiment to Captain Clarke. Several days were passed in turning over our horses, arms, and equipments to the several depots, and in drawing the camp equipage necessary for a permanent camp. We had hardly established ourselves on a beautiful hillside, on the western slope of the Valley, when Major Starr returned from Washington and took command of the Remount Camp, relieving Major Leiper, who rejoined the regiment.

1864.

A remount camp is a rendezvous for all straggling cavalrymen, whether coming from the front with worn-out horses, or returning to duty from hospitals, or arriving as recruits. Every cavalry soldier looking for a resting-place goes to Remount Camp; there he knows that if he wants to go he will be sent to his regiment, and if he wants to skulk he has a better chance there than anywhere else; if a recruit, he goes there simply because he is sent. Connected with this camp was a large corral of horses, an ordnance and a clothing depot, and a commissariat of course. There were always from 1000 to 1500 men in the camp, made up of squads and individuals from every cavalry regiment in the Eastern army. And though in the month that Major Starr commanded it, over 1500 men were sent to the front, well mounted and completely equipped and re-clothed, new-comers filled their places. The command of such a camp was no sinecure. To preserve in it such discipline as our regiment was accustomed to, was an impossibility with the means at hand. Fearing the effects of its evil example on our men, Major Starr moved our camp a mile further up the Valley, where it remained until the 15th of November, the officers and men being mustered out as their several terms expired, and a strong recruiting party being sent to Philadelphia.

The news of the splendid victories of General Sheridan came promptly to our camp and was received with the greatest enthusiasm. But our joy was moderated when the list of casualties was reported, and especially

1864. when we heard that Dr. Coover, who had been our surgeon, was lying mortally wounded at Sandy Hook Hospital, two miles below us.

SURGEON JOHN B. COOVER was born in Cumberland County, Pennsylvania, January 20th, 1834. In his medical studies he entered the office of Dr. Ira Day, of Mechanicsburg, and graduated from the 'Jefferson Medical College in Philadelphia, in March, 1857. In the spring of 1862 he entered the service as assistant surgeon in the 46th Pennsylvania Infantry. In consequence of faithfulness in field service and attention to our sick and wounded while a prisoner in Libby, he was promoted to surgeon, and in December was transferred to the 6th Pennsylvania Cavalry, which then had a vacancy in that position. During his connection with the Reserve Cavalry Brigade, composed of the 1st, 2d, 5th, and 6th U. S., and the 6th Pennsylvania and 19th New York Cavalry regiments, he acted as chief medical officer of the brigade for more than a year.

A short time previous to his death, he had been appointed Medical Inspector of the Middle Military Division, under General Sheridan. The term of service of the regiment having expired, he had expected to be mustered out also, and to accept an appointment in the Surgeon-General's Office of Pennsylvania; with orders on his person for muster out, he generously stayed at Winchester when the regiment was ordered to the rear, that he might assist in taking care of the wounded in Sheridan's brilliant fight.

When the press of work was over, he left for Harper's Ferry, on the 26th of September, in company with 1864. Surgeon-General Phillips of Pennsylvania. Between Charleftown and Halltown they were attacked by guerillas, who fired upon them from both fides of the road. The fmall guard that was fent with them for protection being recruits, were fo frightened that they did not return a fingle fhot. The entire company attempted to efcape by flight, and when nearly beyond range of the enemy, and by the laft fhot fired, Dr. Coover received a mortal wound in the abdomen, the ball paffing through his body; he kept his feat in the faddle, clinging to his horfe, until the purfuit ceafed, and the party came to our infantry picket lines, when an ambulance was fent for, and he was taken to Harper's Ferry, where his injuries received attention at the hands of Dr. Phillips. The next morning he was removed to the hofpital at Sandy Hook.

From noon until the evening he had moments of confcioufnefs, in which he recognized Major Starr and Major Leiper, who were at his bedfide, but after funfet his mind wandered, his breathing became lefs regular, and about midnight he died, as peacefully as if paffing into fleep. He was buried at Cheftnut Hill Cemetery, near Mechanicfburg, Pennfylvania. Dr. Coover was always remarkable among us for his cheerful and buoyant fpirits, which never feemed to fail him; he was enthufiaftic in the caufe for which he gave up his life, and energetic and faithful in the performance of all the duties his different pofitions prefented to him. His memory will ever be cherifhed by his fellow-officers of the 6th Pennfylvania Cavalry.

CHAPTER TWENTY-SIXTH.

Record of Officers muftered out in 1864, and of Promotions and Changes omitted in the Narrative.

1864. IN clofing this portion of our annals, which completes the ftory of the original regiment, there remains only to mention the fervices of thofe officers who were detached at different times from the regiment, and to fupply the omiffions in the military records of others, which have been made in the courfe of the narrative.

John H. McArthur, Captain 5th U. S. Cavalry, affifted in organizing the regiment, and was muftered as Lieutenant-Colonel, September 11th, 1861. He moved the firft detachment to Wafhington, and remained with the regiment until the end of March, 1862, when he was ordered back to the 5th U. S.

Charles Rofs Smith ferved in the three months' campaign of 1861, as Firft Lieutenant of "A" company (Wafhington Grays of Philadelphia), 17th Pennfylvania Infantry, Colonel F. E. Patterson. Joined the regiment as Captain of "A" company, which he recruited and organized, and was muftered as its Captain, Auguft 27th, 1861. Promoted to Firft Major and muftered October 1ft, 1861. Promoted to Lieutenant-Colonel *vice* McArthur, and muftered March 29th, 1862. Commanded the regiment at Harrifon's Landing, and during General

McClellan's retreat in 1862. Served with the regiment 1864. until the organization of the Cavalry Corps, when he was appointed Provoſt Marſhal on the ſtaff of General Stoneman, commanding the cavalry, February 15th, 1863. July 29th, 1863, was appointed Chief of Staff to General Pleaſanton, who was put in General Stoneman's place. Served in that poſition until April 28th, 1864, when he was appointed Provoſt Marſhal to General Sheridan, then put in command of the cavalry, and filled the ſame office in the Middle Military Diviſion under the ſame General until he was muſtered out at the expiration of his term of ſervice, October 2d, 1864, holding at the time the commiſſion of Colonel of 6th Pennſylvania Cavalry, dated September 30th, 1863.

Henry C. Whelan ſerved in the three months' campaign of 1861, as Firſt Lieutenant of "F" company (Waſhington Grays of Philadelphia), 17th Pennſylvania Infantry. Joined the regiment as Captain of "C" company, which he recruited and organized, and of which he was muſtered Captain, September 10th, 1861. Promoted and muſtered Major, February 10th, 1863. Major Whelan was with his command in moſt of the engagements, raids, and marches, during the firſt two years of the war. The expoſure of the campaign of 1863 proved too great for his conſtitution, which was never ſtrong, and he was obliged to leave the field in the winter, ſoon after the Mine Run campaign. He never rejoined the regiment, but died of a pulmonary diſeaſe in Philadelphia, on the 2d of March, 1864. Major Whelan was diſtinguiſhed in the regiment for his ſoldierly qualities, his manly preſence, and courteous manners; he was a ſtrict diſciplina-

1864. rian in camp and a brave and judicious leader in the field, a man in whom the war developed great thoughtfulnefs of character and earneftnefs of purpofe. He had before been obliged to take leave of abfence on account of ill health, and had returned to duty againft the advice of his phyfician and friends. His death was fincerely and deeply felt throughout the regiment, where he had won the efteem and refpect of all, and to which he left a confpicuous example of felf-facrifice and devotion to duty.

Benoni Lockwood, a graduate of the Univerfity of Pennfylvania, recruited and organized "H" company, and was muftered as its Captain, October 12th, 1861. He ferved faithfully with the regiment with this rank, commanding in feveral engagements, as has been before mentioned, until March 15th, 1864, when private reafons compelled him to refign. At the time of his refignation he held a Major's commiffion, bearing date September 30th, 1863.

James Starr, a graduate of Harvard College, and a member of the Philadelphia bar, ferved in the three months' campaign of 1861 as private in "F" company (Wafhington Grays of Philadelphia), 17th Pennfylvania Infantry. Joined the regiment as Captain of "I" company, which he recruited and organized, and was muftered as its Captain, October 14th, 1861. Served as aide-de-camp to Major-General Franklin at the firft battle of Frederickfburg. At the opening of the campaign of 1863 was ordered to report with his fquadron, I and E companies, to Major-General Hooker, as efcort to headquarters, Army of the Potomac. The fquadron was retained at headquarters by General Meade, when he took command of the army. Captain Starr ſerved as 1864. ſpecial aid to that General at the battle of Gettyſburg. Rejoined the regiment with his ſquadron in October, 1863. Promoted to Major on the death of Major Whelan, March, 1864. Muſtered out at the expiration of his term of ſervice, October 14th, 1864. Has ſince been breveted Lieutenant-Colonel "for highly gallant conduct at the battle of Todd's Tavern, Virginia," and Colonel for "meritorious ſervices during the campaign in the Shenandoah Valley, and while in command of the Remount Camp at Pleaſant Valley, Maryland."

R. Walſh Mitchell muſtered as Firſt Lieutenant of Company " B," September 2d, 1861. On the 25th of April, 1863, was appointed Captain and aide-de-camp, under the act of July 17th, 1862, and ordered to report to Major-General Reynolds, with whom he ſerved until the death of the General at the battle of Gettyſburg. On his return to the army from eſcorting the body of General Reynolds to his grave, Captain Mitchell ſerved on the ſtaff of Major-General Meade until February, 1864, when he rejoined the regiment and was promoted Captain. Served with the regiment in the Wilderneſs campaign and in the Shenandoah Valley, and was muſtered out at the expiration of his term, in the autumn of 1864.

Samuel Hazard, Jr., entered the regiment at its organization, and was muſtered Firſt Lieutenant of Company "D," on the 12th of September, 1861. Served with it until April 30th, 1862, when he was forced to reſign on account of ill health, after repeated and moſt praiſeworthy endeavours to overcome the evil effects on

1864. his conſtitution of the expoſure of camp life. In September, 1862, his health being ſufficiently reſtored, he recruited a company for the 152d Pennſylvania Volunteers, 3d Artillery, Colonel Roberts, and was muſtered as Captain, February 11th, 1863. Served with his company at Fortreſs Monroe during 1863. During the Peterſburg campaign of 1864-65, commanded a detachment of his regiment at Fort Converſe in the line of the Bermuda defences, under General Charles K. Graham, where his command was remarkable for its diſcipline, neatneſs, and preciſion of drill. Reſigned, on ſurgeon's certificate of diſability, February 13th, 1865. Breveted Major, March 13th, 1865.

Charles E. Richards ſerved in the Firſt Troop of Philadelphia City Cavalry, as private, in the three months' campaign of 1861. Joined the regiment as Firſt Lieutenant of Company "F." When the two new Companies, "L" and "M," were organized, in the autumn of 1862, he was promoted to be Captain of Company "M." He ſerved faithfully with the regiment until 16th March, 1863, when he reſigned, for private reaſons.

Charles E. Cadwalader, a graduate of the Univerſity of Pennſylvania, ſerved in the three months' campaign of 1861, as private, in the Firſt Troop of Philadelphia City Cavalry. Entered the 6th Pennſylvania Cavalry as Firſt Lieutenant of "H" company, and was muſtered October 3d, 1861. Was promoted Captain of "D" company in June, 1862. Served with the regiment through the Peninſular and Maryland campaigns of 1862. After the battle of Antietam, ſerved with his company for a ſhort term at General McClellan's and at General

Reynolds's headquarters. March 17th, 1863, was appointed aide-de-camp by General Hooker, and in this pofition ferved at Chancellorfville. When General Meade was affigned to the command of the Army of the Potomac, June 28th, 1863, Captain Cadwalader was retained on the ftaff and ferved in this pofition at Gettyfburg and through the Wildernefs campaign, and at the fiege of Peterfburg. Was muftered out by reafon of expiration of term of fervice, October 3d, 1864. Received a brevet as Major, on General Hooker's recommendation, "for fpecial gallantry and meritorious fervices in the battle of Chancellorfville, May 3d, 1863, and in the cavalry fight at Brandy Station, June 9th, 1863;" and, on General Meade's recommendation, a brevet as Lieutenant-Colonel "for diftinguifhed gallantry and good conduct at the battle of Gettyfburg, and in fubfequent operations, including the campaign from the Rapidan to the James, in 1864, and the fiege of Peterfburg."

1864.

Ofwald Jackfon ferved as private in "F" company, 17th Pennfylvania Infantry (Wafhington Grays), in the three months' campaign of 1861. Entered the 6th Pennfylvania Cavalry as Firft Lieutenant of "I" company, and was muftered, October 2d, 1861. On the 27th February, 1862, was ordered to report to Brigadier General E. D. Keyes, for ftaff duty, and on the 20th Auguft, 1862, was appointed Captain and aide-de-camp. June 23d, 1862, promoted to Major on the fame ftaff. Was muftered out Auguft 20th, 1863, under the act of July, 1862, by S. O. 354, A. G. O.

John W. Williams, a graduate of the Univerfity of

1864. Pennfylvania, and a member of the Philadelphia bar, entered the fervice of the United States as Sergeant of "A" company (Wafhington Grays), 17th Pennfylvania Volunteer Infantry, Colonel Frank Patterfon, in which pofition he ferved during the three months' campaign of 1861. October 24th, 1861, was muftered Firft Lieutenant "K" company, 6th Pennfylvania Cavalry, and ferved with the regiment until April, 1862. On the 14th April, 1862, was commiffioned Captain in the Adjutant General's Department, and ferved with General Ricketts's Divifion at Cedar Mountain, Rappahannock Station, Thoroughfare Gap, and Bull Run No. 2. Served as aid to General Meade, then commanding 2d Divifion, 1ft Corps, Army of the Potomac, at South Mountain and Antietam, and at Chancellorfville and Gettyfburg with General Sykes, commanding 5th Corps. Refigned July 30th, 1863.

W. W. Frazier, Jr., joined the regiment as Second Lieutenant of "B" company, and was fo muftered, September 3d, 1861. Acted as regimental commiffary at Camp Barclay in the winter of 1861–62. March 26th, 1862, promoted and muftered Firft Lieutenant and Adjutant, *vice* Newhall, promoted Captain "K" company. Promoted and muftered Captain "B" company in November, 1862. Served faithfully with the regiment until February 22d, 1864, when private affairs compelled him to refign.

Emlen M. Carpenter ferved in the three months' campaign of 1861, as a private in the 1ft Troop Philadelphia City Cavalry, attached to General Patterfon's command. Joined the 6th Pennfylvania Cavalry as Second Lieutenant of "D" company, and was so mustered 1864. on the 13th September, 1861. Promoted and mustered First Lieutenant, June 22d, 1862. Detached as special aid to General Franklin at the first battle of Fredericksburg; rejoined his command after that engagement. Promoted Captain of "E" company, *vice* Hazleton promoted, February 5th, 1863. In March, 1863, his company was detached with "I" company, forming Captain Starr's squadron, as body guard to Major-General Hooker, then commanding the Army of the Potomac. Served in this capacity at the battle of Chancellorsville, and did efficient service in assisting to check the rout of the 11th Corps in that engagement. On the night of the 17th of June, 1863, accompanied Captain Starr and 12 picked men from their squadron, carrying despatches from General Hooker at Fairfax Courthouse to General Pleasanton at Aldie, and served on the staff of the latter at the battle of Upperville on the next day. Served on the staff of General Meade at Gettysburg. Rejoined the regiment October 17th, 1863, and served with it until the 7th May, 1864, when he was taken prisoner at the fight at Todd's Tavern.

Captain Carpenter was incarcerated in Libby until the end of May, and was then shipped by rail to Macon, Georgia, where he met his brother, a prisoner since Gettysburg. About the end of July, 1864, he was shipped by rail for Charleston. Before reaching Charleston, he escaped by jumping from the cars, and got within five miles of the Union lines, when he was hunted down by bloodhounds and recaptured. He was then taken to Charleston and thrust into jail, from whence, after three weeks of ter-

1864. rible suffering, he was sent to Roper Hospital. Yellow fever breaking out among the prisoners on the 5th of October, 1864, they were shipped by rail for Columbia, S. C. Near Orangeburg, Captain Carpenter, this time accompanied by his brother, again succeeded in escaping by jumping from the cars, and set out for East Tennessee. After many trials they were tracked by the hounds and recaptured in a swamp and taken to Columbia. December 12th, the prisoners were moved from the camp outside of the town to the Insane Asylum and located in the yard of that institution. Learning the approach of General Sherman, Captain Carpenter and a few others cut holes with a saw-knife in the wooden ceiling of a frame building in the yard, and when the prisoners were removed they concealed themselves between the ceiling and roof. From this retreat they were driven by the firing of the buildings by the departing rebels, and Captain Carpenter succeeded in getting concealment from a lady in the town, who hid him in her cellar; next day at daylight a negro took him to an empty house next door, from which in a few hours he saw the glorious sight of Sherman's column advancing into the town, and his deliverance was completed. In a few moments he met the head of the column, and was recognized by a friend on General Sherman's staff. Being ordered to report to General Howard, he was at once taken into his military family, appointed an aid, and completely re-equipped by the generous staff of the General. Captain Carpenter served with General Howard through the Carolina campaign, and soon after the entry into Fayetteville obtained leave of absence. Captain Carpenter would have been entitled to the rank of 1864. Lieutenant-Colonel in his regiment had he been with it in the fall and winter of 1864, when it was reorganized. He was honourably difcharged May 15th, 1865. He has fince received two brevets, one as Major, "for gallant and meritorious fervices at the battle of Gettyfburg," the other as Lieutenant-Colonel, "for gallant and meritorious fervices at the battle of Todd's Tavern, Virginia," both dated March 13th, 1865.

J. Newton Dickfon, a graduate of Princeton College, ferved in the three months' campaign of 1861, as corporal in the "Commonwealth Artillery," a Philadelphia organization. Entered the 6th Pennfylvania Cavalry as Second Lieutenant of "A" company, and was fo muftered, October 4th, 1861. Promoted and muftered Firft Lieutenant, April 8th, 1862. Promoted and muftered as Captain of Company "C," on the 10th of February, 1863, and was difcharged on furgeon's certificate of difability, January 20th, 1864. Held a commiffion as Second Lieutenant in the 3d U. S. Artillery during his connection with the regiment.

J. Hinckley Clark ferved as private in the "Commonwealth Artillery," in the fpring of 1861. Joined the 6th Pennfylvania Cavalry as Second Lieutenant of Company "F," and was muftered, October 4th, 1861. Promoted and muftered as Firft Lieutenant "K" company, April 19th, 1862, and as Captain of Company "M," March 16th, 1863. Transferred to "C" company, by fpecial order No. 38, September 18th, 1864, Headquarters Middle Military Divifion, and muftered out, September 19th, 1864, with that company. Cap-

1864. tain Clark served faithfully with the regiment in all its campaigns and battles, and has received two brevets, one as Major U. S. Volunteers, March 13th, 1865, "for gallant and meritorious services at the battle of Gettysburg," the other as Lieutenant-Colonel, of the same date, "for gallant and meritorious services in the campaigns from the Rapidan to the James."

William B. Call joined the regiment as Second Lieutenant Company "G," and was mustered, August 8th, 1861. Resigned November 29th, 1861.

Frank H. Furness assisted in recruiting company "I," and was mustered Second Lieutenant, October 14th, 1861. Promoted and mustered First Lieutenant "I" company April, 1862. At the organization of the Cavalry Corps by General Hooker, in the spring of 1863, Lieutenant Furness was ordered to the staff of General Stoneman, and served with the Cavalry Corps as aide-de-camp until after the battle of Gettysburg, when he rejoined the regiment and was promoted Captain of "F" company, with which he served until mustered out with it, October 4th, 1864.

Henry Winser, Jr., enlisted in "I" company on the 14th October, 1861. Promoted and mustered Second Lieutenant "G" company, November 29th, 1861, *vice* W. B. Call resigned. Promoted and mustered First Lieutenant "H" company, June, 1862. Appointed and mustered as Regimental Commissary, February 10th, 1863. Promoted and commissioned Captain of "G" company, April 4th, 1863. October 18th, 1863, ordered to Headquarters 1st Cavalry Division, where he ferved until Auguft, 1864, when he refigned on account of difability. 1864.

Albert P. Morrow, whofe promotions as far as Firft Lieutenant, have been already mentioned, was promoted and commiffioned Captain " C" company, January 18th, 1864.

Samuel Smith, who enlifted in "B" company, in 1861, and ferved as Firft Sergeant of that company, was promoted to Second Lieutenant, his commiffion bearing date April 8th, 1862. Commiffioned Firft Lieutenant, February 10th, 1863, and in the fall of the fame year refigned on account of difability, caufed by the fervice.

John W. Riddle enlifted in "D" company in 1861, and ferved as Firft Sergeant of that company until April 15th, 1862, when he was commiffioned Second Lieutenant. Commiffioned Firft Lieutenant November 1, 1862, and refigned June 4th, 1863, on account of difability.

Ofgood Welfh ferved in the three months' campaign of 1861, in the 1ft Troop Philadelphia City Cavalry. Joined the regiment as Second Lieutenant of Company "G," and was fo commiffioned Auguft 14th, 1862. Honourably difcharged September 19th, 1863.

William White, a graduate of the Univerfity of Pennfylvania, ferved in "F" company, 17th Pennfylvania Infantry (Wafhington Grays), as private, in the three months' campaign of 1861. Joined the 6th Pennfylvania Cavalry as Second Lieutenant of "D" company, and was fo muftered, November 20th, 1862. Promoted and muftered Firft Lieutenant of "D" com-

1864. pany, November, 1863. Promoted and muſtered Captain of "H" company, April 11th, 1864, and was muſtered out with "H" company, October 11th, 1864, by reaſon of expiration of term of ſervice.

Rudolph Ellis ſerved with the 1ſt Troop Philadelphia City Cavalry, in the three months' campaign of 1861. Joined the regiment as Adjutant, and was ſo muſtered, November 20th, 1862, at Frederick City, Maryland. Promoted and muſtered Captain, April 11th, 1864, at Culpepper, Virginia. April 22d, 1864, ordered to report with his company to General Torbett, commanding 1ſt Cavalry Diviſion, and ſerved on his ſtaff as aid until 20th Auguſt, 1864, when he was appointed Aſſiſtant Inſpector General on the ſame ſtaff; ſerved in that poſition until December 28th, 1864, when he reſigned.

Thomas J. Gregg was commiſſioned Second Lieutenant of "F" company, November 1ſt, 1862. On the 3d June, 1863, he was ordered to the ſtaff of his brother, General D. M. Gregg, commanding 2d Cavalry Diviſion, and ſerved with him throughout the war.

Thompſon Lennig enliſted in the 6th Pennſylvania Cavalry on the 13th September, 1862, and was muſtered Second Lieutenant of "M" company, November 20th, 1862. Was honourably mentioned by General Buford, for ſpecial ſervice rendered on Stoneman's raid. At the fight at Beverly Ford had two horſes killed under him, and he was taken priſoner. Was exchanged in the ſpring of 1864, after an impriſonment of nine months in Libby, which ſo injured his health that he was forced to reſign April 11th, 1864.

RECORD OF OFFICERS.

Samuel R. Colladay, who enlifted in the regiment in 1864. 1861, was promoted to Second Lieutenant, and fo commiffioned, January 30th, 1863. He was taken prifoner, as before ftated, at Beverly Ford, June 9th, 1863. November 1ft, 1863, he was commiffioned Firft Lieutenant. He was fo debilitated by his fufferings as a prifoner, that when liberated he was not able to endure the rigours of fervice, and was forced to refign June 3d, 1864. He rejoined the regiment when it was reorganized in 1865, as Captain of Company " E."

John Hendricks enlifted in "E" company in 1861. Was commiffioned Second Lieutenant, November 1ft, 1862. Commiffioned Firft Lieutenant " H" company, February 10th, 1863. Refigned in the autumn of 1863.

William Sproul enlifted in " F" company, and ferved as its Firft Sergeant until April 1ft, 1863, when he was commiffioned Second Lieutenant. Died at Bell Plain, Virginia, May 8th, 1863, of difeafe contracted in fervice.

Theodore J. Wint enlifted in " F" company in 1861. Was commiffioned Firft Lieutenant, June 22d, 1864. Muftered out with " F" company in October, 1864. Has fince been appointed Firft Lieutenant in the U. S. Cavalry.

Michael Towers enlifted in " I" company in 1861. Was commiffioned Firft Lieutenant of " D" company, March 25th, 1864, and muftered out in September, 1864.

G. A. Priefen was commiffioned Affiftant-Surgeon, Auguft 1ft, 1861. Joined the regiment, after the feven

1864. days' fight, at Harrifon's Bar, July, 1862. Refigned October 10th, 1862, by reafon of difability.

George S. Engler was commiffioned Affiftant-Surgeon, March 17th, 1863. Was obliged to leave the field in the fpring of 1864, on account of difability, and refigned in the fummer of the fame year.

The following are the records of thofe officers who were not muftered out with the original regiment, but who remained in fervice with the regiment when reorganized, and whofe records have been omitted.

Charles B. Coxe, muftered Captain "K" company, July 19th, 1864.

Richard M. Sheppard enlifted in "A" company in 1861. Was commiffioned Second Lieutenant, February 10th, 1863. Commiffioned Regimental Quartermafter, November 25th, 1863.

Philip H. Ellis, Jr., enlifted in "B" company in 1863. Commiffioned Second Lieutenant, April 4th, 1863. Promoted and commiffioned Firft Lieutenant, Auguft 13th, 1863.

Archer Maris, promoted and muftered Firft Lieutenant, April 1ft, 1864. Served on the ftaff of the Cavalry Referve Brigade from November 7th, 1863, to November, 1864, when he rejoined the regiment.

Abraham D. Price, promoted and commiffioned Firft Lieutenant "I" company, March 16th, 1863. Promoted and commiffioned Captain "I" company, March 19th, 1864.

Bernard H. Herknefs, promoted and commiffioned Firft Lieutenant, January 18th, 1864.

Edward J. Hazel was promoted from the ranks and 1864. commiſſioned Firſt Lieutenant, March 19th, 1864.

Iſaac T. Moffat enliſted in "H" company in 1861. Was promoted and commiſſioned Firſt Lieutenant, July 19th, 1864.

Lewis Miller, Jr., was promoted from the ranks and commiſſioned Firſt Lieutenant, June 22d, 1864.

James H. Workman enliſted in "H" company in 1861. Was promoted and commiſſioned Firſt Lieutenant, June 22d, 1864.

Rev. S. Levis Gracey ſerved faithfully with the regiment in all its marches, raids, and fights, until the ſpring of 1864, when he was aſſigned to duty as Poſt Chaplain at the priſon camp at Rock Iſland, Illinois, where he remained until the ſummer of 1865, when he rejoined the regiment, and was muſtered out with it, Auguſt 7th, 1865.

CHAPTER TWENTY-SEVENTH.

Winter Operations of the Army—The Beginning of the End —Destruction on James River—Last of Jubal Early— Charlottesville—Duguidsville—Amherst Courthouse—Arrival at White House—Rejoining the Army of the Potomac.

1864.   DURING the winter of 1864-65, active operations of great importance were pushed forward in other parts of the immense field covered by the armies. General Sherman, with his army in splendid fighting trim,
Nov 14th. left Atlanta on the 14th of November, to "move through Georgia, smashing things, to the sea," as he expressed the object of his expedition, when proposing it to General Grant. He emerged from the cloud that enveloped his operations, at Fort McAllister, on the Georgia coast, and occupied Savannah on the 21st of December.

Dec. 15th.   On the 15th of December, General Thomas, after a two days' battle, near Nashville, completely "used up" Hood's army, driving it from the field in utter confusion, and taking many thousand prisoners, including four general officers.

Dec. 25th.   On Christmas Day, an attempt was made at Fort Fisher, in North Carolina, by General Butler, but was such a wretched failure that no officer has yet been found to bear its responsibility. A second expedition

GENERAL OPERATIONS.

was, however, at once fitted out, which reached its def- 1865.
tination on the 13th of January, 1865. On the day Jan. 13th.
fucceeding, a reconnoiffance was pufhed up to within
500 yards of the Fort, and on the 15th it was taken by Jan. 15th.
affault, with its entire garrifon and armament, after the
moft defperate fighting.

Although it is not within the fcope of the hiftory of
a fingle regiment to detail the operations of our immenfe
army, yet this brief outline is in fome fort neceffary to
enable us to underftand the pofition of affairs at the
opening of the fpring.

During the month of January our regiment was increafed by the addition of about 100 recruits, and on the
26th of that month was relieved at Hagerftown, where Jan. 26th.
it had been in winter quarters fince November 16th, by
the 2d U. S. Cavalry.

On the 28th, we rejoined our brigade, near Winchef- Jan. 28th.
ter, and fet to work in the beft of fpirits to prepare our
fecond fet of winter quarters, in which we remained
comfortably until the 27th of February.

While in this camp our number was increafed by the
arrival of 800 recruits, by fpecial favour of General
Sheridan, and on the 10th of February, Major Leiper
was muftered as Lieutenant-Colonel, and Captain Morrow as Major.

On the 20th of that month Sheridan received the following inftructions from General Grant:

"As foon as it is poffible to travel, I think you will
have no difficulty about reaching Lynchburg with a cavalry force alone. From there you could deftroy the
railroad and canal in every direction, fo as to be of no

1865. further use to the rebellion. Sufficient cavalry should be left behind to look after Moseby's gang. From Lynchburg, if information you might get there would justify it, you could strike south, heading the streams in Virginia to the westward of Danville, and push on to join Sherman," who had been marching northward, "smashing things" in the Carolinas.

The final campaign against the Confederacy was opened when Sheridan broke camp near Winchester, and set out with his troopers in accordance with the instructions he had received from General Grant.

Feb. 27th. In the gray dawn of the 27th, we left Winchester, Major Morrow in command, with the 1st Cavalry Division, under General Merritt, the 3d Division, under General Custer, and one brigade of the old army of Western Virginia, under Colonel Capehart, and two sections of artillery.

For several days the roads had been in process of preparation for a soft, if not an easy, march, by a continuous fall of rain, which also melted the snow on the mountains, swelling the streams in the valleys until they were almost impassable.

We had an excellent turnpike road to favour our advance, and pushed rapidly forward with the advance brigade through Middletown, Strasburg, and Woodstock to Edinburg, doing a march of thirty-five miles, a good old Virginia storm beating down on us all day, by way of keeping up our spirits. The enemy were in front of us in small force during the day.

Feb. 28th. At 4 o'clock the next morning, we took up our march for Mount Jackson, skirmishing all the way with a small force of the enemy, and the ufual rain. At Mount 1865. Jackfon we croffed the North Fork of the Shenandoah, which, by this time, was in a fearful ftate, between the melting fnow of the mountain and the rain of the valley. Here feven troopers were drowned in croffing, including one of our own men. After croffing we rode through New Market to Sparta, where we got about two hours' fleep.

The following day we marched about thirty miles, Mar. 1ft. and encamped within a few miles of Staunton. While we refted that night, General Devin was fent with his brigade through Staunton on a reconnoiffance. The night was very dark, and of courfe it was ftill raining. They pitched through the pickets of the enemy and advanced through the town to Chriftian's Creek, feven miles beyond it, where they deftroyed a treftle bridge of the Virginia Central Railroad, and returned, joining the column at Staunton.

On the 2d, we marched in the rear of the wagon Mar. 2d. train through Staunton to Fifherfville, where we found it raining, as it had been all the day.

At Fifherfville, Cufter having the advance, ftruck the rebel pickets, and drove them upon their main force, which was forced back to Waynefboro. On the arrival of our entire force, a reconnoiffance developed the enemy advantageoufly pofted on a range of hills fkirting South River, with feven pieces of artillery, in moft provokingly good pofition—for the enemy.

Two regiments were immediately deployed as fkirmifhers, and advanced, firing brifkly; they were foon joined by the entire line in an impetuous charge upon the

1865.
Mar. 2d.
enemy's pofition. They held the line only long enough to deliver a fingle volley, when they fled precipitately; but in their efforts to efcape, they met with flight impediments in every direction; the "Yanks" were everywhere, and they were "bagged." This being an operation of which we had heard much in the early part of the war, but not much practifed until 1864-65.

General Early, placing a proper eftimate upon the value of his perfonal fervices to the Confederacy, thought it prudent to abfent himfelf from his command about this time, and haftened off to Charlottefville ("to rejoin his command"), and what became of him for the next three months "nobody knows and nobody cares."

In this engagement we captured eleven guns, two hundred wagons and teams, feventeen battle flags, and fixteen hundred prifoners, all of which were fent back to Winchefter.

General Cufter's three brigades purfued the ftraggling rebels; Capehart's brigade, croffing the South River, marched to Greenwood Station, where a large depot was deftroyed, and a train of wagons filled with commiffary ftores and ordnance fupplies; fix pieces of artillery alfo fell into his hands; the guns were fpiked; the gun carriages, and all the wagons, ambulances, and ftores were burned. Completing their work of deftruction, they pufhed on rapidly to Charlottefville, which they occupied on the 3d of March.

Mar. 3d.
We had not the pleafure of affifting at this fight, but when we reached Waynefboro on the 3d, we amufed ourfelves by deftroying the iron railroad bridge over the South River, and making a fire with a hundred or fo of

the wagons which Cuſter had captured. We croſſed 1865. the South River during the night, marched through Rockfiſh Gap, and went into camp a little before daylight on the 4th.

On the 4th we left camp at 9 o'clock in the morning, and had another tedious march, in the rear of the wagon train, to Ivy Hill, and on the 5th reached Charlotteſville, where we went into camp, and drew our ſcanty rations.   Mar. 4th.

At Charlotteſville, General Sheridan divided his force into two columns; ours, under command of General Merritt, proceeded to Scottſville, on the James River. Here we were detailed to deſtroy the aqueduct, about ten miles down the river; but on reaching it we found it to be built of heavy ſtone, and as we had nothing but our finger nails and carbines to work with, we ſpared the ſtructure, but burnt four canal-boats and deſtroyed three locks before returning to Scottſville.   Mar. 6th.

We marched the next day along the James River Canal, cutting its banks in every available place, and deſtroying all the locks and boats as we paſſed. At New Market the column was halted, and we were ſent twelve miles up the river to Duguidſville, to try and ſave the bridge over the James River at that place, but we found the enemy had deſtroyed it before we arrived.   Mar. 7th.

We remained here until the next day, when the reſt of the column came up and joined us, and we marched back to New Market—through the rain, of courſe.   Mar. 8th.

The other column, under General Cuſter, which we left at Charlotteſville, in the meantime had proceeded down the Lynchburg Railroad, deſtroying the road as far

1865.   as Amherſt Courthouſe, ſixteen miles from Lynchburg,
Mar. 8th. and then joined us at New Market.

   At this place General Sheridan had determined to croſs the river and move rapidly to the Southſide road at Farmville, intending to deſtroy it towards Appomattox Courthouſe. But the river was very high, and the pontoon bridge not long enough to reach acroſs, and as time was valuable, he decided to move down the left bank, and "ſtrike a baſe at the White Houſe." So, on the 9th we marched down the canal, through Warren and Scottſville, to Columbia, which place we reached on the 10th, *en paſſant* ſtopping at Rockfiſh River to blow up the bank of the canal, and at New Canton to deſtroy the guard lock. This let the James River into the canal, changing its ſluggiſh flood to a torrent, which ſwept away the banks in many places, rendering it ſomewhat inconvenient as a medium of tranſportation.

Mar. 11th.   On the 11th, we croſſed the Rivanna River, by the aqueduct, and on the 12th ſtruck acroſs the country to near Louiſa Courthouſe, on the Virginia Central Railroad, where we picketed during the night.

Mar. 13th.   The next day we devoted to deſtroying the Virginia Central Railroad from Tolerſville to Frederick's Hall Station, and on the 14th marched to Taylorſville on the Richmond and Potomac Railroad, and deſtroyed the treſtle bridge over the South Anna River at that point.

Mar. 15th.   The following day, anticipating an attack by Pickett's Diviſion of rebel infantry, we threw up a line of fence-rail breaſtworks, but after waiting in vain for them all day, towards evening we moved acroſs the North Anna River at Oxford, where we went into camp.

WHITE HOUSE.

We marched on the 16th to Monangohick Church, one of our foraging parties being attacked during the march, and one man being killed and feveral captured. The next night we camped at King William Courthoufe, and on the 18th, reached the Pamunkey, at White Houfe, where we found an infantry force, which had been fent on the 12th, by General Grant, to that place in anticipation of our coming. 1865. Mar. 16th.

Here we had a good reft of five days to prepare for the tough work that awaited us on the fouth fide of the James. The expedition had been eminently fuccefsful, and had been accomplifhed with but flight lofs to our force, and great lofs to the enemy in the fhape of canals and railroads. Mar. 19th.

From the White Houfe Captain Coxe was granted leave of abfence, on account of ficknefs, and, while abfent, received his commiffion as Major of the regiment, and was muftered in as fuch on the 21ft of March.

On the 25th, we left White Houfe, to join the Army of the Potomac in front of Peterfburg, where we were joined by Lieutenant-Colonel Leiper, who refumed command of the regiment, and the regiment being entitled to a full field and ftaff, he was then muftered as Colonel, Major Morrow as Lieutenant-Colonel, and Captains A. D. Price and B. H. Herknefs as Majors. Mar. 25th.

CHAPTER TWENTY-EIGHTH.

Reconnoiſſance toward Five Forks—Charge of the Regiment—Dinwiddie Courthouſe—Five Forks—Laſt Fight of the Regiment.

1865.
Mar. 26th.

ON the 26th of March, we croſſed the river James by a wooden bridge, above City Point, and entered again into the domain of General Lee; for it can hardly be ſaid that we were in his domain before we croſſed the river, as we held almoſt undiſputed poſſeſſion of the country through which we had raided. But the mere occupancy of territory was not our aim, though it is undoubtedly pleaſant to roam at will over an enemy's country; ſo we paſſed on to new fields gladly enough, being confident now that the ſun of the Confederacy was about to ſet, and we hoped to have our ſtandard gilded by its laſt declining rays.

The river was gay with tranſports and iron-clads and all ſorts of water-craft, whoſe colors were ſtreaming in the wind; and the wind was a gale, by the way: you could "lean your back againſt it like a poſt." The monitors were formed in a ſort of naval cloſe-column, and, pointing their ſharp prows toward Richmond, kept a keen look-out with their turret-eyes upon the hilly battlements beyond, which, on either bank of the James, ſtood ready to bar the road to the Capital with their plunging fire. Every now and then, as if to give warning, theſe would ſpeak in dull, land-muffled roar, and the echo would be buffeted from ſhore to ſhore until it died away in Richmond.

1865.
Mar. 26th.

On the north bank of the James we left Butler's army, whoſe coloured troops looked ſtrange to us who had been fighting only among ſun-burned white men; and on the ſouth bank we found the long-extended lines of the Army of the Potomac, each army being confronted by heavy fortifications and ſuch force as the laſt efforts of the Confederacy had been able to gather together. In all the camps there was a buſy air of preparation, and even inanimate things had caught the ſpirit of reſtleſſneſs peculiar to the moment. Nobody could doubt it who ſaw the tents flap their white wings, as if angry at the long reſtraint. They ſeemed to have caught the univerſal feeling: Lee was to be vanquiſhed, his army to be broken up or captured; then why delay? Everybody was afraid that Lee would eſcape, ſteal away in the night and be far on his road to North Carolina before we could let ſlip our forces in purſuit; and ſo the army was ſtraining at its leaſhes, eager to cloſe with the enemy before he ſhould break out of the lethargy which ſeemed juſt then to enthrall him. The cavalry of General Sheridan, freſh from ſucceſsful campaigning, was not the leaſt confident of ſpeedy victory; and on the 27th we moved to the left of the Army of the Potomac, to be ready for a burſt into the enemy's country when the commanding General ſhould give the ſignal for the combat to begin.

Mar. 27th.

1865. Meanwhile our regiment was getting ready for the fray as beſt it could. We were not very ſtrong, except in faith and ſelf-reliance, only 100 men being found to
Mar. 29th. ſtand to horſe on the morning of the 29th, when, at the founding of "the general," we fell in and waited for the order to march. But this ſmall number was mainly owing to the dearth of horſes, for at diſmounted camps we had plenty of men, and we might have ſhown a ſtrong front ſtill if horſes could bear the work which our cavalry had been called upon to do. A man may ride from Wincheſter to Peterſburg, through rain and mud and cold, and get little to eat and little ſleep, and yet not ſuffer in health very much: after one ample dinner and one good night's reſt, he will very likely be getting uneaſy and bored with the quiet life, and be longing for more rides. But the horſe that carries him on the trip is apt to reach his journey's end in pitiable plight. Hunger and cold have ſtarved him, pitileſs rain has pelted him, deepening mud has mired and tired him. His back has been galled with pinching ſaddle or frozen blanket; he is leg-weary and foot-ſore; decrepitude is in his gait and dejection in his eye; great ſcars are ſcalded on his weather-beaten front, and on his ribs and rump famine might hang her banner. Some indomitable wills bear up through it all, though, and theſe deſerve to be rewarded of their country, for they rendered poſſible the deeds of Sheridan's cavalry. To this brave hundred of ours, then, let us affectionately look back, for they breaſted many waves of trouble and outrode many ſtorms. They winced a little as they were mounted, perhaps, but ſoon ſtood firm on their legs again, and ſet

out cheerily with the column which General Sheridan was leading to new and final glories.

1865.
Mar. 29th.

He had been ordered by General Grant to get out to the enemy's right and rear, without confining himself to any particular road or roads; and so he rode as the crow flies and we all followed, straining through the crusted muck of the open fields. The command consisted of the cavalry from the Shenandoah Valley, under General Merritt, Custer and Devin commanding the divisions, and of General Gregg's old division, now commanded by Major-General Crook: in all, 9000 effective mounted men; and it seemed almost as if the 6th Pennsylvania Cavalry might be crunched under foot by that struggling multitude, and never be missed. After a while we got upon a road at Reims's Station, on the Weldon Railroad. Here there had been repeated fighting, and all the region round about was seamed with the scars of it. Massive lines of earth-works stood out like veins on the face of the country, and in so many directions did they run that the fortune of war seemed to have boxed the compass. Mementoes of battle lay scattered about, here a broken musket, there a ruined caisson; through the empty window-frames of the few buildings there, the wind whistled plaintively; the 5th Army Corps, with grim humor, had left its mark in iron badges wrought of the rails of the Weldon road; ruin and desolation everywhere. Beyond the railroad we crossed the Rowanty Creek, after the head of our column had repaired the bridge and given chase to a party of rebel cavalry who had destroyed it, and so passed on to Dinwiddie Courthouse, where another little picket

1865.
Mar. 29th.
party of the enemy fired a few shots at us before galloping away to report our sudden coming. Here the cavalry went into camp on the various roads which radiate from the Courthouse, and a part of our regiment went on picket for the night. Everything was quiet, and sleep in camp would not have been disturbed if rain had not poured down so violently.

Off on our left flank, across Stony Creek, the enemy's cavalry was known to be moving to get between us and the Southside Railroad, which we threatened by our movement to Dinwiddie; but this hostile force was intent upon getting into position rather than encountering us just then. From Dinwiddie Courthouse there is the Boydton Plankroad leading to Petersburg, distant some fifteen miles; a dirt road leads to the Southside Railroad by way of Five Forks, on the White Oak Road; another road runs in the same direction across Chamberlaine's Bed, a small stream winding about Dinwiddie; and two or three avenues, of more or less importance, diverge from these. Toward the James River there are two main roads; and the Boydton Plank of course pursues its way to Boydton, seventy miles or so from Petersburg, southerly. These roads made Dinwiddie Courthouse an important point in a military view (it is a poor affair of a town), and we all knew well that night, that, early in the morning, we might look for something to do. It was only a question of time. As soon as the enemy in strong force should get across our path to the Southside Railroad, we might expect to hear of him. Our regiment was on the road to Five Forks, through which we must pass to gain the railroad. We were in the extreme advance of General Merritt's com- 1865. mand, and therefore the nearest to the Forks, the point that the enemy must hold to protect the Southside Railroad, and to guard the right flank and rear of Lee's army covering Petersburg. Here, then, it was evident, the fight would be hottest, if there were any fight at all.

When the morning of the 30th broke, it was dismal Mar. 30th. and gloomy enough in the pine woods, where we camped and picketed. The rain came down relentlessly, and the loamy soil was frail and porous as a honeycomb; the horses crushed it under their feet and seemed hardly to find a footing anywhere. But about 9 o'clock an aid of General Sheridan came to General Merritt to order a reconnoissance toward the Forks. General Merritt's map was almost ruined by water before he had glanced at the geography of the position, and then he started us forward through the storm to find the enemy. In front of us a stream, called Gravelly Run, dashed across the road, too large for its bed, since the rain had swollen it, and soon after we had waded through it and deployed into line, we encountered a small brigade of rebel cavalry, lying quiet in the woods. The enemy was in our front, then, and we were to have the honour of opening the campaign. Colonel Leiper immediately advanced his men, and rapid firing at once ensued, and was sustained until we drew close to the opposing force, when prudence called for a halt for assistance, the enemy greatly outnumbering us. Soon the 2d Massachusetts came up, and then the 1st United States and 7th Michigan regiments, and, as soon as they had formed, Colonel Leiper, in command of this impromptu brigade,

1865. advanced again, this time with confidence, and by a sudden charge, scattered the enemy's troops, who fled away toward Five Forks, and took refuge behind some infantry rifle-pits, which were seen to be briftling with the muskets of a strong force posted there. Obviously our men could do nothing more, and so we were withdrawn, without moleftation, and refumed our several places behind Gravelly Run. In the fight we killed and captured forty of the enemy, and loft but a few wounded ourfelves. It was a horrid day, and enough of itfelf to quench the ardour of anybody, but the men behaved in the moft fpirited way, and Colonel Leiper added a frefh leaf to his laurels, and was brevetted a Brigadier-General for his conduct and good management on the field. In the afternoon there was a little fkirmifh on our left, where our regiment joined Colonel Fitzhugh of the 6th New York, but it did not amount to much; and when the miferable evening fell, we very uncomfortably went into camp to find rations all foaked, and blankets all wet, and spongy beds under leaking fhelters. Those who had the heart to whiftle, whiftled " Home, fweet Home," and the reft of us lay ftill under the trickling canvas, hungry, cold, and tired, coveting our neighbour's houfe.

Mar. 31ft. Before morning the rain ceafed, and we got an early breakfaft, to be ready for fuch events as daylight might ufher in. It was likely to be a campaign of fudden moves on both fides, and we were not going to be caught napping if we could help it; the enemy might expect to find us up and dreffed at almoft any hour of the morning. More reconnoiffances were ordered for this day, and this time General Devin went to the front with

Fitzhugh's brigade, and repeated our experience of the day before, except that he was not allowed to retire unmolefted. The enemy's cavalry had early attacked Crook's Divifion in front of Dinwiddie Courthoufe, on our left, and had been repulfed; then they moved up toward Five Forks, and, uniting with their infantry troops (two divifions of Anderfon's Corps), preffed back Davies's brigade from Crook's extreme right, and foon got upon the flank of Devin and Fitzhugh, bearing Davies before them. Meanwhile our brigade had been withdrawn to a fork of the Five Forks Road, nearer to Dinwiddie, and here we ftood to horfe, while the events juft defcribed were progreffing; and, as the country was denfely wooded, we were utterly ignorant of what had been done or how our troops in front were faring. The point where we ftood was admirably adapted for a force in referve, as ours was, for the right or left of the main line could from here be promptly reinforced by us as occafion fhould require. From the firing we heard and from the general afpect of things about us, it was now eafy to be feen that our turn would be foon; and perhaps each one of us was fpeculating as to whence the call for help would come, when a ftaff officer of General Sheridan rode rapidly into the thicket where we were, and faid a few words hurriedly to General Gibbs, commanding our brigade. No more fpeculations, then, and no longer to wait. *Prepare to mount! Mount!* and then *Forward!* There was good caufe to hurry, for we happened to be ftanding on the threfhold of a crifis. Davies and Devin had been pufhed back from the Five Forks Road altogether, and were now making the beft

1865.
Mar. 31ft.

1865.
Mar. 31st.
fight they could, as they fell flowly back to the Boydton Plankroad on our right and rear. The enemy was purfuing with heavy lines of infantry, and by his fuccefs had made a great gap in General Sheridan's line, entirely ifolating Devin and Davies from the two brigades of Crook's Divifion on the left. Into this gap the enemy had boldly pufhed, and were now feeking to break up our force, and drive us away from Dinwiddie, and fend us reeling back upon the left of the Army of the Potomac. They were making good headway, they thought, in this intent, when we were ordered to the refcue. They were fweeping acrofs the Five Forks Road directly in our front, when General Sheridan's aid rode up to General Gibbs, and were prefling hard upon Devin and Davies. As we moved forward we took the trot and foon reached the Dinwiddie Road, where we were ftopped by a fence and thick woods beyond, quite impaffable for horfes. We quickly difmounted, to fight on foot, while the tramp of the enemy's troops through the undergrowth could be plainly heard, and before we got over the fence we could fee that the woods were gray with them. They faw us, too, juft then, and halted to look to this new and unexpected enemy, and foon volley was anfwering volley, and we found ourfelves hotly engaged with fome of Lee's beft infantry. There had been a time in the war when this fort of unequal fight would have been confidered madnefs for cavalry to enter upon, but now the troopers made it a rule to engage whatever oppofed; and fo we mounted the fence and went into the woods with a will, making the beft of the advantage we had in the furprife and confufion which

for a moment ſtaggered the enemy's lines. As we drew nearer they turned and confronted us, and the fight waxed hot all along the front of our brigade. Almoſt the firſt to fall in our regiment was Lieutenant-Colonel Morrow, who was badly ſhot in the thigh, as he was leading on the men with that remarkable coolneſs and courage of his which no emergency could ruffle or diſmay. A good many men were hit, and it was too one-ſided a thing to laſt long, after the enemy became ſteady and turned his whole attention to our attack; and we muſt have been driven ſpeedily back to our horſes but for the timely reinforcement of Gregg's Brigade of Crook's Diviſion, which had been holding the croſſings of Chamberlaine's Bed, on our left, and now moved up and joined us. Between our two brigades the rebels were then kept buſy for a little while, but we were ſtill too weak to do more than divert them from Davies and Devin, who now, entirely relieved, got together their troops as ſoon as they could, and marched down to Dinwiddie by the Boydton Plankroad. Fortunately for us the enemy's lines now moved away from our front and felt to their right towards Chamberlaine's Bed, to ſee if there were not ſtill lying there a reſting brigade or two that might be ſent to take them in flank as ours had done. They had not far to go before they found Smith, of Crook's Diviſion, and with his freſh and capital brigade they had a deſperate ſtruggle before they drove it back toward Dinwiddie; and meantime Gregg's Brigade and ours aided Smith as much as poſſible, by moving along parallel with the enemy and annoying their flank with a conſtant and heavy fire. When Smith was com-

1865.
Mar. 31st.

pelled to give way he took post on the high, clear ground in front of Dinwiddie, where one of Custer's brigades had already established itself behind some rude works of fence rails.

General Custer had been in charge of the wagon trains all this time, which were hopelessly fast in the mud about Reims's Station, and his troops had been sent for by General Sheridan, late in the day, to take part in the final scene about Dinwiddie Courthouse. We ranged ourselves now on the right of Gregg, Custer and Smith prolonging the line on the left; and here was a fair field and no favour, and the enemy might get Dinwiddie if he could. Evidently he was about to try, for, after reforming in the low grounds where Smith had been fighting, his lines emerged from the woods and began to ascend the slope, on the top of which our troops awaited him. At this moment another of Custer's brigades reached the front, and came trotting over to us with ringing cheers. Davies and Devin had not come yet, and so five dismounted brigades of cavalry were now to withstand the onset of two divisions of infantry, or be swept back in disorder and defeat. Some rebel cavalry there was, too, but not of much avail; and it was soon put out of the contest. Just as the enemy's infantry came into view, a sudden charge of their horsemen was made from Chamberlaine's Bed to the open ground in front of Gregg and Custer, on our left, and, while we wondered at this bold dash, those who made it were staggered and blinded by the hot fire which met them, and in an instant they had scattered in every direction, in the utmost rout and panic.

It was twilight, and almost dark, when the advancing 1865. infantry line fired its first shot, the flash twinkling like Mar. 31st. a spark in the edge of the woods. Generals Sheridan, Merritt, and Custer, with some staff officers, rode up the line as the bullets began to hiss, and with cheers and shouts our men braced themselves for the encounter, and poured forth a rattling welcome to the oncoming enemy, the guns of our artillery joining in the chorus of our volleys. It was soon too dark to see far, but we all grew conscious that each moment the enemy's ardour was dying away, and that he had abandoned his purpose of driving us from the field. In a close defensive fight, he found, no doubt, that carbines, well handled, are a merciless foe to face, and, so reflecting, he paused and ceased firing; and when we were satisfied that he declined the combat, we leaned on our arms and rested from the turmoils of this hard day. In our regiment it had cost us Lieutenant Magee, killed, besides Lieutenant-Colonel Morrow and the men who were disabled, none of whom, happily, were mortally wounded. Lieutenant Magee had just been promoted; he had distinguished himself on many fields, and had won an excellent name for all soldierly qualities. He fell in the front of his men, doing his duty manfully, and bearing his part in upholding the honour of his regiment and the cause for which he fought.

We slept that night soundly and well, near to where we had fired our last shots; and the enemy lay down in our front, across the Five Forks Road, intending then, no doubt, to renew the fight at daybreak, if we should still audaciously remain at Dinwiddie. Davies and Devin

1865. joined us after dark, and General Sheridan had his command together for the morrow, not at all the worfe in fpirits for this day's hard fighting.

The Army of the Potomac, under General Meade, had moved out on the 29th from its old lines in front of Peterfburg, and was now in part advanced nearly to the White Oak Road, on our right front. A divifion of the 5th Corps, fent to us as a reinforcement, marched down the Boydton Plankroad as we lay fleeping on the night of the 31ft, and this movement coming to the ear of the enemy fcared them away in the early morning of

Apl. 1ft. the 1ft of April; and when we awoke, before day, the rebels were already on the march. The laft of them difappeared in the woods as we moved down to the fork of the road, where General Sheridan's aid had found us the day before; and juft as the head of our column reached that point, the divifion of the 5th Corps, under General Ayres, gained it alfo. They fat down to reft and get breakfaft, while we pufhed on through the mud and trees on the trail of the retreating enemy.

Weakened by the loffes of the previous day's fighting, the 6th Pennfylvania Cavalry numbered hardly a handful now; but we preffed forward with the brigade, to bear our fhare of whatever the fates had in ftore for us. Fighting there would furely be, and fome glory we hoped. We were not long in overtaking the rebel rear-guard, which came to a ftand in every favorable place, and fought to delay us by boldnefs. But our cavalry moved up as fteadily and fpeedily as the very bad ground would permit; and, after one or two efforts to check us with volleys from haftily conftructed works, the enemy was forced to a quick retreat, and halted again only when he had sheltered himself behind his strong fortifications on the White Oak Road, above and below Five Forks. Our regiment was in the advance, and when, in front of these formidable lines, the 6th Pennsylvania Cavalry for the last time dismounted to fight on foot, there stood in the ranks but 48 men bearing carbines. These all went into the fight. There were no Nos. 4 left behind to hold horses that day. Every man was willing and eager to do his part, and the horses were given in charge to officers' servants and such other peaceful followers as could be borrowed for the occasion. Taking a small cow-path on the right of the road to Five Forks, we trudged on till we encountered the enemy's skirmishers in a belt of woods, just in front of their main line on the White Oak Road, and then we deployed and commenced firing, the rebels retiring before us as we were reinforced by the rest of our brigade. When they were safe behind their earthworks, we secured the best cover we could find, and kept up a sharp skirmish fire, and made feints of attack, to distract the enemy's attention from the flank movement of infantry that General Sheridan was planning on our right.

All of the 5th Corps, under Warren, had reported to General Sheridan since we left Ayres's men by the road-side, and now a movement was on foot to burst suddenly upon the enemy's left flank with that corps, while we of the cavalry assailed him in front. We could see nothing of this infantry, but the orders were that when we should hear heavy musketry firing on our right, this would be our signal to assault. So we skirmished and

1865.
Apl. 1st.
coquetted with the unsuspecting enemy, keeping up an appearance of intention to attack; and still the signal did not come. We might have been ourselves attacked, and may be driven away, had the co-operating movement come to the knowledge of the waiting rebels; but fortune was smiling upon us, and they contented themselves with such stray shots as some of their anxious marksmen thought fit to favour us with.

Either by accident or design the woods caught fire while we were waiting in their shelter for the signal to advance, and blinding smoke was added then to the enemies which we had to encounter. The thick undergrowth burned briskly, and threatened to make our places too hot to hold us; but each man for himself made a clearing about him, and kicked away the dead leaves underfoot, and stood to his post firmly, using his carbine as often as there seemed to be a chance to do any harm with it.

About 4 P.M. there was a slight pattering of musketry where we thought to hear the signal volleys, and in a moment they came too. What a terrific roar! The woods rang with it as the 5th Corps, on our right, swept over the White Oak Road, and the battle of Five Forks was begun. This thundering salute, so welcome to us, was a shock of surprise to the enemy in our front. Once or twice they had moved out strong columns on our right, as if to penetrate the woods in that direction, to see if they were as empty as they were still; but a few shots from us had caused them to withdraw, as if ashamed of suspecting us of any hidden strategy. Now that their worst suspicions were to be more than realized,

they were all unprepared to meet this great emergency; 1865.
and as the rattling mufketry came clofer and clofer upon Apl. 1ft.
us, a cloud of gray foldiers rolled heavily back before it,
along the White Oak Road. Without further orders
the cavalry advanced at once, we in our place, of courfe,
and getting acrofs the path of the retreating rebels,
brought them to a ftand. Our infantry now appeared,
and joined us on our right, and while the confufed and
broken enemy ftood aghaft at the fudden difafter, they
were enveloped on every fide, and had no choice but
furrender.

Leaving this detachment in the hands of an infantry
guard, we then turned up the White Oak Road, and, in
conjunction with Ayres's and Griffin's Divifions, of the
5th Corps, preffed on toward Five Forks, where the enemy's battery was, and where already there was a heavy
fight raging, as the cavalry of Cufter and Devin on our
left attempted to gain the works. As we neared the
Forks our forces alfo became hotly engaged, and the
enemy, forely befet, made defperate efforts to keep poffeffion of this key of his pofition. But his gallantry and
defperation were foon feen to be futile, and not long
after we opened fire on his flank, the brave cavalrymen in
his front were fwarming over the earthworks in the teeth
of his guns, fome on horfeback and fome on foot. We
hurried on, too, enfilading his line with a very warm fire,
and gained the battery, in company with Griffin and
Ayres, almoft as foon as our fellow-troopers who charged
it. The enemy broke in great confufion, abandoning
their artillery and throwing away their mufkets, and fled
in every direction which feemed to offer the means of

1865.
Apl. 1st.
escape. Some went by the Ford Road and tried to get across Hatcher's Run, and so to the Southside Railroad; but these were quickly turned about by Crawford's Division of the 5th Corps and MacKenzie's Division of cavalry, which by this time had gained that road in their rear. Some went up the White Oak Road, and these were speedily captured by the mounted regiments of Custer, which, as soon as the battery was carried, dashed into the road and galloped away in pursuit.

We saw them ride off, but were not able to join them, for our horses were still far back in the rear, waiting for their riders patiently. It was almost dark as we stood among the captured guns; and the broken enemy offered no more resistance where we could help to engage him. The battle died fast away about us, and in a few moments was borne far off into the sombre woods and came to an end in their gloom. We got up our horses then and went into camp on the battle-field, congratulating each other on the glorious victory and on the safety of our little party; for in spite of the stirring fight and the random firing through which we had passed, nobody of ours was killed, and a good Providence seemed to have watched over us all day.

This was the last battle in which we took much part, for the next morning General Merritt, thinking us too weak to do a regiment's duty in the brigade, ordered us to his headquarters as escort and guard, and we marched with him for the rest of the campaign, and our carbines swung idly over our shoulders from Five Forks to Appomattox Courthouse. Our men were actively employed, though, and did a great deal of hard work on that long ride. We were used in all sorts of ways, for all sorts of things, and found that an escort is not the easiest place to serve in through a cavalry campaign. We saw about as much of the finish as any one saw, and bore our part in whatever was done. We were almost constantly in the saddle, by night as well as by day; we rode to the front when there was fighting, and did duty in many capacities on the field; and after a hard day's work, when the most of the cavalry were sleeping, we often were up and about.

1865.
Apl. 1st.

CHAPTER TWENTY-NINTH.

The Purfuit and Surrender of Lee.

1865. THE battle of Five Forks was the fignal for a general attack on Lee's lines by the Army of the Potomac; and by daylight next morning, General Meade's troops were fwarming over the enemy's earthworks at Peterfburg, capturing thoufands of prifoners, who had no time to efcape. Getting an early breakfaft on the 2d, we, of General Merritt's command, pufhed acrofs Hatcher's Run, and advanced toward the Southfide Railroad, driving in our front a fmall force of the enemy's cavalry, which diffolved at our approach, without refifting us. At the railroad we found no oppofition; and there we turned to the right and followed the track toward Sutherland's Depot, where General Sheridan, with the 5th Corps, already was. Turning to the left, here, we moved in the direction of the Appomattox River, and went into camp that night at a little place called Scott's Corner. There were broken, fhattered parties of the enemy all about us, who had drifted away from the late difafters in their lines at Five Forks and Peterfburg; but we had no fighting to fpeak of: indeed thefe parties were much more anxious to give themfelves up than to give battle.

Apl. 2d.

Richmond, as well as Petersburg, fell into General 1865. Grant's hands this day, and all reasonable hope for General Apl. 3d. Lee now lay in his chance of escape to Danville, to join General Johnston, where he would try to retrieve his fortunes by mingling them with others equally desperate; for Johnston's army in North Carolina was beset by as many difficulties as now encompassed the Army of Northern Virginia. But General Sheridan, bent on dissipating even this small ray of hope which remained to General Lee, started his cavalry forward next morning, the 3d, before the larks were up, to gain the Danville Railroad in advance of General Lee, or interrupt the march of his retreating troops in that direction. We had the shorter line of march, and bearing to our left we moved rapidly upon the Namozine Road, skirting the right bank of the Appomattox River.

Early on the 4th we encountered at Tabernacle Apl. 4th. Church the enemy's columns and trains, pressing on hurriedly toward Amelia Courthouse, a point on the Danville Railroad where Lee was concentrating his forces. General Merritt attacking vigorously and capturing many prisoners and wagons, delayed the enemy's march; and it seemed likely at one time that he would effectually put a stop to it on this side of the Appomattox. But Lee was compelled by his necessities to keep this road open, and so he sent to oppose our cavalry a force of infantry so strong in numbers that our men were unable to break through it; and with his success of the morning, General Merritt was obliged to be satisfied. After dark we were recalled from this errand, which promised to be a fruitless one, and were ordered to follow

1865. the line of General Sheridan's march with the 5th Corps, toward Amelia Courthouſe. *En route* we encountered the 2d Army Corps, which was haſtening on to reinforce him, and we had a moſt tireſome ride all
Apl. 5th. night, ſtriving to make headway in a crowded road walled in by impenetrable woods. At Jeterſville, five miles below Amelia Courthouſe, we found the 5th Corps and General Crook's Cavalry in line of battle, and General Sheridan ſent us out to the left of the line after the 2d Corps had formed on the left of the 5th. Meantime Crook's Diviſion, which had gone on a reconnoiſſance toward Amelia Courthouſe, and had captured a wagon train, was violently attacked by a ſtrong body of the enemy's infantry and driven back rapidly toward Jeterſville. We ſtood to horſe in General Merritt's command, hearing the firing, that was coming cloſer and cloſer, and expecting every moment to ſee the enemy come over the brow of the hill in our front, when there would be ſtirring work for our cavalry to do, as the ground was open and gave us a chance to ride horſes into a fight. But the enemy did not crown the creſt, and we ſoon were trotted over to the extreme right of our line by an order from General Sheridan, who was planning a cavalry movement there in caſe Lee's troops ſhould continue to advance. It is a pity that they halted where they did, for there was a little valley winding along the front of the 5th Corps, through which our troopers could have ſwept like a wind upon the flank of any force that had come down to attack our infantry. With Crook's return, however, the fighting ended for the day, and darkneſs came on ſoon after.

We were undisturbed that night by any of war's alarms, and woke next morning, the 6th, to find work to do, soon after daylight, on the Deatonsville Road, five miles on our left, as we looked toward Amelia Courthouse. General Crook's reconnoissance of the day before had shown that the enemy was trying to steal a march by passing our left flank and avoiding a fight for the railroad lines: so at earliest dawn General Sheridan sent Crook out again on our left, and before the sun peeped over the murky horizon his cavalry had begun to worry the flying trains and troops which General Lee, by this new road, was seeking to pilot to Danville. General Merritt moved up in support of Crook, and we got the entire benefit of a very brisk shelling intended by the enemy for him. When General Sheridan came up he sent us all off to the left, to try for a better opening, this one of Crook's not promising well, owing to the heavy force that the enemy showed on the flank of his wagons here. We rode on then parallel to the Deatonsville Road, where the hurrying trains could be plainly seen, and Merritt and Crook were instructed to pass each other from time to time, while each should seek a chance to gain a footing in the enemy's column. For a good while no favourable opportunity for an attack was seen, and by the afternoon our flanking movement had carried us over a little stream, called Sailor's Creek, that runs into the Appomattox.

Feeling then along the line of the enemy's march beyond the stream, and there seeming to be some prospect of success at last, a handsome effort was made by Crook's Division to get possession of the Prince Edward Court-

1865.
Apl. 6th.

1865. house Road, into which the enemy now had struck.
Apl. 6th. They failed at first to make an impression, as well they might in the face of such a warm reception as they met; for the enemy guarded the road with a heavy infantry force, and was evidently disposed to fight desperately for the right of way. But General Devin soon came up on the left of General Crook, General Custer was soon charging gallantly on his right, and then General Ewell's troops found it impossible any longer to hold our brave cavalry in check: the impetuous troopers swept over the temporary earthworks which lined the road, and, riding down all opposition, were soon among the coveted wagon trains. They captured many officers and men and much spoil of guns and vehicles and mules (the latter two somewhat the worse for wear); but hurrying the prisoners away to the rear and burning whatever was combustible, they pressed on still through the enemy's column and sought to make a junction with General Sheridan, who was thought to be near by, somewhere on Sailor's Creek, with the 6th Army Corps, which had temporarily reported to him, the 5th Corps having been returned to General Meade. As we gained a crest overlooking the creek, the rear-guard of Ewell was seen just below us, warmly engaged with the gallant 6th Corps, which had crossed the water and was trying to drive Ewell's men from their strong position on the hillside. Our cavalry meanwhile was pressing on, and, to the utter astonishment of our enemies, now burst into view from among the pine trees on the crest. There was no time to form a line to meet them; there was not a moment from the first alarm till they were riding pell-

mell through the enemy's ftaggered troops, which in another moment, completely hemmed in and panic ftricken as they were, threw down their arms and furrendered. It was a thing of an inftant almoft: each man had feen for himfelf what needed to be done and had not faltered in the doing. It was one of the fineft of our cavalry fucceffes, and to our men it was almoft a bloodlefs victory, for in the rufh of their bold charge they had trampled all danger under foot.

It was quite dark before the infantry and General Sheridan reached the ridge from which our troopers had borne down fo refiftleffly, and here, by this time, were gathered the fhattered remnants of Ewell's force, including himfelf and his generals; for, to the great honour and glory of the 6th Corps and the cavalry, hiftory has to tell that, fo far as is known, Ewell's whole command, some 10,000 men in all, it is thought, fell into the fnare which General Sheridan fpread fo fuccefsfully on the banks of Sailor's Creek.

Lee, with the remnant of his army, recoiled before this heavy blow, and, forfaking now the highroads to Danville, reeled back towards the headwaters of the Appomattox, and croffed that river at Farmville, hoping perhaps to find fome refpite from purfuit or to miflead the relentlefs flankers who were fruftrating all his devices of efcape. But on the morning of the 7th our cavalry ftill bore to the left as it marched, without regard to Lee's backward movement, and paffing through Prince Edward Courthoufe, a little town on the Richmond, Prince Edward, and Danville Pike, we left Farmville and General Lee far away on our right and preffed

Apl. 7th.

1865. forward to Prospect Station, on the Richmond and Lynchburg Railroad—a march of nearly thirty miles—before we called a halt. It was thought that General Lee's army would soon be compelled to seek this railroad for supplies, which now could be drawn only from Lynchburg; and so General Sheridan determined to keep his cavalry in hand on this line, feeling certain that before very long it would encounter here the head of Lee's retreating column.

Apl. 8th. Early on the 8th we set out again, marching now with our faces toward Lynchburg, and, following the railroad, still disregarded the momentary whereabouts of General Lee. To Appomattox Station, some twenty-five miles in our front, comes the Cumberland Road, a good broad highway, which Lee might easily gain from Farmville; and our march to-day was for that point, where it was hoped we might intercept him. Late in the afternoon, as we were riding behind General Merritt, between his two divisions, General Custer, in advance, struck the enemy at the station, and the evidence of their presence there was borne back to us on the wind in rapid reports of artillery. We hurried on to see what sort of fight the impetuous Custer had found, and just as we gained the station some of his leading regiments were surrounding four heavy supply trains, that had lately arrived from Lynchburg by rail with rations for General Lee, while across the track and up the road and through the woods a perfect storm of shells was hurled from some unseen source. Custer's men rapidly disappeared among the trees, where, for a moment, there was a fearful fusilade of musketry and heavy guns; but as Devin came up on Cufter's right, and difmounting his men advanced to his fupport, the firing ceafed; and as the fun went down, his laft blink over the hills faw us peacefully gathering in the fruits of a brilliant little victory. Some of the trains and fupplies were burned, and fome were run off to Farmville; twenty-five guns and as many wagons rewarded Cufter's dafh at the artillery parks, and to him and Devin more than one thoufand prifoners were to be credited.

1865.

Night found us on the road to Appomattox Courthoufe, toward which place a demoralized remnant from the ftation had flown, and we lay down here for our laft fleep in the lap of actual war; for, though we hardly hoped for fuch good fortune then, the morning would fee us toffed fuddenly into the arms of peace.

Shortly after daybreak on the 9th of April—a day to be always remembered with pride and pleafure by all of us—we became aware that heavy reinforcements had come to our fupport, and, as the enemy came down from Appomattox Courthoufe and opened their fierce attack on General Crook, in our front, it was pleafant to fee that long lines of our infantry were forming in the woods behind him, and before very long would confront the ardent troops of General Lee, who feemed confident of breaking through to the railroad. Meantime General Merritt's command was not engaged, and our men fcouted about everywhere to learn what was going on, and here and there one got himfelf among the enemy.

Apl. 9th.

Sergeant Golden went into a fight with one of Crook's brigades, on the left of the line, and charging in the

1865.
Apl. 9th.
woods, wounded himſelf in the face with his own ſabre, which rebounded from the branch of a tree as he cut at a rebel who was galloping away. Soon General Merritt was moved out to the right, and he advanced toward the Courthouſe leiſurely, while Crook gave way in the ſame direction to unmaſk the infantry, which now was ready to take his place.

As the cavalry thus withdrew from the enemy's front we could hear the cheers of Lee's tried troops, who thought that at laſt they ſhould make good their eſcape; but in a moment they were ſtruck dumb with ſurpriſe as the grand line of the 5th Corps and General Ord's command ſurged forward to the open fields and preſented its impaſſable front. From this new and unexpected calamity the enemy fell back amazed; our infantry followed them ſilently, in battle array, and our cavalry, with Cuſter in advance, puſhing rapidly out on the right, ſoon caught ſight of Lee's trains and guns lying almoſt unprotected in the valley beyond the Courthouſe. Regarding theſe with eager eyes, and joyfully noting the ſteady advance of our infantry line, General Merritt's command was gathering up the reins for what would doubtleſs be a final charge, when an order to halt paſſed along the column. In a moment it was known that a flag of truce had been received, and then, after a rouſing cheer, each man dropped his reins from his hand, and diſmounting from his horſe ſat quietly down by the roadſide to await the ſurrender of Lee.

In an hour or two General Grant came up and rode rapidly paſt our column on his little black pacer, and ſtruck acroſs lots to the Courthouſe, where he expected to find

THE SURRENDER. 351

General Lee. Generals Sheridan and Merritt and a great number of officers were affembled on our infantry picket line, juft at the edge of the town, but none from the cavalry, except General Sheridan and a few of his ftaff, accompanied General Grant when he went up to the houfe where the terms of furrender were fettled. We learn fomething, however, from one of thefe officers of what tranfpired there. He says: "The town confifts of about five houfes, a tavern, and a courthoufe, all on one ftreet, and that was boarded up at one end to keep the cows out. On the right hand fide as we went in was the principal refidence, owned by Mr. McLean, and to his houfe General Grant was conducted to meet General Lee. At the fence the whole party difmounted, and walking over a narrow grafs-plot to the houfe noticed General Lee's gray horfe nibbling there, in charge of an orderly, who was holding his own as well. General Grant entered the houfe with one or two of his ftaff, and the reft of us fat down on the piazza and waited. Mr. McLean was out there, too, but was fo much excited by his appreciation of paffing events that he did not know where his pump was, or if he had any, and if not could not tell us where there was a fpring. In a moment Colonel Babcock came out fmiling, whirled his hat round his head once and beckoned Generals Ord and Sheridan to come in. They walked the floor filently, as people do who have first peep at a baby, and after a while General Lee came out and fignalled to his orderly to bridle his horfe. While this was being done, he ftood on the loweft ftep of the piazza (we had all rifen refpectfully as he paffed down), and looking over

*1865.
Apl. 9th.*

1865.
Apl. 9th.
into the valley toward his army, ſmote his hands together ſeveral times in an abſent ſort of way, utterly unconſcious of the people about him, and ſeeming to ſee nothing till his horſe was led in front of him. As he ſtood there he appeared to be about ſixty years of age, a tall, ſoldierly figure of a man, with a full gray beard, a new ſuit of gray clothes, a high gray felt hat, with a cord, long buckſkin gauntlets, high riding boots, and a beautiful ſword. He was all that our fancy had painted him ; and he had the ſympathy of us all as he rode away. Juſt as he gathered up his bridle General Grant went down the ſteps, and paſſing in front of his horſe, touched his hat to General Lee, who made a ſimilar ſalute, and then left the yard and returned to his own lines with his orderly and the ſingle ſtaff officer who had accompanied him to the interview, and who was ſaid to have been Colonel Marſhall, his chief of ſtaff, a quiet-looking man in ſpectacles, more like one of thought than of action. General Grant preſented ſomething of a contraſt to General Lee, in the way of uniform, not only in colour but in ſtyle and general effect. He had on a ſugar-loaf hat, almoſt peculiar to himſelf, a frock coat unbuttoned and ſplaſhed with mud, a dark veſt, dark blue pantaloons, tucked into top-boots, muddy alſo, and no ſword. His countenance was not relaxed at all, and not a muſcle of his face told tales on his thoughts. If he was very much pleaſed by the ſurrender of Lee, nothing in his air or manner indicated it. The joyful occaſion did not ſeem to awaken in him a reſponſive echo, and he went and mounted his horſe and rode away ſilently to ſend off a diſpatch which ſhould electrify the North, and ſet all

the church bells ringing jubilant vefpers on this happy Sunday evening?"

1865.
Apl. 9th.

Peace, then, had come at laft. No more need for pickets and fcouts; no more weary raids and dufty marches; no more need for fighting on foot in tangled woods; no more wounded, and no more killed. The Great Rebellion being dead, fome troopers that we know of had much better chance of their lives thenceforth, and were duly thankful, let us hope, as they went to bed that night.

When Lee furrendered the war was over to all intents and purpofes, and it would needleffly prolong this hiftory to dwell at length upon the fubfequent movements of our regiment. It only remains to touch upon the flow march back to Peterfburg—the pleafanteft march we ever made—to mention merely that we then accompanied General Sheridan on his delightful trip to the border of North Carolina and back—a ride that had for its object the reinforcement of General Sherman had Johnfton perfifted in fighting after he heard of Lee's furrender; and to record our journey to Wafhington, where we fhared in all the glory of the Grand Review. Here, as the 6th Pennfylvania Cavalry turned out of Pennfylvania Avenue, where the great throng had greeted us with fuch a fplendid outburft of applaufe, it may be faid that our glorious old regiment ended its career; that with the cheers of the crowd ftill ringing about us we furled up the tattered colours which had ftreamed over us fo long.

When the review was over we were fent acrofs the Potomac and confolidated with fome other regiments,

1865. and as part of the " 2d Provifional Pennfylvania Cavalry," we drifted flowly out of the fervice; not, however, before we had travelled to Louifville, Kentucky,

Aug. 7th. where the muftering officer, on the 7th of Auguft, 1865, excufed us from further duty, and fent us home rejoicing.

CHAPTER THIRTIETH.

Conclusion.

AT the close of this record of work and war, we are tempted to set out from home again and wander once more over the old fields and roads, to see if there be not some berries of memory worth the picking, that are not white with the dust of marches or bruised with the shock of battle. We could laugh now at the troubles of our youth, "sit and grin" on the old stumbling-blocks, and make a pleasant ramble of what was once a weary journey. If we were game for the tramp there ought to be plenty of berries; but there is hardly room for them now in the basket.

Old Camp Meigs, though, is not very far, and we cannot resist just looking over the fence for a minute, to recall the happy time when with awful gravity we mounted guard with hickory sticks over its company streets, that lay so silent and peaceful in the moonlight. Those were pleasant days and restful nights, and may be we have looked back upon them since and sighed; but we were in deep earnest then, and more anxious for coming events than to bask in the sunshine that surrounded our daily life. It was only when we got into shadows that we felt all the sunshine's worth.

How full the old camp is of remembrances! Mists rise all about it and float over it, taking form here and there of some long-forgotten scene or pleasant reminiscence of a fellow-campaigner; and it is pleasant to find it peopled with so many who proved themselves to be thorough good fellows in all our hardships and perils. In those early days it was only the perils of organization that beset us, and these hemmed us in on every side. Did not they knock at our tents with the earliest dawn and hardly leave us sometimes till midnight? but it is true that in spite of them we were not long in making ourselves formidable to our friends, whatever we might have proved to our enemies. Our soldier-growth was gradual, though, and it is good fun to recall its development.

The emotions of the first day in camp can hardly yet be stifled in any of our breasts, as our company filed in from the recruiting station and was assigned its place; very accurately assigned, too, and not to be departed from by a hair's breadth. Then those white tents were pitched, the like shimmer of which was seldom seen again by those who slept in them there; sometimes afterward we had dusky canvas, and sometimes shelter of sky and forest trees, but this first snowy white was only renewed in memory. The sunshine seems to beat on them now glaringly; the red stitching trickles down the seams, and the tent-maker's name in stencil-work is quite fresh in our recollection. And these were stalwart recruits who pitched the tents. They bore the bone and muscle of the land, no doubt about that; but how fearfully and wonderfully their uniforms were made! If the eyes of most of us had known what a foldier ought to be, we might have fhuddered to remember that the apparel oft proclaims the man. Certainly it was fome time before ours proclaimed us to be foldiers; but after awhile we did find out that a No. 2 man in a No. 4 jacket, with the collar chafing his ears and a loofe overloaded belt dragging it awry; in troufers a world too large, a flouching cap and enormous boots, is not feen to the beft advantage. Even to our early ignorance fome remedy feemed needful, and fo we began at the top of the fubject to improve it. After much confultation, the officers adopted a lovely hat, with feathers for themfelves and for the men without. What a dreadful load it was to carry, and how the wearer's head would throb under the weight, we remember with pain even now. The ftouteft knight of old could not have hewn through this helmet, had he hewn with all his might, any more than he could have carried it about on his head all day; fo, of courfe, fuch an inftrument of torture could not laft very long. Among other gorgeous but inexpedient ornaments they were in good time given up, and all being gently packed into barrels were turned over to the Quartermafter's Department at Wafhington. If they have not gone there they are doubtlefs ftill; and fhould any one care to rummage the ufelefs lumber of the war, perhaps he will find them in fome Wafhington wareroom whirling playfully upon the difcarded lance-points which lie alfo fomewhere in oblivion. After this fingle attempt at improvement we wifely left it to time to foften the outline of the foldier, and to harmonize the difcordant elements which at firft confpired againft his noble form;

and, indeed, we had hardly time to bestow this thought upon the man before the horses were upon us demanding our attention.

Shall we ever forget those first bounding geldings neighing and stamping and pawing the ground? They cost $135 each; and he who had a horse that had the glanders, or the heaves, or was spavined, or was going blind, brought him to the government, and the government purchased him. What a delight to see them feed, tossing the half of their oats skyward, far over the beautiful nose-bags! At night we wished we were Arabs, that we might take them to bed with us; and their pleasant whinnying called us out early in the morning. That was like cavalry, indeed, when they came, and the whole air was filled with the fragrance of the stables. The effect was quite intoxicating. Some men hung round the horses' necks, and some tried if their tails would bear a man's weight. In "A" company, which got the first issue, there was mounting in hot haste, even before the saddles arrived; and meantime there was some rapid dismounting, too, of luckless riders pitched over picket ropes as the horses came galloping madly up from watering.

When the mounted drill began, was such a gallant sight ever seen as First Lieutenant Treichel's platoon careering across the sward at a very slow trot, some of the men more diligent to keep their seats than to observe the instructions which Treichel thundered forth, spurring nervously at his charger. The rest of us used to stand by on our legs and watch him, saying it over after him to ourselves from first to last: *Attention!* *In each rank count fours!* Steady there! The rear-rank will count as well as the front. *In each rank count fours!* Very well! At the command *Prepare to mount*, Nos. 1 and 3 will lead forward, &c., &c. Pay attention there! Eyes to the front! *Prepare to mount! Mount!* And then there would be a jangling of fabres, and jingling of curb-chains, and reftlefs moving of horfes all huddled together, one of which at leaft would gallop off to the picket rope, with wildly-clutching rider ftriving to catch up the reins. Then more orders would ring out, and the platoon would move off by twos or fours, and form compactly or lengthen indefinitely at the word of command. It was a ftirring fpectacle, and fo we all thought, hide it as we might from the civilians who looked on. Meantime we moved with bufy feet all day; and what with policing and fweeping, burnifhing, cleaning, and drilling, we brufhed the dews off the morning grafs, and the laft rays of the evening fun fhot through the duft that followed us. Anybody was at liberty to lounge about in the intervals of leifure, if he could find any; but fomehow from funrife to funfet there was not time to fmoke a pipe, while the Colonel endeavoured to get us into form by word and example, aided in chief by Lieutenant-Colonel McArthur, who was alfo from Weft Point (as any one would know at a glance), and by Major Morris, poor fellow, who feemed to know all about foldiering without learning.

We had called ourfelves "The Philadelphia Light Cavalry," and after a while we got the ladies to chriften us fo; and then we flaunted their pretty guidons in his Excellency the Governor's face, with our title emblazoned on them. Very naturally he did not like it, as he wanted to number us with the regiments from the State; but we did not want that, and we worſted him, utterly vanquiſhed him, in the correſpondence on the ſubject. Then two of us went up to Harriſburg and put our caſe before Mr. Meredith, the Attorney-General, who was thought to be a reaſonable man and a friend of ours, and he got up from bed to hear us, and ſent us away wiſer if not ſatisfied. Finally we yielded gracefully and came under the banner of the State, and perhaps were none the worſe for it, eſpecially as everybody had to do the ſame. But in one point we triumphed: the appointment of officers remained with the Colonel; two doctors who were ſent to us by his Excellency were handſomely bowled out, and we were afterwards left to our own devices.

It was in the height of the complications of our organization that the telegram came from General McClellan aſking us to adopt the lance. Moſt of us heard of it with enthuſiaſm; and thoſe of us whoſe opinion was aſked pondered how the points ſhould beſt be ſharpened and how the ſhafts ſhould beſt be tapered to the downfall of all oppoſers. And how beautiful they looked when we got them! how the points glimmered in the ſunlight, and how bravely the pennons ſtreamed! They were a trifle awkward to handle at firſt, perhaps, and we uſed to wonder how St. George managed to kill the Dragon, but we made no doubt that in time we ſhould be able to ride a tourney with great ſucceſs. Lieutenant Furneſs made a picture to illuſtrate the ſuperiority of the lance to the ſabre. A cavalryman with a sabre rode into a charge and pierced one foe and carried him off in triumph on his sword, but a lancer rode in by his side, and transfixed half a dozen foes, and bore them all off on his lance gayly. That would have settled the question, perhaps, if any grave doubts had surrounded it.

We were mightily pleased with ourselves when we were all mounted and armed; and not to keep our glory and splendour under a bushel, we illuminated the city one day with our pennons, and woke its echoes with our new brass band, making a most beautiful parade in column of *play-tunes*, poor Whelan said. And nobody knew that we were not the best of cavalry, fit to gallop and charge; for we rode at a slow walk, like Aladdin, and people took us for the bold riders that we looked to be. One horse reared and his rider fell off; but that of course was accidental, and might happen to any man quizzing pretty girls at a window.

The citizens were certainly very much impressed by us in those days, and if any of us has found less of glory since than he expected, he got then rather more than he was entitled to. Most of our visitors at camp, especially among the ladies, saw in every man a hero, not in process of formation, but complete already; and whether his clothes sat well upon him or he could fit his horse they seemed never to know, and they would exclaim how well an officer or man could ride though he might look like a mounted windmill, wildly flapping his legs and arms. The Colonel, by the way, was much afraid that our friends would take us at their own valuation, and expect great things of us accordingly. Look at his speeches to the ladies and the Governor, and see how anxious he is that we shall not be overestimated; how he insists, in effect, that brass bands and pennons do not make cavalry. But the civilians did not believe in that, and flocked to the camp as before. Some came early and stayed all day, never weary of watching and prying into the secrets of war, and solving the mysteries that lay hidden in tents. It is true that sometimes a tent-fly suddenly thrust aside would reveal to women's eyes appalling sights; but that was their fault and not ours, and they knew then to respect the sanctity of our canvas homes.

Our busy days carried us into the autumn fast, and the woods on the border of our camp were painted with brilliant hues. Then the leaves fell, and we nestled under the shelter of the great trees from the chill November gales. Then mud came, and cold, and the fair-weather friends of summer left us almost alone. Then we began to look for orders to move, and to wonder what part we should have to play in the war; for as yet we had not been assigned to any command, and had no idea what niche in the army we should fill. Our feelings were somewhat mixed, perhaps, owing to our isolated condition and the sort of arms we carried, and we did not know whether to take it for granted that we should be a centre from which all other troops would radiate, or to fear that General McClellan would move away with the rest of his army and forget us. There were some scoffers among us who held to the latter opinion, but for the most part we looked up to General McClellan with abiding faith. He had put the lances into our hands, and so became our patron, and we had

CONCLUSION. 363

little doubt that in all the viciffitudes of coming campaigns he would keep one eye always on us. We rather expected to be held in referve near him for emergencies. We knew that critical moments come to every battle-field when guards and efcorts are hurled at vital points. We had read this in hiftory and romance; and for fuch moments we fhould perhaps be held in hand. It was eafy to fancy glorious battle-pieces, in which, through clouds of fmoke and duft, fquadrons of lancers were feen for a moment in the thickeft of the fight, and then to bear away the laurels of victory upon their lance points. But we could not then have believed that we fhould fet out like Don Quixote to break many lances with little good refult, and that they would prove as harmlefs to our enemies in the woods as was the lance of the angry Don to Sancho's enemies who toffed him in a blanket in the yard of the inn, caring little for Don Quixote and his lance on the other fide of the wall.

Early in December we began to move away to Wafhington, and in two or three days Camp Meigs, of pleafant memory, was quite forfaken. It was fummer-time when we faw it again, and the old field was hardly to be recognized. A waving crop was bending over it, and nothing remained to tell that it had borne the foot-prints of a thoufand horfes. The trees about it were all again in leaf, but nothing told that the tents of a thoufand men, making ready for battle, not long ago lay in their fhadow. The ftream was flowing by in the hollow ftill, but the well-worn banks were overgrown, and all the paths were peace.

It is a long road we have travelled fince leaving here,

and the foldier who returns in 1865 is not much like the recruit of 1861. He has parted with his picturefque lance, and carries a practical carbine in place of it; he wears his cap on the fide of his head, and the vifor turned up with a jaunty air; his fhort blue bloufe is a perfect fit, and his tight-drawn belt does not give to the piftol's weight; his troufers are clofe about the thigh, and fpring over the foot a little; his fabre is ftrapped under his faddle-girth, and he knows how to fit his horfe; he is neat and ftraight and feels himfelf to be a man; he has felf-refpect and pride in his regiment; and when he is muftered out of fervice he is a better civilian than ever he was before.

But there are many who ftarted with us, and many who joined us later, who have fallen by the way. Let us give our laft thought to the memory of thefe, as we bid farewell to the gallant old regiment, and put away the torn ftandard and the trufty arms.

ROSTER

OF OFFICERS OF SIXTH PENNA. CAVALRY MUSTERED OUT, AUG. 7, 1865.

Colonel—Chas. L. Leiper.
Lieut.-Colonel—Albert P. Morrow.
First Major—Abraham D. Price.
Second Major—Chas. B. Coxe.
Third Major—Bernard H. Harkness.
Adjutant—C. A. Newhall.

Quartermaster—J. W. McElhenny.
Commissary—Chas. White.
Surgeon—D. D. Swift.
Assistant Surgeon—Jos. J. Yocum.
Chaplain—Samuel L. Gracey.

A.
Captain—T. Camp Oakman.
1st Lieut.—Michael Golding.
2d "

B.
Captain—Wm. R. Wright.
1st Lieut.—
2d "

C.
Captain—Isaac F. Moffatt.
1st Lieut.—Wm. Scott.
2d "

D.
Captain—Chas. A. Vernou.
1st Lieut.—John Laird.
2d "

E.
Captain—Samuel R. Colladay.
1st Lieut.—Abiah T. Smedley.
2d "

F.
Captain—A. L. Lanigan.
1st Lieut.—Jos. D. Price.
2d "

G.
Captain—Ed. Whiteford.
1st Lieut.—
2d "

H.
Captain.—J. H. Workman.
1st Lieut.—Daniel D. Hurtz.
2d "

I.
Captain—Ed. I. Hazel.
1st Lieut.—
2d "

K.
Captain—Archer Maris.
1st Lieut.—Henry J. Toudy.
2d "

L.
Captain—Levis Miller, Jr.
1st Lieut.—
2d "

M.
Captain—R. M. Sheppard.
1st Lieut.—Wm. Carey.
2d "

INDEX.

A Company, 19, 20, 56, 112, 118, 123, 134, 155
Adams, M. J., 262
Aldie, 177
Aldrick's Houſe, 232
Algie, John, 261
Amelia Courthouſe, 343
Antietam, 93
Appomattox Courthouſe, 349
Aſh, S. F., 262

B Company, 55, 89, 97, 111, 118, 290
Barclay, Clement B., 20
Barnſville, 44
Baynes, J. F., 262
Bealton Station, 153
Beaver Dam Creek, 58
Beaver Dam Station, 240
Bennett, James, 262
Berlin, 192
Berryville, 287
Bertolett, A. F., 120
Bertrand, E. P., 121, 216
Betheſda Church, 252, 256
Beverley Ford, 157, 175
Boon, 236
Boonſboro, 185
Booz, 236

Bottom's Bridge, 246, 257
Bowers, 236
Brandy Station, 194
Briſtow Station, 199
Buford, John, Major-General, death of, 211
Burk, 236
Burnſide's Mud March, 123
Burnſide's Mine, 274.

C Company, 55, 66, 76, 84, 112
Cadwalader, Chas. E , 109, 304
Call, Wm. B., 310
Camp Barclay, 37
Camp Buford, 195
Camp Meigs, 20
Camp at Belle Plains, 129
Camp at White Oak Church, 118
Carpenter, E. N., 130, 199, 235, 306
Carr, John A , 262
Caſſiday, 236
Catlett's Station, 155, 176, 200
Centreville, 198
Chancellorſville, 232
Change of Baſe by McClellan, 83
Charles City Courthouſe, 266
Charlotteſville, 225, 320
Clark, J. H., 219, 224, 227, 235, 254, 260, 281, 309

368   INDEX.

Clymer, George E., 20, 55, 89, 111, 120, 215
Coffee, James, 262
Cold Harbour, 55, 246, 255
Cole's Houſe, 82
Colladay, Samuel R., 164, 168, 313
Columbia on the James, 143
Coover, John B., 162, 214, 298
Coxe, C. B., 122, 236, 265, 314
Culpepper, 194, 205, 207
Cuſter's Raid, 222, 230

D Company, 56, 112, 123, 155
Darby's Houſe, 273
Davis, Charles B., 164, 167, 168, 171
Deep Bottom, 272
Denney, Sergeant, 261
Dickſon, J. N., 46, 309
Dinwiddie Courthouſe, 336
Dobſon, James, 262
Dougherty, D., 262
Duffield Station, 290
Dumfries, 154

E Company, 111, 130, 199
Ellis, Charles M., 77, 219
Ellis, P. H., Jr., 261, 314
Ellis, Rudolph, 164, 167, 168, 312
Engler, George L., 314
Erben, W. B., 120.

F Company, 71, 85, 111
Fair Oaks, 48, 57
Farrell, M., 262
Finney, 236
Five Forks, 336
Frazier, W. W., Jr., 168, 306
Frederick City, 178
Frederickſburg, 113

Front Royal, 285
Funkſtown, 188
Furneſs, F. H., 222, 310

G Company, 20, 55, 89, 97, 111, 118, 183
Gaines's Mill, 59
Gaineſville, 200
Gardner, John H., 62, 217
Germantown, 201
Gettyſburg, 179
Gieſboro Point, 85, 195, 276, 279
Gilbert, 236
Golden, 236
Gracey, S. L., 214, 315
Gregg, Thomas J., 312
Gringee, W., 262
Guinney's Station, 249, 263
Gurrance, W. A., 261

H Company, 55, 66, 76, 84, 112
Hacket, 236
Hagerſtown, 317
Haines, Howard, 130
Halltown, 280
Hanover Courthouſe, 45, 251
Harden, 236
Harkneſs, B. H., 189, 216, 314
Harper, G. W., 261
Harriſon's Landing, 75
Hartwood Church, 153
Haſeltine, J. H., 62, 111, 168, 171, 218
Hawes's Shop, 251
Hazard, Samuel, Jr., 303
Hazel, E. J., 235, 315
Henderſon, 236
Hendricks, John, 313
Hickler, 236

INDEX.   369

Hoap, James, 262
Hoffman, O. A., 261
Hopkins, John, 261
Horner, Charles W., 254

I Company, 56, 89, 97, 111, 112, 130, 199, 227
Irvin, Wm., 262

Jackſon, Oſwald, 305
Jones's Bridge, 266
Jones's Neck, 273
Jones, Wm., 261
Johnſon's Farm, 49
Johnſon, J., 361

K Company, 56, 111
Kelley's Ford, 130
Keyer, 236
Kirk, Sergeant, 236
Kirk, William, 235

L Company, 111, 130
Lance, 26
Lanigan, A. L., 258, 275
Lee's Mills, 275
Leetown, 290
Leiper, Charles L., 90, 110, 138, 164, 167, 171, 235, 255, 280, 296, 317, 329
Leipſen, J. H., 262
Lennig, Thompſon, 164, 167, 168, 312
Lighthouſe Point, 269
Lockwood, B., 66, 194, 201, 223, 302
Louiſa Courthouſe, 140, 322

M Company, 111, 130
McArthur, John H., 19, 300

McCord, 236
McClellan's Addreſs at Harriſon's Landing, 76
McNamee, Theo., 261
McNee, Thomas, 262
Madiſon Courthouſe, 224
Magee, James, 335
Maleſberger, J. C., 262
Maley, Thomas E., 218, 273
Malvern Hill, 72, 247
Maris, Archer, 216, 314
Martin, S. H., 236, 254
Meade, George, 214
Meadow Bridge, 245
Mechanicſville, 58, 244
Miller, 236
Miller, Levis, Jr., 242, 315
Milligan, Robert, 71, 216
Mine Run, 208
Mitchell, R. W., 303
Mitchell's Station, 211, 221
Moffat, Iſaac F., 315
Morris, Robert, Jr., 43, 49, 130, 135, 159, 164, 167, 171, 197
Morris's Farm, 44
Morriſville, 153, 202
Morriſon, T. L., 219
Morrow, A. P., 120, 153, 189, 290, 311, 317, 333
Moſeby's Attack on our Train, 283
Moſs, William, 90
Moyer, John, 261
Muirheid, H. P., 217
Mulberry Point, 43
Murphy, Arthur E., 255

Neill, T. W., 113, 218
New Caſtle Ferry, 44
Newhall, F. C., 111, 215

370   INDEX.

New Market Bridge, 42
Newtown, 282

Occoquan, 119
Odenheimer, William, 213
Old Church, 44, 256
Orange Springs, 139
Original Officers, 36

Pennington, Sergeant, 261
Pepper, George W., 121
Philadelphia Light Cavalry, 19
Piping Tree Ferry, 44
Presentation of Flags by Ladies of Germantown, 21
Presentation of Flags by Governor Curtin, 27
Presentation of Sword to Col. Rush, 38
Price, A. D., 120, 280, 314
Priesen, G. A., 313
Prospect Hill, 40

Reams's Station, 268
Reserve Brigade, 43, 178
Review of Cavalry Corps, 131
Richardson, 236
Richards, Charles E., 304
Riddle, John W., 311
Ruffin's Farm, 44, 251
Rush, R. H., 18, 23, 32, 47, 52, 62, 106, 118, 135
Ruffell, T. L. J., Diary of, 77

Sage, Theo. M., 202
Savage's Station, 67
Saxton, P. A., 236
Scott, 236
Scypes, 236
Shearer, C., 262
Sheppard, Richard M., 314

Sheridan's Raid, 239
Sheridan's Order destroying Crops, 286
Sheilds, Charles, 262
Shriver, Anthony, 262
Simpson, J. C., 262
Smith, C. Ross, 300
Smith, Alexander, 262
Smith, Kirby, 262
Smith, D., 262
Smith, John, 261
Smith, Samuel, 311
Smithfield, 291
South Mountain, 96
Spring Campaign of '63, 133
Sproule, William, 154, 313
St. Mary's Church, 267
Staley, Sergeant, 294
Stannardsville, 225.
Starr, James, 51, 56, 111, 130, 227, 269, 282, 290, 293, 302
Staunton, 319
Stevensburg, 207
Stokes, James, 262
Stoneman's Raid, 136
Stout, George, 261
Strong, E. B., 236
Stuart's Raids, 50, 100
Stuart killed, 264
Surrender, 351

Tevis, E. L., 122
Thomas, Oliver, 262
Thompson's Cross-Roads, 147
Thoroughfare Gap, 177
Todd's Tavern, 235
Towers, Michael, 313
Treichel, W. P. C., 20, 56, 123, 134, 149, 177, 189, 199, 222, 228, 265, 269

Trevillian Station, 259
Tunstall's Station, 44

Wapping Heights, 193
Warrenton Sulphur Springs, 204
Wattis, G., 261
Waynesboro, 320
Weaver, Samuel, 262
Welsh, Osgood, 311
Whalley, Thomas, 254
Whelan, H. C., 51, 62, 85, 160, 168, 301
White House, 44, 249, 264, 323
White, William, 168, 189, 214, 222, 311
Whitehead, G. I., 85
White Oak Swamp, 68, 247

White Post, 281
Whiteford, E., 189, 219
Williams, John W., 305
Williamsport, 183
Winchester, 318
Windmill Point, 268
Winsor, H. Jr., 310
Wint, Theo. J., 258, 313
Winter Quarters of 1862-63, 118
Winter Quarters of 1863-64, 211
Workman, James H., 315
Wright, Joseph, 121
Wright, Samuel, 227

Yorktown, 43
Yellow Tavern, 244

ERRATA.

Page 20. For "Clement C. Barclay," read "Clement B. Barclay."
Page 100. For "2d Pennſylvania," read "4th."
Page 100. For "4th Indiana," read "3d."
Page 118. For "Profeſſor Bache," read "Charles M. Bache, of the Coaſt Survey."
Page 120. For "George W. Clymer," read "George E. Clymer."
Page 122. For "Edwin L. Teirs," read "Tevis."
Page 138. Lieutenant T. Lennig captured at Beverley Ford, June 9, 1863.
Page 154. For "Elk Run," read "Elk Town."
Page 178. For "Middletown," read "Middleburg."
Page 216. Captain R. Milligan reſigned on account of diſability cauſed by field ſervice.
Page 218. For "Thomas O. Mailey," read "Thomas E. Maley."
Page 222. Firſt Lieutenant White promoted Captain at this date.
Page 259. For "South Anna," read "North Anna."
Page 310. For "Henry Winſer, Jr.," read "Henry Winſor, Jr."

ERRATA.

Page 20. For "Clement C. Barclay," read "Clement B. Barclay."
Page 100. For "2d Pennſylvania," read "4th."
Page 100. For "4th Indiana," read "3d."
Page 118. For "Profeſſor Bache," read "Charles M. Bache, of the Coaſt Survey."
Page 120. For "George W. Clymer," read "George E. Clymer."
Page 122. For "Edwin L. Teirs," read "Tevis."
Page 138. Lieutenant T. Lennig captured at Beverley Ford, June 9, 1863.
Page 154. For "Elk Run," read "Elk Town."
Page 178. For "Middletown," read "Middleburg."
Page 216. Captain R. Milligan reſigned on account of diſability cauſed by field ſervice.
Page 218. For "Thomas O. Mailey," read "Thomas E. Maley."
Page 222. Firſt Lieutenant White promoted Captain at this date.
Page 259. For "South Anna," read "North Anna."
Page 310. For "Henry Winſer, Jr.," read "Henry Winſor, Jr."

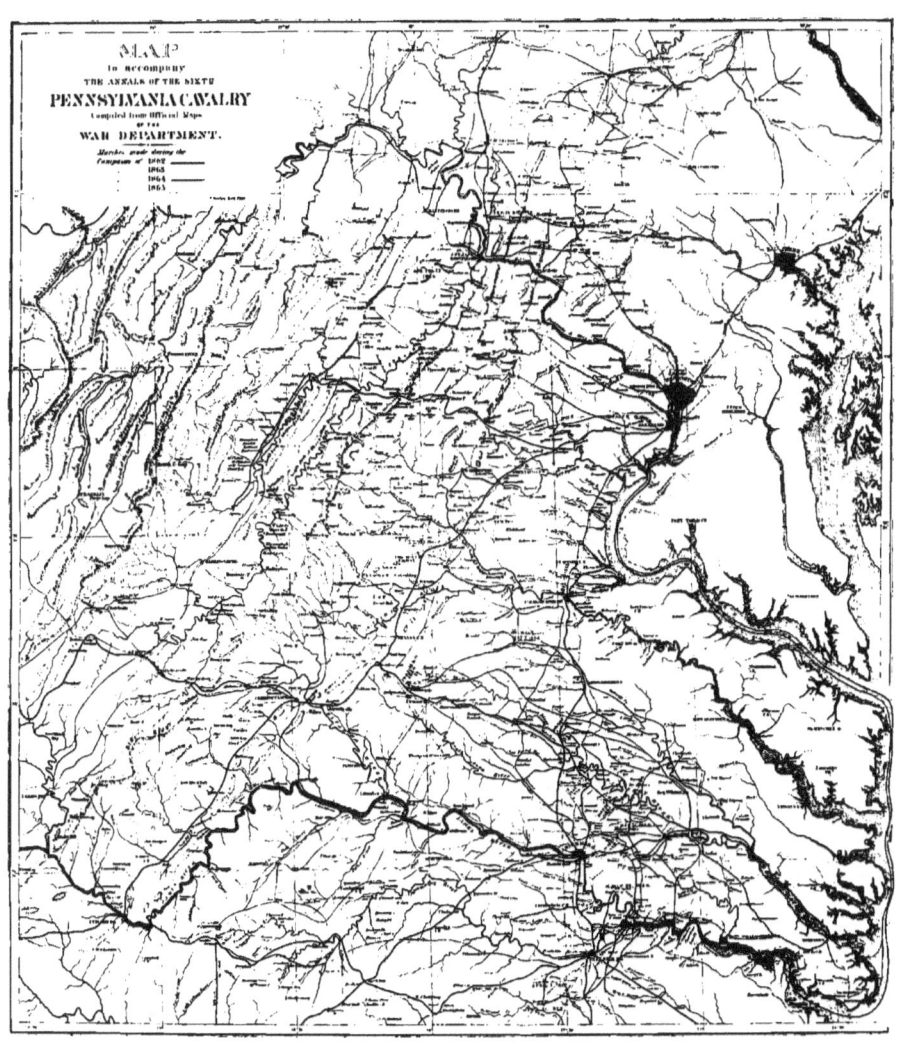

www.ingramcontent.com/pod-product-compliance
Lightning Source LLC
Chambersburg PA
CBHW020308240426
43673CB00039B/743